Dear Maxine

Dear Maxine

Letters from the Unfinished Conversation with Maxine Greene

EDITED BY

ROBERT LAKE

FOREWORD BY

SONIA NIETO

Teachers College
Columbia University
New York and London

Published by Teachers College Press, 1234 Amsterdam Avenue, New York, NY 10027

Library of Congress Cataloging-in-Publication Data

Dear Maxine : letters from the unfinished conversation with Maxine Greene / edited by Robert Lake ; foreword by Sonia Nieto.
    p. cm.
  Includes bibliographical references.
  ISBN 978-0-8077-5137-4 (pbk. : alk. paper) — ISBN 978-0-8077-5138-1 (hardcover : alk. paper) 1. Education—Philosophy. 2. Education—Social aspects—United States. 3. Educational change. 4. Greene, Maxine. I. Lake, Robert (Robert Lewis), 1951–
  LB885.G682D43 2010
  370.1—dc22

                      2010026338

ISBN 978-0-8077-5137-4 (paperback)
ISBN 978-0-8077-5138-1 (hardcover)

Printed on acid-free paper

Manufactured in the United States of America

17 16 15 14 13 12 11 10   8 7 6 5 4 3 2 1

Contents

Foreword

Just yesterday, I participated in a symposium on the social imagination and education, dedicated to Maxine Greene. She was there, in all her glorious 91 years of elegance and power. Maxine started the panel off by reading a reflection she had written for the occasion, holding slightly crumpled papers with lipstick stains along the bottom. As inevitably happens, Maxine stunned everyone with both her intoxicating ideas and the gorgeous language with which she expresses them. I am always impressed that instead of intimidating people with her eloquence and her presence, Maxine inspires those around her—students, colleagues, artists, teachers—to rise to the occasion.

The panelists, led by Herb Kohl, reflected deeply on Maxine's words, on how we need the arts more than ever in our schools, and how so many schools are bereft of creativity and imagination. At the end of the discussion, Herb asked her to summarize our conversation. In her distinctively throaty, New York–accented voice, Maxine said, "Well, you know, I believe in unanswered questions," once again becoming our teacher.

It is with that image of Maxine reading her piece yesterday that I begin this Foreword, which I present not only as a beginning to this book, but also as a way to understand the power of letters, particularly in this age of e-mails, tweets, and blogs.

A number of years ago, I undertook a project to compile and publish a series of letters to Paulo Freire. I had actually been collecting them from my students since 1980, when I started teaching at the University of Massachusetts. We read Freire's *Pedagogy of the Oppressed* (1970) as the text for my Introduction to Multicultural Education class. Although Freire never mentioned the words "multicultural education" in his groundbreaking book, I always thought his ideas reflected how I conceived of this field.

Because his ideas and writing were challenging to some students, especially undergraduates, I began asking them, toward the end of the semester, to write a letter to him. I wanted them to explain how his ideas had instructed, inspired, angered, or moved them to action, and how their teaching might change as a result. I envisioned this as a good way to have students reflect on Freire's philosophy, and for me to make sure they were "getting" his ideas.

It was many years later, in 2005 to be exact, when I finally got around to compiling the letters. Since I didn't have too many of the original letters, I decided to augment them by contacting former students, many of whom were now teacher educators in their own right, and asking them to compose letters as well. Then it occurred to me that other teacher educators I knew might also like to contribute and, while I was at it, I decided to ask some Freirean scholars and others who had been inspired by his work to do the same (Maxine was among them, and, of course, her letter was magnificent).

And so emerged my book *Dear Paulo: Letters from Those Who Dare Teach* (2008), its title fashioned after his book *Teachers as Cultural Workers: Letters to Those Who Dare Teach* (1998). The book, with letters ranging from a paragraph to a dozen pages long, written by a diverse group, from frightened first-year teachers to seasoned educators who had spent their lives working for social change and educational justice, was a labor of love for Paulo, a man who had inspired so many throughout the world to think of education, and indeed of life, as beyond their "limit-situations." Through the words of teachers, scholars, teacher educators, artists, and even a farmer educator (a former student of mine), readers of *Dear Paulo* have participated in a private/public act of love and appreciation for Paulo Freire, a man most of them never met but who has nonetheless taught them many things.

I am certain that Maxine has felt affirmed and appreciated when reading the letters in this book, although I am equally certain that she questioned whether she deserves the accolades and what she may perceive as the exaltation in them. About a decade ago, Bill Ayers and Janet Miller organized a book inspired by Maxine's ideas (Ayers & Miller, 1998), and they faced a similar conundrum.

In inviting us to write something, they cautioned us that Maxine did *not* want this to be a book about her, but rather a book built on ideas important to her, and to us. Maxine Greene is humble and, yes, even insecure in her own brilliance, so this was not surprising. As Bill Ayers writes in his letter for this book, Maxine posed what he called that "crazy question" after a lecture she had given. "Was it okay?" she asked, a question she has often repeated, and one that never fails to astound those of us who hear it. It is difficult, then, to write a book in honor of a person as humble, as concerned with others more than herself, as is Maxine. In spite of this tension, *Dear Maxine* is a valuable undertaking because it makes these conversations part of the public discourse, it lets others "in" on the beauty and virtuosity of Maxine's ideas, and it may even change how readers live in the world.

The power of the epistolary genre resides in precisely this: it makes a private act public, and it gives others access to insights and wisdom that might otherwise be inaccessible to them. In the process, it allows readers to see the interactions between two people who have a personal connection, one of whom has agreed to let others listen in on the conversation. While the private letters of many famous people have been published (although they might never have been meant to see the light of day), books such as *Dear Paulo* and *Dear Maxine* are different in that they are meant, from the outset, to be public encounters that go beyond the writer and the addressee. These letters are meant to illuminate, teach, and inspire, and to help us face life with some new meanings and motivations. In this, they may also be problematic, because although they are not meant to be doting or adoring, they may end up being just that, a result that Maxine would never approve of.

But Maxine, dear, we hope you do approve, because our intention has been quite different. The letters in this book are written not by your "fans" but by your students (not just those who happen to have taken classes with you) and colleagues (not just those who happen to work with you). In their tender tribute to a remarkable woman, the letters also help to teach and encourage others to take on the challenge of looking beyond our individual lives and to build community. Robert Lake has brought together the various pieces of Maxine Greene's life in these pages: here are teachers, dancers, graphic artists, educational philosophers, and others. No one in these pages is content with things as they are; we have learned from life, and from Maxine, that there are always unanswered questions.

—Sonia Nieto

Acknowledgments

I am extraordinarily grateful to all the people who have helped me complete this book of letters. First and foremost, I thank all of you who set aside time to write for this project, when each of you already had so many other deadlines and commitments. I also wish to thank my family for their personal support and encouragement while I have been engrossed in this task.

I want to thank Sonia Nieto for planting the idea in my head for a book like this, after reading her book, *Dear Paulo: Letters from Those who Dare to Teach* (2008), and for her contribution. Thank you, Nel Noddings, Michelle Fine, and Janet Miller, for your wonderful contributions to the prologue and epilogue. I am very grateful to Graeme Sullivan and Nisha Nair for their wonderful artwork for the book covers. I also want to thank Ming Fang He and the curriculum studies guys named Bill—Schubert, Ayers, Pinar, and Reynolds—as well as Clyde Coreil, Jim Garrison, and Craig Kridel, for their encouraging words, advice, and e-mails. I also appreciate the outstanding help with copyediting that I received from our graduate assistant, Lacey Prine.

Finally, I want to thank Carole Saltz, Emily Ballengee, Judy Berman, and all of the staff at Teachers College Press for their amazing help and excellent advice, not only on the logistical aspects of publishing, but for their vision and comprehension of the immense significance of the life and scholarship of Maxine Greene.

Publisher's Note

Dear Maxine,

Please note: This is a note and not a letter. Over the years—more than a quarter century of them—there have been many notes back and forth: thank yous, feel betters, celebrations, even yellow sticky notes with editing marks on manuscripts. To and fro they went, some by hand and some electronically. Years of work and love with time always passing. Notes to confirm dinners, breakfasts (never too early), lunches, teas (coffees for you). Indignant, furious notes (like Lear, we rail at the heavens and the politicians and the mess), loving notes (after happy triumphs or sad endings), and funny notes (even a poem or two, usually sent late at night in instant-messaging fashion). Notes with just enough text in them to tide us over until the next bracing conversation. Notes to keep me going until there was time for more talk and, amidst the wonder and whine, comfort.

So, while this may be a publisher's note and *not* a letter, there are wonderful letters in this book and they are all addressed to you. Let me be very clear—this book is not a *festschrift*. *Festschrift*s are eye-rollers—works of dutiful attentiveness and reverent praise. That's not right for you: too starchy and boring; too irrelevant by far. The writers don't want to praise you; they want to relish in your intellect and pass it on to others just as they themselves have been seized by it. As editor, Robert Lake has brought together some really interesting people who have wondered, turned, started, looked at, revised, transformed, acted, changed, and questioned because of you, Maxine. In his book, artists and writers; public school, university, and museum educators; students; and others write to you about your work and theirs and the spaces between.

Later, I know we will talk about *Dear Maxine* and unpack it slowly. I imagine (and I use that word with caution) that first we will ponder your profound unease with being venerated before you've even gelled! I think you will let go of that as your interest in the ideas this book has pushed out from its various contributors take hold. We will twist and turn, let things go, and worry about them later. You will look up at me from your musings—balefully at times, appreciatively at others—and, we will also gossip. There will be threads of memory and coffee and laughter and gorgeous lines of poetry that you will share with me and that will help me to understand what you think. Final note: One thing your appraisal will not be is uncritical, because that is unthinkable.

—Carole Saltz

Prologue

Dear Maxine,

Those of us who write have caressed the pages of this volume with love, kisses, hugs, envy, and laughter. The Maxine Greene volume of letters and notes honors your intelligence, generosity, wisdom, and courage.

As you read through, you may smile and weep to realize all you have touched. Then, do a simple math trick and multiply each letter by the hundreds of students with whom each of the writers has worked. Then multiply that number by another 100 (to be conservative) to estimate the students that our students have taught. Your final sum will escort you to the conclusion that so many of us have already reached: *You are a social movement with thousands of grandchildren.*

But before you dive too deeply into letters from the well-known, I offer you notes from a set of girls and women for whom your words have been balm for the soul, inspiration for a different tomorrow, oxygen that circulates where the air is dead.*

Dear Maxine,

Hi! My name is Pecola. I don't know if you remember me. I am the little girl in Toni Morrison's *The Bluest Eye* (1970). Maybe you will remember that I wanted to be Shirley Temple.

> Pecola Breedlove, an unloved Black child made to believe she is ugly, yearns to have blue eyes, pretty blue eyes. She thinks that "if those eyes of hers were different, that is to say beautiful, she herself would be different." Her mother and father would be different. Maybe they'd say, "Why look at pretty-eyed Pecola. We mustn't do bad things in front of those pretty eyes." Unable to see her own beauty she wants to look like Shirley Temple. (Greene, 1995b, pp. 118–19)

---

* These are of course fictional notes, written with the ink of love, drawn from the words that Maxine herself has placed on the page and into the hands and hearts of so many readers.

That's so embarrassing to read 40 years later. But now that Michael Jackson has died, I realize I wasn't alone in my yearnings. It just seems so sad that we cried for white skin, blue eyes and straight hair and . . .

Maxine, I am writing to say thank you for knowing that, really, I didn't want the skin or the hair or the eyes. I just wanted to be loved, to be noticed, to be known—I was a little girl and all I saw was how much Shirley was loved by everybody. I thought that if I could only paint my skin, curl my hair, then I would be worthy. You understood it wasn't about hating myself, but about desire.

And then you made a miracle. You made me worthy, with my dark skin and kinky hair and my brown eyes. You made me something!

You put me in stories with famous people like John Dewey, Deborah Meier, Mike Rose, and Toni Morrison. You told your readers that they should see the world through my eyes, through my skin, with my hair. You said, "It would appear that there are few more potent ways of relating to the hopes and sufferings and misconceptions of young people like Pecola, strangers to many university people, strangers to their own teachers, who may need to be urged at last to imagine" (Greene, 1995b, p. 1).

Maxine, you yanked my body out of a sewer of shame and honored it as a temple of wisdom. I have a feeling that maybe sometimes, in the dark night, you wish you were somebody else, too. But I'm glad you're not. Thanks from the bottom of my loving body and soul.

—Pecola Breedlove

Dear Maxine,

When you walked into the prison college room, in 1999, I admit I was suspect. A fancy Columbia University professor of philosophy coming to talk to us. I knew that Michelle usually brought us good people but, well, trust me, I had my doubts.

But then you spoke.

You read aloud from Tillie Olsen's *I Stand Here Ironing*, and you asked us about the pain of losing our babies when we got locked up. You told us about the pain of losing yours. And you cried. You didn't talk down to us, you just talked with us. You even made an "us," a group of women, reading, speaking, crying, writing, thinking together. Like those salons you say you have in your living room.

You told us that John Dewey considered democracy to be community always in the making. So, Maxine, you entered our lives in that horrible, little room in the middle of hell, and you were like a midwife, giving birth to a community in the making.

Now that I am out of Bedford, whenever I enter a room, well, I always feel out of place. I try to reach back in my memory to conjure you up, and then, with hesitation and enormous fear, I speak.

If I say what is rumbling in my belly and careening through my nerves, I connect up with the rumblings in the empty bellies of other women. And soon we all feel full. And together. If just for a moment.

Thanks,
—Sara (You'll remember my story
about my daughter, aged 2 when I was incarcerated)

Dear Maxine,

I saw you in the auditorium at Mamaroneck High School in June 2000. We were watching *Exclusions and Awakenings: The Life of Maxine Greene* (2001), the film that filmmaker and producer Markie Hancock made about you. Afterward, my daughter introduced us. You were then—and I guess still are—about my age, maybe a few minutes younger. But you had accomplished so much. You are a professor, famous, my daughter loves you. I was speechless when I met you. All I could say is, "You are almost my age. How do you know so much?" And you were so gracious. You smiled and said, "Rose, it's true that what I know, you don't. But what you know, I don't. We could teach each other a lot."

You made me feel not so small and very, very proud to know you, and that you know my daughter and that she loves you.

Thanks,
—Rose Fine

And so, Maxine,

So many thank you for your fierce mind, your gifted pen, your eloquent talks. But, for a moment, I want to appreciate your grace, your generosity, the dignity you bring to all whom you touch, the light you shine on those around you. In your own words, you refuse to engage others "with the one-dimensional vision" but you "look, instead, toward might be and what ought to be"—a humanity not yet (Greene, 1993a, p. 213).

Thank you indeed for a lifetime of friendship and love.

—Michelle Fine

Introduction

Maxine Greene and Human Freedom

Preparing to write this Introduction gave me an opportunity to reread parts of Maxine's beautiful book *The Dialectic of Freedom*. It is well worth reading again today—to be reminded of how far education has fallen from the vision she articulated in 1988. Her hope was to open possibilities for all students to achieve some measure of freedom in recognizing possibilities and directing their own lives. In contrast, today's policies aim to control the lives of students through uniform preparation, uniform achievement, and uniform futures.

The Dialectic of Freedom draws skillfully on existential philosophy, but it resists the temptation to describe freedom in absolute terms. Instead, it embraces a view of freedom as achievement, a view closer to that of John Dewey. In "the relation between subject and object, individual and environment, self and society, outsider and community, living consciousness and phenomenal world" (1988, p. 8), there is a dialectical relation, a relation inviting mediation. To understand an object or another person, one must communicate, make connections to past and possible future encounters, receive what is there, and respond. One must be at least somewhat free in order to do this. And the result of such thoughtful, free encounters is further freedom; new possibilities arise.

How do we prepare young people to achieve a capacity for the freedom that is rightfully theirs as existential beings? Even Sartre, who posited an absolute freedom, realized that people have to recognize their capacity to choose before they can exercise it. A society that oppresses its citizens economically and politically does not encourage the exercise of freedom as Greene has described it. It is not only that people are deprived of the material goods needed to liberate their intellectual capacity but, worse, that various bureaucratic powers define the possibilities for their futures. Young people in highly coercive educational settings are told specifically what to see, what to learn, what future to seek, and how to satisfy the benign powers coercing them. Many educators today believe that preparing all students for college by requiring them to study academic subjects and forcing them to pass test after test on material for which they have little interest is actually providing them with opportunities for a better life. Maybe. But Greene has eloquently expressed some reservations.

To achieve and exercise freedom, Greene writes, one must be wide-awake and cultivate a passion to see. This means that the young must be *invited* to engage with the worlds of people, objects, and ideas. They must be allowed to communicate in ways that open up spaces instead of closing them down by prescribing beforehand exactly what should be learned in every encounter. Without attributing evil motives to today's "reformers," Greene warns that policymakers may be "deliberately or incidentally" making the school system into a machine "geared to training instruments for the state" (1988, p. 13). The U.S. Bureau of Labor Statistics tells us that most of the job openings in the next decade will be in occupations at the lowest or next-to-lowest pay scale. Many new college-graduate assembly-line workers will wear white collars and work in cubicles, their work prescribed step by step, much like Charlie Chaplin's in *Modern Times*. Only the setting and the color of the collar will be changed. Surely, as Maxine recommends, policymakers should recognize that there is more to genuine education than preparation for occupations, and students should be prepared to live fully human lives, whatever their eventual occupations.

Greene uses literature powerfully in making her arguments, and she would like schools to offer all students rich opportunities to engage in the arts—not to memorize who wrote this and who said that, but to awaken their imaginations. The object is to widen perspectives and increase perception. Like Virginia Woolf and, more recently, Susan Sontag, Greene believes that the visual arts and literature possess the power to move emotions and open new vistas. Both artistic forms open spaces. No one human being can participate directly in all of the activities depicted in literary works, but we can engage vicariously in a host of them, and as our perception and understanding grow, we may choose more wisely those to which we will commit ourselves. Moreover, as we share in a wide range of perspectives, we should gain greater appreciation for the diversity of human experience.

These anticipated benefits are beautifully expressed by Greene:

> And there is the notion of consciousness, our way of thrusting into the world, of grasping its appearances. Acts of believing, perceiving, thinking, wondering, imagining: all are among the acts of consciousness; all exist in complex relationship. It is the hope of those engaged in aesthetic education to free others—teachers students, creative artists themselves—to reach towards a reciprocity of perspectives. . . . Of all human creations, works of art are most likely to resist fixed boundaries, even as they resist one-dimensionality. There are no fixed boundaries between illusion and reality, between the visible and the invisible:

illusion awakens us to aspects of the taken-for-granted we never were aware of before; art, many have said, makes visible what was never visible before. Most significant for me is the capacity of an art form (when attentively perceived, when authentically imagined) to overcome passivity, to awaken us to a world in need of transformation, forever incomplete.... There is always, always, more. (2007a, p. 660)

—Ned Noddings

Dear Maxine

Chapter One

The School and Society

Imagining and Reshaping Public Spaces

In this time of increased passivity when "spectacle is preferred over dialogue" (Fruchter, 1998, p. 229), the following letters sound a call to participate anew in public spaces. In this chapter the writers reach beyond imagination as a theoretical concept, to one that gives voice to the silenced and vision to the hopelessly lost. This is certainly one of the central motifs in all of Maxine Greene's writing and in all that is implied in "social imagination."

Imagining the Possible

MIKE ROSE

Dear Maxine,

We've corresponded since meeting in 1995—I'm holding that first note in my left hand as I write this—but before that I knew you through your writing, particularly *The Dialectic of Freedom*. The book couldn't look more unassuming: dark blue cover, no illustration, the title and your name in simple white lettering. It is a thin volume, a collection of lectures you gave for the John Dewey Society. I can't recall how I got it or who might have recommended it. But it came along at such a crucial time, and it shaped how I would know you. So let me go back to that book as a way to celebrate you and your work.

We met right after the publication of my *Possible Lives* (1995). That book got us talking, and I would like to take this opportunity now—this letter of tribute and affection—to tell you how much *The Dialectic of Freedom* meant to me as I tried to bring *Possible Lives* to an end.

I don't know about you, Maxine, but for me conclusions are harder than hell to get right. Openings are no picnic, but conclusions—that right mix of summary and tying ideas together and giving the book a lift, an opening-out while closing down—boy, that calls on everything I've got. And this was one of the times when I feared I didn't have the goods.

As you know, *Possible Lives* is a documentary of good teaching in public schools across the country, one-room schoolhouse to urban academy. I had spent over 3 years visiting communities, talking to people, observing classrooms, reading student work. The book was nearly done, the chapters in each setting complete, and I was embarking on the conclusion. The conclusion: Just sit down and pull the big themes together. Apply the seat of the pants to the seat of the chair, as some writer once admonished. Sit on down, son. It'll come. Weeks passed, then a month, then more. I had words on paper, but no real *ending*, nothing that brought ideas together in a way that led to something greater than its parts. There were nights—honest to God—when I would wake up certain that I couldn't do it, that after all this time, I'd fail. How could I tell all those people I observed and interviewed? I was going through heavy Woody Allen angst, without the jazzy soundtrack.

More time passed. I wrote, but the writing was flat, mostly summary. Then some people and books intervened. During a visit with a buddy in Santa Fe, I talked the thing through several times during long rides across the desert. Later, on a trip to Philadelphia, the urban historian Michael Katz had an extended conversation with me about the meaning of "the public." And around that time, my reading opened up: Jane Jacobs's *The Death and Life of Great American Cities*, Patricia Williams's *The Alchemy of Race and Rights*. Your *The Dialectic of Freedom* (1988).

As I said, I can't recall if someone recommended the book to me or if I already had it—but in the moment it took on special meaning. Here was rich discussion of freedom, and possibility, and imagination. You wrote about "imagination as a vision of the possible," about "looking at things as though they could be otherwise," and about public space and the public sphere.

This was a warm and compatible vocabulary. I had been writing about the need in our education debates for portraits of good classrooms, for images of what's possible. I had been writing, too, about teachers being creative within institutional constraints (like your notion of "situated freedom"). I kept writing about seeing things another way, taking another line of sight—and all your wonderful passages on imagination were resonant here. But now it was time to bring all this together, and it felt encouraging, confirming, to read you. There's nothing like finding someone who has already thought things through. A companion. A hand on the shoulder.

The other idea I drew from your book is that imagination can be an element of social policy. This wasn't the traditional use of imagination in the artistic sense or imagination as fancy. And it wasn't Wallace Stevens's force of the mind that protects us from harsh reality. It *was* a force, all right, but imaginative power turned outward toward the social order. Or maybe another way to say it is this: Envisioning a better world—those possible lives I was championing—has an artistic as well as sociological dimension to it: imagination as an aid in creating the future.

That stalled conclusion began to come alive, to direct itself with the aid of these powerful conceptual tools: an enriched sense of "the public" and the use of imagination as a mechanism of public policy. So thank you for that, Maxine.

I keep correspondence from writers in their books. It's my simple filing system. *The Dialectic of Freedom* is much scribbled on and beaten up by now, but the spine holds despite the letters wedged in the middle of the pages. The letters are beautiful, a blend of literature and social science and politics—and great generosity of spirit. They contain your concerns about possibility and dignity and justice, and they are rich with detail from both books and your city, with teaching and students, with new projects. You "flunked retirement." You "remain obsessional about possibility." Ideas are imbued with feeling. The letters give a script, a voice to this vibrant blend of cognition and affect. When I needed it most, I found in your work ideas with a heartbeat.

—Mike Rose

Walking the Dialectic of Freedom

JIM GARRISON

Dear Maxine,

I was walking aimlessly in the shadows of the early afternoon sun until I met you. This is literally true. The year was 1988, and I was attending the annual meeting of the American Educational Research Association. Like many, I find this annual event disassociating. It was early in my career, and while things were going well professionally, the person within was unsteady and unsure. Academic ritual and enterprise remain strange and somewhat alienating to me, but they were especially so in the early years, and particularly at these pretentious and imposing summits. We were in New Orleans, the tourist trap that we all like so much because it allows us to walk mildly on the wild side without wandering too far and falling into the abyss. Of course, Katrina has since blown the cover off my romance, exposing the horror hidden below, but that is commentary. The point is in the time and place.

As I walked through the lesser-known streets of the French Quarter, I realized that the Quarter itself is much larger than the one defined for tourists. Rooms, alcohol, and alternative attitudes appeared cheaper here beyond the usual bounds. Emptiness, dizziness, strangeness, and the bottomlessness of being only express abstract "existential" ideas. They state the condition, but fail to capture the feeling. It became clear that something was missing in my life. It would not come closer, and I could not continue toward it. In such wild pursuit or evasion, we all stumble. Sometimes we fall; sometimes we, and those we love, do not rise up again.

Such distress comes when the center will not hold; in such places at such times, there is no center. Images melt. Colors blur and blend. Smells merge. Even the welcoming touristy part of the Quarter stinks. Everything smells rotten. The sounds fuse and the beer begins to taste sickenly sweet. A confused queasiness takes hold. Rock and roll intermingles with the blues; country-western winds its way through the jazz. Meanwhile, the soundtrack of my life also jams across genres. It all reaches me with a physical impact. I realize that this is the land of adjectives, verbs, and adverbs. Nouns know it not. Human beings cannot BE here. They can only keep walking.

You, Maxine, know primary phenomenology well and weave it wonderfully into your narratives. I give you the previous three paragraphs as a small gift of my "self," such as it flows in return for all that you have given me. That and gratitude are all I can offer.

In such untethered emotional spaces, nothingness is the only *that* that will stand in place. Hell, nothing noths itself here, if we can trust the thought of Heidegger. Heidegger! There is a noun!! Now I can name it!!! As Dewey says, "Intuition precedes conception and goes deeper." I got it—almost, but not in my own words.

I walk out of the Quarter, back to the conference, into the book display, and I swear, Maxine, I walk right into the large display for your book, *The Dialectic of Freedom* (1988), just out. The opening sentence of the Introduction immediately seizes me: "This book arises out of a lifetime's preoccupation with quest, with pursuit." Yeah! I get that! The next sentence tells me that it is deeply personal, about "a woman striving to affirm the feminine." Hmmm! Not me! I continue: "On the other hand, it has been in some sense deeply public as well: that of a person struggling to connect the undertaking of education, with which she has been so long involved, to the making and remaking of a public space, a space of dialogue and possibility." Damn! Change that "she" to "he" and "long involved" to "briefly involved" and that is me, and that clause, "a space of dialogue and possibility," pretty much describes my walk of the last 3 hours. I can "get" this a little bit. I keep reading. I can understand the "reaching, beyond the limits imposed by the obligations" even if I cannot comprehend the "of a woman's life" part.

Your book educated me about "the achievement of freedom by people in search of themselves." It taught me that I had lived my life trapped in the confines of my ego. (I fear it is still where I find myself most of the time.) It told me that there are contexts of another kind, that "where persons attend to one another with interest, regard, and care, there is a place for the appearance of freedom." No one in the Marine Corps ever mentioned that to me; we just marched in rank and file. While we should sometimes walk alone, as I had much of that afternoon, we should much more often stroll with others, especially those who are different from us, and be wary when we walk in drumbeat rhythm in the uniform of our supposed nature, fate, or calling.

Your first chapter taught me to walk beyond the "autonomous and independent" state that is "the American dream" (or nightmare). You talk about how young (our students) and old (ourselves) are "immersed in the taken-for-granted and the everyday" and how this leads to "unreflective consumerism; for others, it means a preoccupation with *having* more rather than *being* more." Academia has its own consumerism, and we often confuse having more knowledge with becoming wiser, which lies beyond knowledge alone. It was the academic consumerism and the preoccupation with having rather than with being, a concept so manifest at academic meetings and one that I found also within myself, that I was struggling with as I walked that day, although I did not know it until we met.

You taught me to walk out of the nihilism of false autonomy and false free will, to move beyond negative freedom from constraint, by naming what oppresses me, and into the positive freedom of disciplined goal-seeking. You inspired me to keep walking until I made community with others, while also striving to name how my actions might oppress them and learning to appreciate differences that I do not understand. For these gifts, I am thankful.

I have taught *The Dialectic of Freedom* many times, and on every occasion, I come upon some new paradox that entangles the class and me. The ordinary discursive logic of identity cannot handle these paradoxes; it only evades them. Every time, you teach my students and me how to embrace these paradoxes of freedom and cultivate them for meaning and growth (although such growth often requires painful but necessary pruning). Too often, I have taught selfishly. From you, and from my students, I have learned that what frees me does not free others, and that my freedom project can actually harm the freedom projects of others. I guess it is this kind of fecundity that keeps your book in print after all these years. I am sure it is what gives it and your other writings, and, even more, your vivacious personality and presence, a kind of immortality.

You know what, Maxine? I have come to think that freedom means being bound in love to others who fertilize our growth. Often, fertilizer stinks, and pruning away that which heretofore seems a vital part of us is always painful. Seeing, feeling, smelling, touching, and even tasting the flavors of otherness and difference can be as strange and dizzying as was staggering around New Orleans slightly drunk, but it can also be intoxicating in the grander sense.

Thank you, thank you, and thank you, Maxine. Beyond that, words fail. I have hugged you upon our meeting more than once. Now, today, please accept this verbal embrace and thank you yet again.

With deep affection and appreciation, for your words and your wisdom, I am cordially yours,

—Jim Garrison

Imagining Things Being Otherwise

PATTY BODE

Imagining things being otherwise may be a first step toward acting on the belief that they can be changed. And it would appear that a kindred imaginative ability is required if the becoming different that learning involves is actually to take place. A space of freedom opens before the person moved to choose in the light of possibility; she or he feels what it signifies to be an initiator and an agent, existing among others but with the power to choose for herself or himself.
—Maxine Greene, *Releasing the Imagination*

Dear Maxine,

I am "imagining things being otherwise" in our public schools today, where the eradication of the arts in schools is threatening a generation of youth to grow up with little or no access to arts education. I believe this threat can be changed into a call to action with your work as a guide. We have reached this point because the policies and practices of No Child Left Behind have catapulted a deliberate assault on arts education, resulting in the repression of cultural knowledge, the constraint of students' vocalization of identity, and blocked access to their communities' histories. Yes, I agree: "Kindred imaginative ability is required" to reconceptualize the role of arts in schools and bring democratic support to teachers of the arts through funding and community engagement (Greene, 1995, p. 22).

I was a public school art teacher for 16 years and now, in teacher education, I work with pre-service visual art teachers. My life's work is to participate in and help to bring light to the environment of student knowledge and teacher knowledge, student inquiry and teacher inquiry, that fuels imaginative participation in a democratic society. Watching art programs exterminated from schools across the nation is like watching a destructive wildfire consume old-growth forests. Rather than hover over the smoking ashes with regret, I hope to rally our kindred imaginative ability to fight the fire and plant new growth.

I have heard the phrase "Art is always the first to go" countless times when the topic of budget cuts in the public schools is discussed. It is often stated with the sad, wistful tone of conventional wisdom, and with the certainty of common knowledge, often followed by "it's a shame." Yet the arts are essential to education. A visual art program makes the schools look good. It makes the students feel good, and it makes the families feel welcome and affirmed in our learning communities. That could be reason enough to keep art programs pulsating and growing. However, there is much more to quality art education programs. Your work, Maxine, asks that we imagine the multifaceted dimensions of art education by reconsidering that common phrase: "the first to go."

Would we say the same thing about other aspects of learning? For example, when considering the cognitive development and reflective understanding that the study and practice of visual art promotes, we might say, "It's a shame, critical thinking is always the first to go." Likewise, when students demonstrate their academic understandings and philosophical questions in visual forms through painting, printmaking, sculpture, ceramic pottery, stained glass, technological media, photography, mixed media, video, electronic images, Web communication, and more, we might say, "It's a shame, learning that expression and communication are multimodal and dynamic is always the first to go."

When peering into the art room in K–12 schools, we see students working together in a common visual language. We see English language learners; a broad range of academic achievers; students receiving special education support; students new to this country and others several generations American-born; children of domestic laborers, college professors, and tradespeople sitting beside one another. We might say, "It's a shame that when kids develop emotional and intellectual understanding across social groups, it's always the first to go."

When we hear youth discussing the impact of popular culture in their art classrooms, learning that most social scientists agree that children are "reading" more visual imagery than text-based communication, while cultivating consciousness in surfing Web pages, clicking on pop-ups, reading magazine ads, studying television production, creating video, posting on YouTube, examining billboards, walking through shopping mall design, we might say, "It's a shame, learning to be critical consumers of our visual environment is always the first to go."

When perusing the topics investigated in visual art curriculum we see traditional works of art, museum collections, indigenous arts, family photographs, media coverage of current events, video blog postings, graphic design productions, street art, community exhibits, picture book illustrations, digital photography and much, much more. As students develop knowledge across the history of countries, cultures, and subcultures on human concerns that span beauty, violence, science, and humanity, we might say, "It's a shame, learning to be socially conscious, politically active citizens is always the first to go."

While reviewing recent national educational research, we learn of academic achievement related to the arts, with an especially significant impact on student populations who come from economically disadvantaged families, that indicate dropout rates decreasing and test scores soaring. The National Latino/a Education Research and Policy Project (Pedraza & Rivera, 2005) and AERA's Commission on Research in Black Education (King, 2005) have both insisted that participation in the arts is central to increased achievement. College admission rates also increase when students have a strong arts curriculum, regardless of the prospective college major. Perhaps we should say, "It's a shame, our democratic commitment to equal and equitable education is always the first to go."

The presence of a vibrant visual art curriculum is a signifier of overall excellence and health of school systems' and districts' curriculum. The loss of art teacher positions in America's public schools over the past 5 years and a reduction of the art teacher staffing in the elementary schools, middle schools, and high schools eliminates a great deal of curriculum; it illustrates the serious blow to school systems suffering under these budget cuts. In all grades and all subject areas, class sizes are increasing, support staff is being reduced or eliminated. Students will suffer in every curriculum area. This did not happen overnight, and the communities of U.S. public schools need to develop a proactive stance for change. Such a stance requires honestly confronting the ugly realities and consequences about making such dramatic reductions in art curriculum.

Your life's work provides us with the vision, courage, and politically active stance we need to confront the policies of No Child Left Behind that are driving the national public school system into a privatized enterprise. Action requires targeting misinformed legislators about the negligence of the state and the underfunding of our public schools. Can we ever imagine telling them, "It's a shame that the overuse and exorbitant cost of standardized testing is always the first to go"?

You asserted in *Releasing the Imagination* that the "learner must approach from the vantage point of her or his lived situation, that is, in accord with a distinctive point of view and interest" (Greene, 1995, p. 31). So, too, I argue that all educators, all community members, all concerned citizens of a democracy must engage our collective imaginations to thoughtfully reenvision what schools are for, what counts as art, who counts as artists and what counts as knowledge. Such collective imagination also allows us to reposition our perspective and envision with empathy, as you, Maxine, so aptly explained:

> It may well be the imaginative capacity that allows us also to experience empathy with different points of view, even with interests apparently at odds with ours. Imagination may be a new way of decentering ourselves, of breaking out of confinements of privatism and self-regard into a space where we can come face to face with others and call out, "Here we are." (p. 31)

Maxine, your work flies in the face of the conventional wisdom, and the certainty of common knowledge that sadly nods "it's a shame" about our current crisis and future arts education. My experience as an art teacher and teacher educator makes me feel "what it signifies to be an initiator and an agent" (Greene, 1995b, p. 22). I embrace a vision of schools pulsing with vibrant ecosystems of expression, understanding, and inquiry. I thank you for your inspiration and for your hopeful vision.

In Solidarity,
—Patty Bode

Stargazing, Wide-Awakening, Cultural Imagining

MING FANG HE

Dear Maxine,

I am going to share with you my stories of stargazing, wide-awakening, and cultural imagining. I first heard about your work when JoAnn Phillion and I worked as doctoral students with Michael Connelly at the University of Toronto. Like many thirsty doctoral students, JoAnn and I were eagerly planning our trips to AERA annual meetings to stargaze: to see and to hear famous people like you, known to us only from our reference lists. We sat in economy class on the airplane, frantically highlighting the sessions given by stars from the AERA program catalogues. Bustling out of our hotels with empty stomachs in the early morning, we determined to gaze at as many stars as possible. Sweaty and out of breath, we slumped in our chairs, stared at the podium, and identified which star we wanted to track. And then we followed you from session to session, each one packed with people sitting or standing in the hallways. In 2001, JoAnn and I, the co-chairs of AERA's Division B Equity Committee, organized a panel for you, Chris Carger, Lourdes Diaz Soto, and Guadalupe Valdés. Prior to or after the panel, you greeted and hugged almost every single person rushing in the hallways or magnetized to the lunch table where you were surrounded by a group of stargazers.

Your inspiring words, hilarious comments, and the gripping stories you told during your talks and walks captivated me and many others. Those of us who were once content merely to stargaze began to read your writings. The epiphanies I experienced from your brilliant lines were constantly interrupted by an ocean of references in literature, art, and philosophy, which provoked me to delve into a river of great literary works that I may never finish reading in my life. These include John Steinbeck's *The Grapes of Wrath*, Ralph Ellison's *Invisible Man*, Richard Wright's *Native Son* and *Black Boy*, Virginia Woolf's *A Room of One's Own* and *Moments of Being*, Toni Morrison's *The Bluest Eye* and *Beloved*, Alice Walker's *The Color Purple* and *Meridian*, Wallace Stevens's "The Man with the Blue Guitar," Walt Whitman's "Song of Myself," and many more.

Poetics of narrative you illuminated in your works made me "wide-awake to the world" (Greene, 1995b, p. 4) filled with contradictions, diversities, and complexities, and released my cultural imagination. My imagination traveled from British and French literature, to American literature, to an experience and reexperience of Chinese and Chinese American literature written by people in exile at home or abroad such as Amy Tan's *The Joy Luck Club*, *The Kitchen God's Wife*, and *The Hundred Secret Senses*; Maxine Hong Kingston's *The Woman Warrior*; Gao Xingian's *Soul Mountain*; Hong Ying's *Daughter of the River*; Ha Jin's *Waiting* and *Ocean of Words*; Dai Sijie's *Balzac and the Little Chinese Seamstress*; Da Chen's *Sounds of the River* and *Colors of the Mountain*; and more.

This cultural imagination was extended to an exploration of the works of those whom you have influenced tremendously, such as Bill Ayers's *Teaching toward Freedom*, Bill Schubert's *Love, Justice, and Education: John Dewey and the Utopians*, Janet Miller's *Sounds of Silence Breaking*, and Craig Kridel, Robert Bullough Jr., and Paul Shaker's *Teachers and Mentors: Profiles of Distinguished Twentieth-Century Professors of Education*.

Your literary imagination has also led to my collaboration with JoAnn on the development of courses on multicultural education at Georgia Southern University and Purdue University. We infuse our multicultural teacher education curricula with life-based literary narratives in which our students experience vicariously the lives of diverse communities, families, and students they rarely encounter in life.

Rather than relying solely on theoretical literature, we eclectically combine life-based literary narratives with autobiographies, narrative inquiries, and ethnographies to bring experiential qualities to abstract multicultural theories, with the intent of developing students' narrative imagination—the ability to reflect on experience, question assumptions, and actively empathize with others. The life-based literary narratives "help the diverse students we know articulate their stories . . . [and] pursue the meanings of their lives—to find out how things are happening and to keep posing questions about the why" (Greene, 1995b, p. 165). The focus is on the power of narrative as a means to increase knowledge of ways diverse students experience the world, both inside and outside schools and classrooms, to make sense of lived worlds, to see themselves in the stories of others, and "[to enter] into their realities by means not solely of our reasoning power but of our imagination" (Greene, 1995, p. 3).

In these courses students first read Martha Nussbaum's *Cultivating Humanity* to study the key concepts of *narrative imagination, self-examination,* and *world citizenship.* They also read your *Releasing the Imagination* to explore ideas of literary imagination, creating possibilities, and expanding community. We invite our students to read such life-based literary narratives as Patrick Chamoiseau's *School Days,* Eva Hoffman's *Lost in Translation,* Toni Morrison's *The Bluest Eye,* and Maxine Hong Kingston's *The Woman Warrior.* We use your philosophical framework and that of Nussbaum to relate life-based literary narratives (Phillion & He, 2004) to students' lives and to the lives of diverse cultural and ethnic groups. We explore autobiographical work such as Vivian Paley's *White Teacher;* narrative inquiry research such as Chris Carger's *Of Borders and Dreams;* cross-cultural narrative research such as my *A River Forever Flowing;* and ethnographies such as Lourdes Diaz Soto's *Language, Culture, and Power,* Guadalupe Valdés's *Con Respeto,* and Angela Valenzuela's *Subtractive Schooling.* Through an exploration of autobiographies, memoirs, novels, films, paintings, poems, songs, and artworks created by people from different cultural backgrounds, students are encouraged to reflect on their backgrounds and experiences, and critically examine their values and beliefs to develop understanding of the ways in which their personal histories, cultures, and experiences affect who they are, how they interact with others, and how they perceive the world.

These literary texts help not only to develop empathetic understanding toward others but also to make a transition from "imaginary" characters in the literary narratives to real-life situations of students in diverse classrooms, schools, communities, and neighborhoods. These literary and theoretical texts expand narrative imagination that "enables us to perceive the normal in the abnormal, the opposite of chaos in chaos" (Greene, 2001, p. 83), to understand ourselves and others, and to see ourselves as agents of social justice, to build "a democratic community, always a community in the making... energized and radiated by an awareness of future possibility" (Greene, 1995b, p. 166).

Maxine, from stargazing to diving into a deep ocean of your wisdom to becoming wide-awake in between seas of Eastern and Western languages, cultures, and identities, your narrative imagination has impelled me to explore the "trembling South" with my colleagues and students at Georgia Southern University through personal-passionate-participatory inquiries. Your work on cultural imagination has also inspired me to create a course on the narrative of curriculum in the South. In this course, we explore the narratives and experiences of repressions, suppressions, subjugations, and stereotypes of Southern women, Blacks, and other disenfranchised individuals and groups. The focus is on the power of narrative as a means to tell hidden and silenced stories of suppressed and underrepresented groups, to counter the official narrative that often portrays these groups as deficient and inferior. We reflect on ourselves—our backgrounds, experiences, and values—and the ways in which our personal histories, languages, cultures, identities, and experiences affect who we are, how we interact with others, and how we live our lives in the South. We use these reflections to extend our understandings of stories of others in literary or theoretical texts regarding various experiences endured in the South such as migration, displacement, slavery, resistance, difference, spirituality, race, gender, class, place, and other forms of oppression.

Maxine, you continue to shine in a galaxy of public intellectual stars and inspire generations of educational researchers to soar into life in schools, communities, and neighborhoods; engage in highly contested forms of inquiry; transcend boundaries; raise challenging questions; transgress orthodoxy and dogma; and work with underrepresented or disenfranchised individuals and groups to build a long-term and heartfelt participatory movement to promote a more balanced and equitable human condition. Such a human condition embodies the cultural, linguistic, and ecological diversity, plurality, and complexity of individuals, groups, tribes, and societies that flood with wide-awakening beams of cultural exchanges and capacities that sustain intellectual, emotional, moral, and spiritual existence of worth, justice, and possibility.

—Ming Fang He

Living Beyond Walls

Robert Lake

These are the good old days.

—Carly Simon, "Anticipation"

Dear Maxine,

Before you could give the keynote address at the 54th Annual Conference of the International Linguistics Association last spring, we had to find a way to get you and your wheelchair down several steep steps that led to an auditorium stage. As I lowered you down the steps backwards in your wheelchair, I am sure you must have wondered if I was the right person for the job as we both kept our precarious momentum. The simple fact that you would not be deterred from sharing your remarks that day, in spite of your physical limitations, provided me with a vivid example of how I have come to view your life as an expression of living beyond walls.

I was first introduced to your work when I applied for doctoral studies at Georgia Southern University. As part of the entrance exam for their program, each applicant had to read and write reflectively on a chapter from *Releasing the Imagination* (Greene, 1995b). From this introduction onward, your writing served to awaken me to many new dimensions of imagination, so much so that my dissertation several years later was called *"A Curriculum of Imagination Beyond Walls of Standardization."* At present, I teach social foundations of education and I am very pleased to know that you also taught this subject for many years.

But just for a moment, let's talk more about walls. Just out of curiosity, I counted the number of times you use several words in *The Dialectic of Freedom* (1988). You refer to "walls" 10 times, "obstacles" 24 times and "barriers" 9 times. Naming limitations of every kind and then resolving to be your own agent in moving beyond them is a theme that occurs repeatedly in your writing. In your philosophy, freedom *starts* by naming obstacles, yet some people are so "afraid of acknowledging structures, they can scarcely think of breaking through them to create others, to transform" (p. 20).

In this present time of crisis on many fronts, there are barriers are too numerous to name. But two of them immediately come to mind that your ideas about personal and social imagination have helped me to either break through or transcend. The distinction between *breaking through* and *transcending* comes from the story you talk about in the documentary *Exclusions and Awakenings* (Hancock, 2001), in which you differentiate between things we can't change and ways that people "lock themselves in more than they have to." In the space where these two aspects overlap, imagination helps us "choose the possible against the limits." I can, for example, strongly relate to your story of making the most of the hours that your daughter was in school by choosing the only courses that were available to you during that time, which happened to be in the field of education.

Ten years ago, my family and I moved to Georgia to help care for my wife's very sick father. The only reputable doctoral program within 250 miles of where we live that I could still attend while helping care for my family was at Georgia Southern University, in the field of curriculum studies. As someone who wanted to continue working in the field of teaching English as a second language, this was not the area I would have chosen. But that changed as I had time to read and ponder what you and others had to say about imagination and aesthetic education. My physical circumstances have not changed, but I have found a *transcendent* dwelling place, rich with meaning, possibility, truth and beauty in a way that I have never known before.

I now cherish your idea of "living to our own mortality ... because you enjoy what there is to enjoy more and not less" (in Hancock, 2001). To me this means living in such a way that we are fully attuned and engaged in the present instead of being preoccupied with the finished past or the unknown future, like someone *doing time* instead of living. There is so much to enjoy in the present when we are not obsessed with the next big event in our future or with the past, like Miss Havisham in Dickens's *Great Expectations*, who wore her faded wedding dress for many, many years and surrounded herself with clocks that were stopped at 20 minutes to 9:00.

As we allow ourselves to wonder, we might be able to understand what Eisner means when he says that "there is more beauty in a rock than any of us is likely to discover in a lifetime" (2002, p. 85). I thank you for continually calling us to attend to the aesthetic present in a time when so much of our culture is focused on the anesthetic.

Another wall you have helped me to *break through* might be called abstraction between the self and the "other." All too often in what has been called multicultural education, one form of essentialism is traded for another, through abstraction and generalization that fails to challenge the invisible norm of whiteness. An example of how this happens comes from curricular materials that lump ethnicities all together in broad stereotypical descriptions. For instance, when people say that all Asians are really good at math or that Scandinavian men don't talk too much, we perpetuate essentialist notions of identity.

On the other hand, the view that identity is a completely fluid and socially constructed reality often misses the mark as well. I was reminded of this when you said in the Hancock documentary that no matter how hard you tried, you "could never be a surfer." I completely get this. Check with my wife, and she will confirm that Frankenstein would make a better tango dancer than me for sure.

Your work helped me break through this false dichotomy by emphasizing the importance of knowing the personal lived experience of others. You state this so clearly in your work: "Without some knowledge of connective details a fearful oversimplification takes over in the blankness; we see only [Russia], [student movement][ethnic minorities]" (Greene, 1995b, p. 95). This was made even clearer to me when on the same page you quoted from the Talk of the Town section of the *New Yorker* (1989):

> Ambiguous and unpredictable, details undermine ideology...If you let in the details of some aspect of life, you almost have to allow that aspect to be what it really is rather than what you want or need it to be.... resisting details is usually an expression of xenophobia. (p. 23)

Thank you for your consistent example of welcoming details, and of resisting what the artistic scientist Bob Miller calls "hardening of the categories" (in Cole, 2003, p. 180). I think that condition is at least as deadly as hardened artery walls.

With love, much respect and immense gratitude,
—Robert Lake

The Consciousness of Possibility

SUSAN MAYER

To recognize the role of perspective and vantage point, to recognize at the same time that there are always multiple perspectives and multiple vantage points, is to recognize that no accounting, disciplinary or otherwise, can ever be finished or complete. There is always more. There is always possibility. And this is where the space opens for the pursuit of freedom.

—Maxine Greene, *The Dialectic of Freedom*

Dear Dr. Greene,

I closed an early paper of mine with words of yours that spoke of consciousness as "embodied," as "thrusting into the lived and perceived," and as opening "out to the common" (Greene, 1988, pp. 20–21; Mayer, 2004). For me, those words carried a personal phenomenal knowing into the living spaces within schools, where democracy is practiced and learned.

I had learned something about embodied knowledge from Eleanor Duckworth years earlier, tracking the moon in relation to the world around me, cobbling meaning together from within (Duckworth, 2006). I had seen how hard people think when you let them think for themselves and how long they will continue when you attend closely to their emerging thoughts and understandings. I eventually felt moved to theorize the depth and the draw of that kind of learning and to justify my conviction that such experiences belong in every classroom.

The Dialectic of Freedom (1988) seemed to dwell within the unbounded space I sought to map, portraying insights that touched on my purposes. The text told of those who had drawn the world by their own lights and whose struggles had set the stage for my own. Naturally, I saw such liberties as the key to luring disaffected students into committed relationships with schools. The freedoms to think and to decide define democracy and provide its power.

Dewey spoke of democracy's hopes and challenges in the lofty language he inherited. He expected so much from the new cultural forms and means that were to call America's diverse souls toward a shared set of meanings (Dewey, 1944). As a modern white man, Dewey had involved himself with the nurturing of the young, entering traditionally female spaces, yet had largely neglected the racial tragedies and turmoil of his time.

Nonetheless, we must begin and end with the commitments Dewey named. I admire your clear regard for the truth to be found in Dewey, and value you as an elder who has breathed her own life into those commitments and so presents them as all the more convincing to me. Your words, such as these below, suggest that while you appreciate the barriers to instituting the daring shifts our schools require, you do not shy away from the obvious need to get on with the project.

> It is through education that preferences may be released, languages learned, intelligences developed, perspectives opened, possibilities disclosed. I do not need to say again how seldom this occurs today in our technicized, privatized, consumerist time. (Greene, 1988, p. 12)

Your quote at the top of this letter implicates the uncertainty that sustains freedom and, in doing so, reaffirms my own efforts to complicate the queries and claims that are entertained in classrooms. We must learn to abide this generative flux and cultivate a willingness to imagine disruptive possibilities.

In beginning your history of freedom with the thoughts of Jefferson and extending through those of Sartre, you situate contemporary conceptions of freedom within their historical conditions. In dwelling upon Sartre's insistence that freedom is only possible in a resistant world, you suggest the deliberative and critical capacities that democratic schools must foster. In short, you remind us that it takes work to achieve freedom:

This book is in no sense the first to try to reawaken the consciousness of possibility. It will not be the first to seek a vision of education that brings together the need for wide-awakeness with the hunger for community, the desire to know with the wish to understand, the desire to feel with the passion to see . . . Confronting a void, confronting nothingness, we may be able to empower the young to create and re-create a common world—and, in cherishing it, in renewing it, discover what it signifies to be free. (1988, p. 23)

You have raised realities that went missing in Dewey and that continue to represent this nation's most profound and persistent challenges. In citing Robert Reich's distinction between the appeals Franklin D. Roosevelt made to national "solidarity" and the appeals Lyndon B. Johnson made, three decades later, to middle- and upper-class "altruism" (1988, p. 50), you have pointed to the work that remains: achieving a felt solidarity with those who, due to their historic oppression and marginalization, choose not to align themselves with any vision that does not recognize and address their lived experience.

Like you, like Dewey, I do not see where this project begins if not in schools. If we cannot learn how to open spaces for the disenfranchised—particularly African American boys and men, who have always been as irrationally feared in schools as elsewhere—to see where their thoughts, desires, and experiences connect to the public interests that schools are meant to represent, I cannot see how America, as a hope and a vision, can advance.

Thank you for carrying forward the hopes and commitments that the greatest in our field have always held dear. Your language has helped me find mine.

—Susan Mayer

Imagining Peace, Nonviolence, and the Life of the Mind

Rikki Asher

We cannot always change the physical conditions of our lives, but we can transform our perception of the opportunities they offer and the obstacles they set before us.

—S. McNiff, *Art Heals*

Dear Maxine,

I was thinking of a former student and wanted to share this with you. Joe (not his real name) was an average 10th grader who was well liked, self-confident, and a star ballplayer. On the way home from a party one evening, he was fatally shot. Classmates wanted to honor his memory in a meaningful way. Fifteen sophomores in my Family Group organized, planned, designed, and painted a memorial entitled *The Mural of Peace and Non-Violence*. The time was the 1980s. The place was the South Bronx, at Bronx Regional High School. The school was located opposite abandoned buildings that doubled as crack houses. Members of the school's community believed that Joe was a victim, of a society that was not allowing young people to grow up in full and healthy ways, of a society that allowed poor education, poor housing, unemployment, and racism to foster lives lost in drugs and without hope.

I was the art teacher; Steve Shreefter taught Social Studies; Candy Systra, English; and Mark Weiss was the principal. As a muralist, I know the power of a work of public art, and I suggested that the class create a memorial mural. The group had initial doubts and little enthusiasm. "What's a mural?" they asked. After a few days of discussion and studying historically significant murals, the entire class agreed to try. They came up with the theme of nonviolence. The more they researched, the more they wanted to incorporate peace into the theme, to build peace and nonviolence into their own lives by talking about them, learning about the history of nonviolence in the United States, and drawing pictures of the people they studied, like Rosa Parks, Martin Luther King, and Gandhi. Eventually, each class member transformed feelings of grief, frustration, anger, and despair at such a tragedy into a constructive and caring expression of hope. One student videotaped the entire process.

You may recall sitting in on my presentation of this mural video at a national art education conference in Atlanta, Georgia. During the question-and-answer period, a man in the audience got angry and asked me what good the project had done for the students' future and how many of them went to college. You stood up and said you were more interested in how many of them were "moved out of their own feeling of hopelessness and are able to see that something came out of their creativity and imagination that will be part of this community and their lives for a long time." Everyone applauded. We left the room together, talking about murals and the students.

Since then, there have been many times when your guidance, inspiration, and belief in the possibilities of learning through the arts have influenced my own teaching. Just last spring you were the inspiration for a mural that graduate art education students painted entitled *The Life of the Mind*. At the mural's dedication, the class read excerpts from your essays and the work of Hannah Arendt and Thich Nat Hahn. The choice to include Arendt's discussion of the mind was inspired by your writing and discussions you and I have had about art and the life experiences of young people.

Unfortunately, you were unable to attend the dedication. In an e-mail message, you wrote:

> I am deeply sorry that a suddenly disabled leg makes it impossible for me to deliver the dedication of the Mural Project which I wrote with regard and enthusiasm and anticipation, because I believe it to be a landmark. I was told the reading should take 15 minutes and I HOPE WON'T BE boring or a chore. With real regret, I am sincerely, Maxine Greene.

Your touching speech was read by my colleague, Dr. Phil Anderson:

> I am most honored to be asked to speak at this dedication, in part because it constitutes the expansion of public space at Queens College and does so by means of a communal work of art. The public space is where people come together to act upon their freedom reflectively, collaboratively, imaginatively and to leave the way open to untapped possibility. The first time I met the lead muralist Rikki Asher, she was a teacher at Bronx Regional High School at the time of one of Rosa Parks' visits to New York and she and her students made a mural for the principal's door showing Parks' bus with a student in each window. Those were the beginnings of a trajectory as Professor Asher and her fellow explorers entered the life of the mind. Most of us are aware that the mind is a function of our physical selves and one of the ways of dealing with and interpreting the natural and human environment. Crucial to the making of choices and the creation of identity, "mind" cannot be empirically or logically defined. It can be sustained among the "voices of silence" which might after all mark some dimension of the arts and open new spaces at Queens.

You have always been an inspiration, a mentor, and a friend who has taught me about the power of the imagination to effect social change. Thank you, Maxine.

> With love and gratitude,
> —Rikki Asher

On Being Wider-Awake in the World

KATHY HYTTEN

True philosophy consists in relearning how to look at the world.
—M. Merleau-Ponty, *The Phenomenology of Perception*

Dear Maxine,

While we have only ever met in passing, as a woman doing work in philosophy of education, I can't help but have been deeply moved by your trailblazing work. Studying philosophy as an undergraduate, I became increasingly disenchanted with the abstract, distant, cold, and often seemingly irrelevant style of many philosophers. I came to philosophy of education because it was a space where philosophy impacted how we actually live our lives, and the choices we make for ourselves and our children.

Reading your work in graduate school many years ago, I was inspired to rethink philosophy, to see it as a place for passion, imagination, hope, vision, possibility, and even joy. Every time I picked up one of your writings, I saw the world differently. I still do. I know many of my students feel the same way. In fact, not too long ago, one of my doctoral students framed a quote of yours as a gift for me when he graduated: "My concern is what can be done by means of education to enable people to transcend their private terrors and act together to give freedom a concrete existence in their lives" (Greene, 1975, p. 4). You inspire us to imagine a more just, fulfilling, and humane world, where individuals can grow and flourish amid diverse, fluid, and welcoming democratic communities. You also constantly remind us of what it means to be wide awake, to recognize that we can indeed see beyond what sometimes seems inevitable and unchanging, that a better world is within our grasp.

While there are so many places to enter your work, I find myself returning to your 1986 *Harvard Educational Review* essay, "In Search of a Critical Pedagogy," again and again. There, you provided an alternative history of critical pedagogy, one that drew on different memories and our unique U.S. heritage. I don't think I really understood critical pedagogy until I saw people like John Dewey, Myles Horton, Elizabeth Peabody, Henry David Thoreau, Martin Luther King, Jane Addams, and W.E.B. DuBois as central to its history and to how we bring education for critical consciousness to life in our present. In contrast to the all-too-common language of doom and despair that often surrounds critical pedagogy, you crafted a genuine language of possibility. At the same time, you also bemoaned the "palpably

deficient" world you saw around you. It seems likely that you were responding to the initial rise of neoliberal ideology, marked by smaller government, diminished social services, extensive privatization, and the growing
dominance of corporate interests in the global sphere. As we see now, in
schools this translates into increased standardization, diminishment of the
arts, excessive competition, widespread disengagement and apathy, and the
disturbing yet pervasive assumption that students should primarily be seen
as resources for expanding economic productivity. Sadly, we still see many
"people living under a weight, a nameless inertial mass," (Greene, 1986,
p. 427) struggling to find a meaningful place in the world.

Perhaps one of the most enduring legacies of your work is that no matter how overwhelmed I can feel by the weight of the world, by the "unwar-
ranted inequities, shattered communities, [and] unfulfilled lives," (1986,
p. 439) your words always give me hope. You inspire me to move beyond
complacency and despair, to collaborate with others, to enter new conversations, to be creatively activist, and to embody my dreams for a better world
in my everyday actions. Moreover, you remind me to support my students
and colleagues on this journey as well. In your words, "to engage with our
students as persons is to affirm our own incompleteness, our consciousness
of spaces still to be explored, desires still to be tapped, possibilities still to be
opened and pursued" (p. 440). My students invariably mention your ideas
as among the most memorable at the end of each semester.

Among the many lessons I learned in reading your work is how to do
engaged philosophy, including how to respond to local, national, and global
challenges. In my current work, I am studying the relationship between
globalization and education, trying to imagine a more compassionate and
democratic globalized world. From your model of embodied scholarship,
I have learned to disrupt taken-for-granted assumptions about the world,
to see where they come from and what other possibilities exist. In terms of
globalization, there are many such assumptions that need disrupting and
that you allude to throughout your work: Capitalism is the one best system.
Success should be measured primarily through economic measures. Free
trade equals fair trade. Happiness comes from material acquisition. Competition is inherently good. Standardization is necessary for progress.

I have also learned to ask better questions about global realities and
what it means to live a "good life" in a globalized world. You remind me
that there are many scholars, activists, poets, artists, and writers in our history who have fought tirelessly for justice and equity, and who have resisted
materialism, conformity, and barriers to freedom. I know we need to remember these traditions and use them as resources in our current efforts.

Finally, from you I have learned the power of the arts in awakening
imagination and visions of possibility. I am not sure I would feel as confident

as I do using visual representations, movies, music, drawings, images, and performances in the classroom if it were not for your tireless efforts to show how important the arts are for releasing students from the confines of the given and for arousing passionate commitments to creating a more just world.

Rereading "*In Search of a Critical Pedagogy*" yet again, I am reminded that if we are to confront the problematic consequences of capitalist globalization, in terms of both the material devastation of the poor and the spiritual devastation of the affluent, we must begin by engaging these issues publicly and passionately. We must follow your lead and renew and expand conversations about suffering, injustice, community, and, ultimately, the meaning of democracy and what will enable us to achieve it. It is only through meaningful and engaged dialogue with family, students, colleagues, and neighbors and in our various communities that we can challenge hopelessness and imagine alternatives to the increasingly soulless world we seem to be creating around us.

Thank you, Maxine, for creating a body of work that I can turn to whenever I need to relearn how to look at the world, "to break with the given...to move towards what might be, what is not yet" (Greene, 1986, p. 427). While I can't speak for them, I know my students thank you, too, for your passionate and inspiring words. You have impacted more people than you can possibly know.

Warmest regards,
—Kathy Hytten

Hiding in the Text: Body and Emotion

DONALD BLUMENFELD-JONES

[M]any of us...lead one-dimensional lives...incapable of seeing the visible surfaces of the world...unlikely to frame the significant questions that move human beings to go in search of meaning, to pursue ourselves, to learn.

—Maxine Greene, *Landscapes of Learning*

The body, from which one cannot strip oneself however one tries, from which one is not freed this side of death...the Swede did not want to pass through life as a beautiful boy and a stellar first baseman, wanted instead to be a serious person...He wanted to be born something other than a physical wonder.

—Philip Roth, *American Pastoral*

Dear Maxine,

I write this letter to you in the spirit of an admiring colleague. Although we have no personal history, I have found your work illuminating over the years and I'm grateful for the opportunity to show you how you have led me to think. I admire your work in particular because there is a natural fit between us in our mutual love of the arts as a means toward the development of free, creative individuals with social imagination.

My idea of freedom stems from Martin Buber's (1958) work. He wrote that freedom is usually thought of as freedom from coercion and that the opposite of coercion is usually thought to be freedom to do whatever you want. This is a misunderstanding of freedom: the opposite pole of coercion is not free to do anything but, rather, communion, the freedom of recognizing connections with others and the world around you. Buber wrote that there are three kinds of communion that lead to freedom. There is communion with nature (recognizing that we live in nature and through nature and we must know our responsibility to nature), communion with our traditions (which provide the ground out of which we initially craft our lives and continue to provide the foil for our decisionmaking), and communion with other human beings. This last is most important: we must always recognize that freedom is set within the fact that we do not have a world in which to live except the one we are always making together.

This idea of "together" connects to Emmanuel Levinas (1969), whose work I'm sure you know. Levinas teaches that we are never alone: the ethical good life begins in recognizing and cherishing the infinite humanity of another person. We make our identity by treating the world around us as a resource for ourselves. Generally the world around us cooperates and yields to our actions. But there is this one "thing" in the world that refuses to be merely a resource, that maintains its own integrity: another person. When we come to recognize the existence of this other person (whom Levinas capitalizes as the Other), we find that the Other is more than simply another being. The categories we use to make sense of most things (what is food, what is shelter, what can support my plans?) cannot capture the Other, who never fits into any category. S/he is more than can ever be described. In this recognition, s/he becomes precious and I feel my responsibility to care for her/him. Ethics is born in this moment, and that is what is freeing: free from simply using the world around me and beginning to fully live in the world.

I think your focus on freedom is parallel; you focus on "being more" (Greene, 1988, p. 7), clearing away the blockages to greater self-determination and self-understanding. Although this seems different from Buber and Levinas, who focus on others, your work is parallel in so many ways, as it flows from the situated self to the "other." Our approaches to freedom share two other dimensions. First, both Levinas and Buber acknowledge that we begin alone, and for Buber, we only occasionally experience connection with another that transcends our self-interest. You, too, reach for that transcendence of self and often do it through encounters with the arts. Second, we both acknowledge that the emotions and the body are profoundly important to freedom. The emotions a person feels are felt in the body and are neither right nor wrong but are only "there." Emotions come from somewhere and guide us somewhere and may, of course, interfere with the connection we can have. To deal with how you feel, to live through the feelings, to understand them, this is the way to confront our blockages to freedom. Our bodies, the space and viscera of our emotions, are the places where we can notice ourselves as actually physically living in the world and are the locations for expanding into greater potentials of humanity through our connecting with others. That is, when we are physically and emotionally present to other people and the world around us through our bodies, we begin to experience the immediacy of connection or communion that is freedom.

You recognized this before others recognized it, although, in your writing, the body and emotions hide in secret places. When I started this letter I thought I would find how you had ignored the body and emotions; I could use this as a launching point for proposing work with the body and emotions. But then I discovered, as those who delve deeply into your work will always discover, that you have already presaged this move in moments of your work. You provided (in the above opening quote) a new critique by already seeing places where there are difficulties and accounting for them.

So what is the new work lurking in your writing? In the above you point to a body "numb to our...bodily rhythms and sensations...incapable of seeing the visible surfaces of the world." By unnumbing the body, there is hope for meaning. We must find what that means and how we do it. I presented the Philip Roth quote above to honor your love of the arts and as an image of our old thought about the body. Roth wrote *American Pastoral* (1997) as a meditation on outsiders (Jews) who seem to "make it" because they can pass as non-Jews and marry into non-Jewish families and yet fail to really become one with their country. His character, the Swede, is a beautiful athlete who succeeds at business and marries into a Gentile family but whose daughter turns into a Vietnam War–era bomber and then disappears from their lives. It is a tragedy that, for the Swede, is connected to his body limiting who he might have been. He feels trapped by his body and how people respond to him (he is athletic and handsome). He believes that had he been able to be other than a beautiful, stunningly able body, he might have prevented tragedy in his life. In Western society we are taught to hate our bodies because only the mind is of value. From you we have, instead of loathing the body, a coming to life (unnumbing), coming to know through the body as well as the mind. And even though you connect unnumbing with seeing (a Western metaphor for the mind), you do bring the body into view and push us forward. You reveal the narrowness of our self-understanding. Is it to be ever our fate to not have a body worthy of the place it already holds (we are not *Donovan's Brain*—that 1950s film in which a brain floats in a tank and controls others).

You have, in those few small phrases in the above quote, opened up the world. You have opened up the world, and had you not done what you have done so well, the world would be a constricted place for us indeed. So it is not the developed work that I praise. It is the continuing potential that you provide so that even now your work moves us forward.

Thank you for who you have been and who, through your work, you will always be.

With great esteem,
—Donald

We Who Are Not Yet

JENNIFER MILAM

Dear Maxine,

As I thought about what I would write to you in this letter, I was again and again taken back to my first reading of your introduction in *Releasing the Imagination* (1995). I returned to the text—riddled with pencil markings, highlights, and notes in the margins—to discover again what I believe to be one of your most incredible statements: the one that I believe makes my work, and that of so many other scholars in our field, real, important, and so necessarily hopeful. Fifteen years ago, you wrote:

> One of the reasons I have come to concentrate on imagination as a means through which we can assemble a coherent world is that imagination is what, above all, makes empathy possible. It is what enables us to cross the empty spaces between ourselves and those we have called "other" . . . of all our cognitive capacities, imagination is the one that permits us to give credence to alternative realities. It allows us to break with the taken for granted, to set aside familiar distinctions and definitions. (1995b, p. 3)

Imagination, framed in this way, allows us the freedom to envision a different world—perhaps (and hopefully) a better world, but certainly something different—to imagine an "as if" world, in a world that is "deficient."

I am a woman, a mother, a teacher, a scholar, and a critical being. I find myself disenchanted and less than encouraged with the way things are in education. I feel the constant nagging of my never-satisfied intellect and unanswered questions, whims of visceral discomfort and anger, and yet I remain forever an optimist—longing for better, for more, for equity, for peace, and for love for all, knowing the eminent and inescapable disappointment of dreams deferred. Your work, your reimagining of imagination, Maxine, suggests that not only *must* we do better, but that we *can* do better. We must only free ourselves from the "nightmare that is the present" (Pinar, 2004) and allow ourselves to imagine, to dream, and to conceptualize something beyond it. As you wrote, it is only when we "think" of better classrooms and stronger, healthier communities that we can really understand the inadequacies and consequences of deficient schools and societies.

Maxine, your life and your work in the realm of the imagination encourage me to ponder a world where we are all different but none of us is oppressed (or oppresses others) through the social scripts and bias that envelope us today and have for the entirety of our past. You write that you employ a mode of utopian thinking, but I do not believe your utopia is impracticable. Perhaps this utopia—both a real and an imaginary place—is a place not where we all "get along" or remain compliant; instead, it could be a dynamic, engaged society that recognizes its possibilities and works tirelessly to realize and nurture the potential of all its peoples.

It is there that I see classrooms where teachers understand, appreciate, and nurture differences, both between and among themselves and their students. I envision curriculum that is responsive to all students all year long, not only on celebratory holidays or during a month marked by superficial historical remembrance. In this moment, the content and context of what and how children learn are more important than the teacher. I visualize a society where women are free of patriarchal oppressions and condescending assumptions and men are respected for the complexity of their spiritual, parental, and emotional natures. I hope for a world where my children, all children, will grow, learn, and love, free of hatred, violence, and ecological destruction. I want them to see green trees, walk barefoot on a beach, and hold their own children close in quiet moments of peace. I wish for a human understanding that the greatest of all gifts is to give love and be loved in return, regardless of gender or sexual orientation. In short, I want all of us the world over, regardless of socioeconomic status or ethnic origin, to be who we are not yet—to break free, to leap, and to question.

And so, Maxine, it is here that I, that we, say thank you. Thank you for your time. Thank you for your thoughtfulness. Thank you for living a public life as an intellectual. Thank you for challenging us. Thank you for writing. Thank you for being vulnerable. Thank you for being strong. Thank you for putting into words the call of our souls, the longing of our hearts, and our deepest desires for hopefulness and love. Thank you for challenging us to *choose* to use our imaginations, our courage, and our life to transform.

The still unfinished, always imagining,
—Jenn Milam

Confronting Exclusion and Racism

JoAnn Phillion

We need to keep the anxious faces of new immigrants in mind. What would it take to understand, to offer help, to open possibilities? Does it not take some intentional action to confront exclusion and racism in a meaningful way?
—Maxine Greene, personal communication, 1999

Dearest Maxine,

It is with pleasure that I write this letter to you. In the 10 years that have passed since you served as external examiner for my dissertation and wrote two dense pages of comments to me, filled with questions such as those in the excerpt above, your scholarship has been pivotal to my teaching and thinking. The questions you posed in my exam commentary and in the "conversation" at the defense have guided my work all these years. The rich discussion you initiated tackled broad aspects of multiculturalism globally and whether or not it was possible to pursue these ideas when racism pervades societies. I was nervous about engaging in the conversation with you, but so proud that it came out of my work.

The questions you posed have guided my undergraduate teaching with the predominantly white pre-service teachers I work with in Indiana. My goal is that my students engage with minority students; that they create opportunities for success for students in their care; that they accept these students as full members of classroom communities; that they understand, offer help, open possibilities; and that they accept the challenge that you posed at my defense: to be actively engaged in confronting exclusion and racism in classrooms, schools, and communities.

Your scholarship has also impacted my graduate teaching. It is difficult for me to imagine where I would start my multicultural education class if I did not have your 1993 article, *The Passions of Pluralism: Multiculturalism and the Expanding Community* (1993b), to set the tone for the course. What would I do without your 1995 book, *Releasing the Imagination*, to create a rational for using literature, memoir, poetry, music, art, and film in the class? I recall a conversation with you at an AERA meeting in which you wondered how we can use works such as Toni Morrison's *The Bluest Eye* without reinforcing stereotypes. Your question still sticks with me.

While I had goals of engendering a form of active empathy in my students through reading and discussing the book, I no longer use it; the issues it raised always seemed too difficult for me to handle. Your question of "intentional action" to confront exclusion and racism has driven not only my teaching, but also my research and my life, especially as I work with diverse graduate students from around the globe. Most of my graduate students are engaged in research with minority students and families; most are concerned with doing more than simply publishing and obtaining a position in a university; most want to make a difference in their communities. They deal with questions about what to do, how to be, on a daily basis. More and more of my students engage in work that confronts exclusion and racism in ways I did not in my early work.

While your scholarship has been important to me, your lived experiences have also deeply impacted my thinking and my way of being. Your personal life story of marginalization in the academy—as a woman, as a Jew, as an intellectual—provides a touchstone for exploring exclusion today. It is you as a person who have made the biggest impact on me.

I recall a session at one of my early AERA meetings in San Diego in 1998. I had written you a letter to ask you to be on a panel. Amazingly, you had written back with a home telephone number and a time to call you. I called you; you were cooking dinner—it all seemed so ordinary— weren't you supposed to be contemplating great philosophical thoughts? You agreed to be the discussant for the panel. Someone whom I had thought of as an icon was a real person who agreed to be at graduate students' sessions!

Ming Fang He and I arranged to meet you earlier to escort you to the session. We had a lovely lunch with you in a quiet restaurant; people stopped by to say hello; you were interrupted every few minutes and barely had a chance to eat! I have never seen anything like what I experienced after lunch: there was a mass parting of the crowds as we went through the hallways and people stopped to greet you, shake hands, give you a kiss on the cheek, or just touch you and smile. You knew so many of them; you recalled so many names and so many previous encounters. When we got to the room assigned for the session, about 20 minutes early, it was already packed, with people on the floor, against the walls, and oozing out of the room into an already crowded corridor. Years later, people would tell me that was one of the best AERA sessions they attended!

Maxine, I have so many stories about you! Going back further in time to what I think was my first AERA meeting, you gave a keynote address for the SIG* *Research on Women in Education*. Your topic was teacher education. The first thing you discussed was homelessness. You moved from that to the environment. From there, you continued to build on issues that were, and are, of pressing concern globally. For you, they were all part of teacher education. That was the moment when I learned how broad and deep the landscape of teaching is, when I discovered that it is our responsibility as teacher educators to speak to the big issues, the seemingly irreconcilable issues, to speak with passion and commitment.

You have taught me a lot, Maxine; you are my teacher, my guide, and my inspiration.

With love,
—JoAnn Phillion

Daring to Dare: Teaching for Wide-Awakeness

PAMELA K. SMITH

Dear Maxine,

As an experienced teacher in an urban setting, I thought that I had a definitive understanding of what and how my students in British literature and composition should learn. However, I recognized boredom, disconnectedness, and a seeming unwillingness from students to connect the curriculum to their lived experiences.

Fortunately, my perception of myself, my students, and what it means to teach authentically changed when I read your book *Landscapes of Learning* (1978). I began to wake, and as I slowly came to consciousness, my teaching underwent a fundamental shift.

Good teaching is difficult in that, as you explain in *Teacher as Stranger*, it is of paramount importance for teachers to confront what it is that we think is necessary to know. The world is, as you say, chaotic and not predetermined; the century past and the one just beginning testify to the uncertainty and confusion of life.

---

*Special Interest Group.

In the world of the present, you stand firm in your belief that dependence upon outside accountability measures is unnecessary. You taught many of us to see that it is not enough to ask only ourselves the existential question of who we believe ourselves to be. Rather, it is imperative for us to consider as well the importance of knowing our students and acknowledging the unique backgrounds that will help to constitute how they view themselves, how we have come to understand them, and how we can work together to create meaning in our worlds. Then we can begin to work with the subject matter we teach in ways that question the marginalization of subordinate groups, hierarchization of content areas that privilege some areas while discounting others, and protect the arts as the "connecting links" that authenticate our work.

We grow when we share our stories. In this sense, we need to talk about successes, question our practices, study our worlds, and reexamine our practices to ensure that we reflect a sense of wide-awakeness. You have done this during your Sunday salons. When you invite people to come to your New York City apartment for discussions generated by the study of art and literature, you set the stage for authentic dialogue that can move in so many diverse directions. You create an enervating environment for rethinking philosophical positions and possible actions that can follow.

Your work moved me to question what had been presented as objective fact. In this sense, becoming wide-awake meant considering how my prior teaching practices had reified dominant ideologies and reproduced the lives students had been assigned by traditional schooling.

During my awakening, I began to question how my understandings of what constituted good art represented a dominantly perennialist mode of thought. I rewrote my English IV course. During the first semester, my students and I studied the traditional canon of British literature, beginning with *Beowulf* and continuing to the moderns. Though I was teaching the dominant code of what counts in literature, I began to do so in a far more discursive manner. I started by teaching my students the language of philosophy so that they could begin to look at the works intensively. They learned how to focus on metaphysics, epistemology, and axiology, and they also came to understand that the meaning of a text cannot be determined through a one-way conversation. As our work developed, their voices grew stronger, their opinions were situated in the logical frames of their own experiences, and their contextual frames of reference grew.

We covered the material in the canonical texts so that none of the students would be denied access to the cultural capital inherent in such study. In too many settings, some students have privilege to literature and art that can move them to more critical thought while others are limited to technical language that limits their worldviews and consigns them to marginalized positions in their lives.

As you have taught, beginning to move through the world in a conscious manner is an individual process guided by group activity. As the students took more responsibility for contributing to their class content, they became active learners. They respected themselves as critical intellectuals, rather than seeing themselves as passive information receptacles.

Our last project for the year was student designed and constructed. Each student chose a form of art that reflected the person they thought themselves to be and opened their work to class discussion.

Our classroom became a hub for the kind of discussion and debate that resembled the interactions that occur in your Sunday salons. Soon, other students became aware of the interactions occurring in the class, and they found a way to join us. We dared to do the different, and we celebrated our community.

I entered into the above undertaking understanding that censure could result. However, having studied your work, I knew that to do less would not only function as a disservice to me as a critical intellectual but also deny my students full access to possibility.

Art was the medium through which we looked at our own existences and the creation of meaning. Today, we inhabit an educational arena in which arts are being removed from the curriculum. We are told that budgets will not support them. My cynical side asks if this is true, or if the arts face removal because they represent human diversity.

Education is a class war, so I'll close with reminiscences of Picasso's *Guernica*, which shows what a government can do to its own people. In April 1937, during the Spanish Civil War, Spanish Nationalist forces bombed the Basque country in Northern Spain, without concern for the village of Guernica's residents.

This painting causes dissonance and demands reexamination. Congruently, you have taught us that when educators acquiesce to the educational practices of an accountability movement that deintellectualizes us, we often feel the same sort of disruption and dissonance. Your teaching us to question means that we will look at these moments with eyes that are fully open.

Thank you for your courage and strength.

Sincerely,
—Pamela K. Smith

Not Turning Away

JULIE SEARLE

Music never stops; it is we who turn away.
—Cage, *Composition in Retrospect*

Dear Maxine,

Though we have not met, your writing has kept me company for 10 years of teaching and living. Initially, I had serious doubts about becoming a full-time public school teacher. At 41, I had a degree in poetry, three daughters, and years of experience doing art with children in the community. Would life in the classroom revolve around coercion and compliance? Would there be room for invention, dialogue, new ways of seeing? I chose a credential program at Mills College that I'd heard had inspired professors and a focus on urban schools. During that 1st year, I read a piece of yours about aesthetic education that was like a letter from a wise and passionate teacher, a person who thought deeply and knew that freedom and education belong together. Now I've been given a chance to offer my thanks.

What I have loved in your writing is the abiding warmth behind the intellectual push, the voice that is critical but not judgmental, both fiercely discerning and endlessly inquiring. I have always hated being a beginner, but embracing life as a teacher makes it clear that there is no more interesting point of engagement than the beginning. The vanity of merely "being successful" as a teacher cannot compare with the satisfaction of living large, taking risks, and paying attention. In light of the idea of being a beginner, of not turning away from the wildly uncertain and compelling truth of daily life, I started the practice of giving myself the writing assignments I gave my students. How could I invite the bravest possible writing from middle school students if I did not also grapple with what I needed most to say? I gave us all the assignment to write about someone who mattered a lot to you but was no longer in your life. I wrote a page about my grandmother, an orphan, a rebel, a person who loved the underdog and had worked on the psychiatric ward at the city-run hospital. I wrote about how she threw her slippers at the television when politicians she didn't trust appeared, and about how she always wore gloves when she drove. The students wrote about great-aunts and neighbors they'd moved away from, aged family dogs and ancestors they had never met in other countries. One student whose mother had died wrote simply of his grandmother, "the second person ever to hold me." As the students read their pieces, the classroom hummed like a live wire.

The expansive and inclusive way you have of pulling in a line of poetry, a reference to a film or conversation is a model for me of what it means to be an engaged teacher and thinker. The message, the example, is about using everything you've got. The artist's practice of making a contour drawing of her own shoe, the poet's understanding that everything is grist for the mill—these are ways of looking, making, forming connections and ideas that are available to all students on any given day even within the classroom walls. How can we think metaphorically about the blue recycling bin that holds the tight, tight ball of a failed test as well as the torn off message that asks, "Do you still like him?" What will happen if we challenge ourselves to write about the familiar corner store? Or what if we try writing long-winded titles, such as Chinese poets wrote in the Middle Ages, as we look out the classroom window at wheeling gulls?

The relentless push for being awake that your writing embodies for me is essential to the vitality of my teaching life. Laden with the district-mandated history text with its cluttered pages and highlighted vocabulary, it is easy to forget why my students and I have gathered in a classroom together. I have to take a deep breath and remember that we are here to discuss something no less powerful than the wretchedness and possibilities of the human condition. Plague and angels. Gunpowder that was once packed into the hollows of bamboo for celebrations. Beccaria's thoughts about justice. Salt and greed. A student who has been in 20 different kinds of trouble this year suddenly observes that a poster of ancient Arabic calligraphy looks like the graffiti he covers his papers with. We have to use all sources, and come at all of this from where we are.

Your references to personal loss remind me that fearlessness comes from encountering fear, that open-hearted teaching truly demands an open heart. Not long before my husband died of cancer, he wrote to me about how he saw me as a teacher who takes on challenges with imagination. Though he could have been referring to his own condition, he chose to write to about the context of teaching. He wrote, "Even with the hardest things to face, there is something to wonder about, something to keep moving with. A perspective, a question, a way in. What can this difficulty reveal better than anything else possibly could?" Being curious, attending to what is before us and around us, is the great antidote to despair.

I have also loved your celebration of the human capacity to grow through work, rearranging language using every tool we've got to say what we mean. As students play with metaphor or work with great focus on specificity of language, as they take the time to look closer, they move toward the deep satisfaction that comes from persisting with something that matters. One day we talk about how at times the beginning or end of a draft turns out to be just a flat explanation, while what we want to keep working at is the beating heart at the center of the writing. A student writes:

> I spend a day
> Making a raft
> I know it will not last
> In this devil stream.
> But still I try
> For the love of my life.

The daily practice of pushing ourselves to notice, to try something new, to ask a different question, makes the classroom a place of possibility, even on a murky day that seems full of discord and confusion.

Thank you for continuing to turn toward the music, listening to poets, philosophers, teachers, cabdrivers, students, and singers. Through your deeply generous writing and speaking, you have offered to me both sustenance and a summons.

With affectionate thanks,
—Julie Searle

Free People Need Public Spaces

DEBORAH MEIER

Dear Maxine,

We've been planning lunch together for too long. It's time for us to do it. But, face to face, it'll be harder to say some of the things I want to say to you. I'm always in a better position for conversing with others when I know that someone is your admirer. It makes it unnecessary to ask them as many irrelevant questions. It sets a kind of platform upon which we stand together. I just open my file of "Maxine's maxims" and can start from there. It so happens that "there" is almost endless.

It took me time to read your work thoroughly. I always was nervous about philosophy, and while I loved to argue about it, I couldn't stay on that "level" of discourse long enough. But there came a moment when I could connect the wonderful phrases, paragraphs, and accounts you presented with my own experience—as a woman and as a teacher.

Your particular intensely focused interest in the teaching side of life, the schooling of the young, was also a reassurance to me, who entered teaching thinking of it as "woman's work" in the old sense of that word: beneath the serious attention of smart people.

You reawakened my first passion and study: history. Connecting Jefferson and Dewey was not my first inclination, but I reread "The American Paradox" in *The Dialectic of Freedom* (1988) with fascination recently, as I pondered the connection between the "small schools" idea and Jefferson's distrust of centralized power. America's early love affairs with both small, self-governing community and individualism help set the stage. I often feel agonizingly stretched between these, and conscious that some concerns require that "small community" (p. 29) to stretch rather widely. Can such trade-offs and tensions be held together? I ask daily. But I am myself often on the side of libertarian individualism, and then go to other extreme in my respect for human solidarity, from wanting teachers to feel free to go their own way, and wanting a coherently packaged schoolwide curriculum and pedagogy. You remind me that they may be intertwined and inescapably inseparable. In the same book, you deepen my appreciation for the connections between the uses (and even the mere existence) of public space and the personal freedoms we cherish. A free people needs a "public"—even as too many conservatives and liberals today seem to have forgotten this.

Commenting on these seemingly "trivial" debates, you help draw us into the larger implications of the daily dilemmas we face, as teachers, parents, and citizens, by way of Hannah Arendt, Henry David Thoreau, and Milan Kundera.

Over the years, I have held a deep concern about the relegation of "play" to a lesser status in schools, as "mere play," an indulgence to rest the weary spirit from more serious endeavors. Your use of the word "imagination"—*Releasing the Imagination*—was a heady addition to my arsenal. It gave me new language for demanding that we recognize the centrality of imaginative play—both the interior, individual kind and collective, social play—which is so critical to early childhood. You gave greater strength to the work of my mentor and ally Lillian Weber, who also took such play seriously, as the distinguishing feature of our potential humanity, and thus also at the root of democracy—which rests upon such habits of openness to "the other." Being able to "imagine" the world otherwise, to see "as if" it were different, and to step into the shoes of others—if only temporarily or incompletely—were at the heart of both democracy and play. As we honor one, we must honor the other.

These days, I reread "The Continuing Search for Curriculum" and "Teaching for Openings" (in *Releasing the Imagination*) as we confront the latest reform work being imposed upon us by harried centralizers fearful of the limitations of ordinary parents and teachers. In their call for a one-size-fits-all curriculum, they dare not look at the passions and curiosities of young people and build up from there, connecting the idiosyncratic to the "academic" in ways that strengthen both. Imaginative endeavors appear inefficient, a waste of time, carrying the risk of creating dissent, not unity.

Keep writing, Maxine, and speaking out. Your voice, in the voices of those you've taught over the years, is essential to the next generation.

—Deborah Meier

Chapter Two

"In a Tune Beyond Us
and Yet Ourselves"

(Editor's note: The title of this chapter is from Stevens, 1982, p. 163.)

Unlike so many in the academy who have sought to maintain an aura of depersonalized and disembodied mystery about them, Maxine Greene has consistently adorned her teaching and scholarship within a situated context of "doing philosophy" that is akin to Dewey's rendering of the "mind as a verb." This is the reason that Maxine has been able to have such an impact on so many practitioners in the field of education, the arts, and social reform. While she continues to reach to become what she is "not yet" and refuses the "stasis and the flatness of ordinary life" (1988, p. 123), her life is a song that affirms us in our moments of "vulnerability and loss" and of seeing "the darkness," as the following letters describe.

On Not Being Directed by Optimism

NANCY LESKO

The time is out of joint.

—Jacques Derrida, *Specters of Marxism*

Dear Maxine,

Your visits to many of my curriculum classes at Teachers College over the last dozen years were opportunities to indulge students' generalized excitement and my particular delight in reconsidering your existentialist influences. On many of those occasions, you recounted your entrance into philosophy of education and your specific interest in Existentialism. My ears pricked up as you recalled your being drawn to the emphasis on the difficulties and darkness of human experiences. Dewey remained too sunny for you, and Existentialists' preoccupation with tragedy drew you in. I have often reread the chapter in *Releasing the Imagination* (1995b) where you dwell in Don DeLillo's (1986) amorphous cloud, just as I eagerly followed your connections with Pecola Breedlove in Toni Morrison's *The Bluest Eye* (1970). Negative feelings and debased situations were not ones to be quickly leapfrogged over in your practice, on the way to an upbeat message.

Sara Ahmed (2008) has written about how "happiness" directs us toward conventional lives and normal stories—how it directs us away from acerbic feminist critique, how it pushes us to go along with the norm, the accepted view, the standard joke, or the formulaic study. I'm persuaded that optimism similarly directs us toward the happy, or uplifting, ending, and a static conception of past, present, and future implicated in such optimism. Teachers and teacher educators are directed by optimism in their positions as protectors and romancers of children and youth. The optimism of education is interwoven with the future and the child.

I find echoes of your refusal to be directed by optimism in contemporary gender and sexuality studies. Lee Edelman (2004), for example, rejects stories that invoke "panoptimism" (a morphing of Foucault's panopticon into an omnipresent policing of and for optimistic feelings). Disgust, misrecognition, and ambivalence are emotions that you've acknowledged, explored, and taught about. As a visitor to curriculum classes, your ruminations on the war in Iraq, the Bush presidency, and economic practices that ignore children and inequality reminded students that you stayed bound to an out-of-jointedness, an off-balance with the commonsense ways of the city, the nation, and the world. Your teaching and writings have explored the times and spaces of "outlaw emotions" (Jaggar, 1989).

I thank you for taking my students and me into the tragic spaces of literature, art, and education. I thank you for not being afraid to linger in ambivalence, in the destabilization of order, and in ruptures of an armored life. You always addressed the difficulties of each day, week, season—difficulties that were regularly pushed to the margins of our daily consciousness and our course syllabi. Traveling with you into contemporary texts has offered phenomenological excursions few other educators have been willing to lead. In *Precarious Life* (2004), Judith Butler writes of establishing political community on the basis of vulnerability and loss; she theorizes that the capacity to be undone by wounds, by love, by loss can become the basis not only for rage, violence, and retaliation, but also for human connection. I understand her, in part, because of your pedagogical and poetic explorations of wounds, loss, confusion, and misrecognition.

Being directed by optimism constrains our understanding of humanity, of difference, otherness, desire, and, of course, learning. Being undone, misrecognizing, and becoming unrecognizable to oneself may be part of submitting to a transformation. Unknowingness, losing ourselves, misrecognizing may all be vital, and politically necessary, to becoming human. Undoing oppressive educational and social practices may simultaneously cause us to be undone. Our normal emotions, perspectives, responses, and beliefs may be undone. To write out dislike and disgust from education is to make sure we never know what about learning and teaching and knowledge will undo us.

Optimism disallows outlaw emotions, such as vulnerability, debility, and misrecognition. The surplus of affect that goes beyond the sociable norms of keeping the faith, reiterating stable identities, being proper, being upbeat and optimistic may be now termed hope (Puar, 2003). Thank you, Maxine, for living, excavating, obsessively revisiting and exploring the outlaw emotional terrain, the terrain of hope. As a teacher, you demonstrated reading and living with difficult ideas and texts. Your narration of phenomenological and educational dimensions of various novels and films helped us to dwell in and consider the moments of undoing and unknowing in the arts and in learning. Blanchot (1980/1995) writes that the disaster *describes*; political and social events that involve violence and hurt and death de-scribe and limit what can be said, thought, understood. You acknowledged yet refused that de-scription and used phenomenology, existentialism, and aesthetics to partially renarrate and redescribe. In your espousal of what could not readily be known, seen, or heard, your scholarship allows for "becoming beyond" what is immediately recognized as human or social (Puar, 2003, p. 216). Your writing and teaching helped students at Teachers College come to experience reality, "not as cold knowledge, but as a transformative recognition" (Gordon, 1997, pp. 7–8).

Thank you, Maxine, for your courage to pursue scenes of vulnerability, loss, and inhumanity. Thank you for your redescriptions of outlaw emotions that remind us to become beyond what has been sketched as an optimistic future by others.

With all my love,
—Nancy

Touching Heaven and Earth: Beyond Philosophy

ROSLYN ARNOLD

> But the difficulty of eradicating memories of the Twin Towers (even in
> the case of the very young) must remind us that our students too have
> a consciousness of vulnerability new in this country and, perhaps, an
> erosion of confidence in the long praised superiority of democracy.
> The young were long protected against confrontation with our nation's
> flaws, either deliberately on the part of the adults surrounding them
> or because of the obfuscations in our history. Teachers today must
> somehow reconcile their own unease and even their own more trou-
> bling insights with their obligation to initiate their students into a civil
> society they consider worthy of membership.
>
> —Maxine Greene, 2007, p. 2

Dear Maxine,

What a challenge it is, and a joy, to reflect upon the contribution your voice and mind have made to education in the United States, England, Europe, Australia, and beyond. Whenever teachers in the arts, literacy education, and the teaching of literature need a wise and powerful advocate for their work and for the fundamental role of imagination in their classrooms, they reach for your work and are never disappointed. The freshness, the wisdom, the aptness of your words, thoughts, and reflections, articulate a way forward. You always manage to create a path through the thicket of competing theories while mentoring and empowering those with a questing mind, an imaginative disposition, and the attunement to dwell in challenging propositions.

It is hard to put into words the essence of your being—that unrelenting spirit that spurs me and countless other pilgrims to journey to Fifth Avenue in New York to engage in a private conversation or to attend one of your Sunday salons. How often I stepped into the elevator from your apartment after a lengthy lunch that passed all too quickly, wondering how I would make sense of all the thoughts tumbling in my head. How quickly could I explore the intellectual and emotional avenues opened up for me by your questing mind? As you remind us, analysis alone cannot explain the phenomena of human engagement. It has to be experienced. Which is why your doorbell keeps ringing, your company sought, and your voice recorded again and again. We need to hear that voice because it speaks to the core of our being, stirring us to reignite those parts of ourselves silenced by routine patterns of living. As I leave the lobby of your apartment building, I look at the Guggenheim Museum. I swear it is spinning. I am intoxicated with possibilities!

I reflect repeatedly on your advocacy for the importance of imagination in a rich and meaningful life. It is all too easy in education to take imagination for granted or to ignore it in deference to cognitive thinking. Yet deeply intuitive and wise thinkers like you understand the primacy of imagination in the development of empathy, in the development of speculative, poetic, and hypothetical thinking, and in shaping aesthetic experiences.

I recall vividly one conversation we had after September 11. We talked about the sometimes catastrophic effects of imagination applied without sensitivity to rights, responsibilities, and justice. We both struggled to apply our own imagination to understand zealotry and inhumanity in its contemporary and historical forms. Most of all, we dwelt on the potential for imagination to influence either transformative or devastating outcomes depending on prevailing passions and the presence or absence of a moral framework. Philosophic ruminations yield few easy answers, but that stimulating dialogue remains vivid and dear to my memory. Clearly, you were rehearsing ideas that would appear in your paper from which the opening quote above was taken.

It is indeed imagination that makes empathy possible. Imagination is a necessary but not sufficient condition for empathy. Empathy in its most sophisticated form as empathic intelligence requires the ability to access and modulate both thinking and feeling in the search for understanding and meaning. In its most sophisticated form, empathic intelligence seeks not to judge but to understand. It can tolerate ambiguities and keep possibilities alive. How well you understand that.

When you speak and write, your sense of wonder and surprise colors your words. This is a timely reminder of the function of feeling in complicating thought. If we don't harness the sense of wonder in children and allow it to nurture imagination, how will they ever imagine how others might think and feel? How will they know in the absence of our encouragement that life is enriched by empathic attunement to others?

The sense of wonder vividly apparent as youngsters gaze enthralled at art, at nature, at falling leaves, reminds us of our responsibility to keep that feeling alive, to amplify and mirror it as valuable and humanizing. Intellectual life is arid in the absence of imagination and a sense of wonder, as you have reminded us so often throughout your lifetime of discourse, scholarship, and writing.

We thrive when liberated by the ineffable possibilities you conjure into being like a benign sorceress. Whether the ingredients for your alchemy are aesthetic experiences, affirmations of democratic participation, advocacy for equity, or calls to dialogue, your audience awakens to possibilities, not, as Shakespeare put it, "dream't of in our Philosophy." The logic of your arguments is embedded in the experiential. Questing individuals like you, imbued with a generosity of spirit that tantalizes others, show by example how to awaken the senses and the spirit of inquiry. Educators need such liberation to acquit their responsibility to encourage students to touch the sublime—that secret part of their yearning souls responsive to altruistic forces.

I am surprised how easy is it has been to write this piece. Your writings read like a continuation of the precious conversations we have had. As I sit at my desk in Sydney, Australia, time and distance are no barrier to memory. Maybe you have already been called "A Woman for All Seasons." You should have been long before this.

I wish I could see the Guggenheim spin again.

—Roslyn Arnold

The Audacity of Eros

Nina Asher

> When I speak of the erotic, then, I speak of it as an assertion of the lifeforce of women; of that creative energy empowered, the knowledge and use of which we are now reclaiming in our language, our history, our dancing, our loving, our work, our lives.
> —Audre Lorde, *Sister Outsider*

Dear Maxine,

Over two decades ago, I came from Bombay (now Mumbai), India, to New York City, USA, to pursue doctoral studies in Curriculum and Teaching at Teachers College. I was inspired then—as I am now—by Freire's (1982/1995) conceptualization of education as a process that leads to "conscientization"—becoming conscious/aware—through dialogue. From day one, it seems, I kept hearing of the legendary Maxine Greene—her engagement with existentialism, phenomenology, philosophy, arts, and culture, not only at TC but also at Lincoln Center and AERA. Over time, I heard you lecture on literature and the imagination, women and education, arts, aesthetics, and curriculum, on campus and at conferences. Stimulated by your powerful vision of how teachers can seek untapped possibilities through participating in dialogue and engaging multiple perspectives and different experiences (Greene, 1995b), for the past decade, I have assigned your work to my master's students at Louisiana State University. And, as an affiliate of LSU's Curriculum Theory Project, I have heard of your visits to campus, of the inspiration you provided to new scholars (many of whom are now legends in their own right) in the early days of the Bergamo conference (associated with the *Journal of Curriculum Theorizing*, and now beginning its 4th decade). Therefore, although our one-on-one conversations have been limited, our paths meet, our interests intersect: the dialectic and the practice of freedom, engaging the imagination, envisioning new possibilities, reaching for the seemingly unattainable, multiplicities and openness, dialogue and democracy, incompletenesses and interstices, struggling to bring new, more equitable, more just realities into being, more opportunities for individual and collective agency. These are our shared passions across different landscapes.

I wrestle with these questions as a postcolonial, queer, feminist academic who is an immigrant from South Asia and, therefore, a "woman of color" in the U.S. context. I continue to draw strength from "impossibilities" realized—be it women's suffrage in the United States or Gandhi's success in employing civil disobedience and nonviolent resistance (which Martin Luther King Jr. later brought to the struggle for civil rights in the United States) to bring an end to colonial rule in India, or the recent election of the first black President of the United States. And I continue to grapple with other "utopian" visions we are still far from realizing—be it guaranteeing universal, free education for all children such that each may be able to look "inquiringly and wonderingly on the world in which one lives" (Greene, 1973, p. 267); ending poverty and hunger, racism, sexism, and homophobia; or eradicating the damaging effects of colonialism and attaining peace on the planet.

Thinkers and activists, border-crossers (whether in terms of nations and communities, disciplines and genres, races, languages, genders, and cultures) willing to work to go beyond either/or binaries toward new *mestiza* (Anzaldúa, 1987) spaces, have been sources of inspiration, reminding me throughout how important it is to feel *and* think *and* act upon the courage of one's convictions, to keep alive, engage, assert, and share the audacity of eros, of one's life force, of the will to reclaim and heal self and society. And this you convey, thoughtfully, compellingly, powerfully, through your writings, which have served to educate and inspire legions of us. Each year, as I share these thoughts with my students, I also remind them that we stand on the shoulders of others—Dorothy Allison, Gloria Anzaldúa, Frantz Fanon, Paulo Freire, Maxine Greene, bell hooks, Audre Lorde, Edward Said, Trinh T. Minh-ha, Virginia Woolf, among others—who have had the courage to speak up, resist, rethink, transform.

It is marvelous, indeed, that after the debacles in 2000 and 2004, in 2008, the United States democratically elected an erudite individual as its President. It is remarkable that, as a politician, he also has had the audacity to be "out" as an intellectual in a culture where intellectualism is often seen as suspiciously close to liberalism and, therefore, weakness. Barack Obama (2006) urges us not to remain "locked in 'either/or' thinking" (p. 40) and advocates that as a nation, we develop a "stronger sense of empathy" (p. 67), so that "the conservative and the liberal, the powerful and the powerless, the oppressed and the oppressor . . . [w]e are all forced beyond our limited vision" (p. 68).

This vision for the nation gives me hope. For instance, perhaps more of us will recognize that the possibility of teachers—of color and White—seeing that they and their students—of color and White—are "at the interstices" (Asher, 2005) in dynamic multicultural contexts is not mere ivory-tower theorizing but, rather, a viable goal toward which we may continue to strive, engaging both intellect and affect, theory and practice, imagination and eros, that perhaps we might actually one day come to see that differences of race, culture, gender, and nation exist alongside shared concerns and hopes, that this whole enriches rather than detracts from the quality of life, internal/spiritual as well as external/material. Perhaps, then, we—educators, theorists, activists, citizens in the 21st-century context of a globalized capitalism—can reaffirm yet again that, through all the struggles of living with and working through messy contradictions, we might take yet one more step toward being "alive among others, to achieve freedom in dialogue with others for the sake of personal fulfillment and the emergence of a democracy dedicated to life and decency" (Greene, 1988, p. xii).

Maxine, thank you for your audacity in insisting—for over 4 decades—that we enhance the education field with the erotic to expand and strengthen the possibilities it offers, envision new realities, and bring them to fruition through our very lives, thought, and work.

Very truly,
—Nina Asher

Seeing the Darkness

LOUISE BERMAN

Go to the limits of your longing. Flare up like a flame.
—R. A. Rilke, in A. Barros & J. Macy, *Rilke's Book of Hours*.

Dear Maxine,

Whenever I think about you, I imagine an extraordinarily passionate person—not one who feels strongly about everything, but one who possesses a selective kind of passion. You are an exemplar of an individual who has given enthusiastic attention to moral and ethical values without being stodgy, who cares deeply about people without being effusive, who ponders deeply without being stymied by inaction. Indeed, you are one of the most active and productive people I know. Long after most people are well into "retirement," you continue exploring issues that have been of concern to you and are certainly key concerns of many in the larger culture. You have added much to conversations about matters of justice without decrying those who hold different opinions. Clearly, you are a citizen of the world, becoming entangled with people of diverse backgrounds and who hold perspectives on what matters.

The first time I met you was at a conference in Puerto Rico over 40 years ago. The meetings were held in honor of Alice Miel, a distinguished professor of curriculum who was retiring from Teachers College. As I recall, you had recently accepted a position at that institution, and Alice very much wanted you to speak at the event. I had the good fortune to ride back to the airport with you, and I appreciate your interest in me as a person. You have a real gift for getting at the essence of a person, for encouraging them, for helping them clarify their ideas. You are never above directly, honestly facing another person and assuming that she will do the same in return. What a great way to skip the small talk in which we spend so much of our short time.

Through the years, we have often met at meetings of a variety of professional organizations. I think you must hold an all-time record for program participation, and yet you do it with such humility. Even though you had such an overwhelming number of writing, speaking, researching, advising, and other professional commitments each year, you always were so present at each one.

Not only are you students of the written word, but you are a passionate student of the face and voice. You see and hear the yearnings and longings, possibilities and concerns of those with whom you associate. Whether you are in the classroom, a conference, or an informal gathering, you do not talk about your many honors and awards, but rather about a scintillating idea from a book you have just read or from a play you have recently seen. The tapestry you help to weave in conversation features many bright colors and designs.

You urge people to forsake the ordinary and sameness to move toward the extraordinary. Perhaps a word from you encourages others to probe the depths of an insight, or to push horizontal boundaries, or to see the stars on a dark night. You walk with us, if not in person, then in recollection, as we feel a loving discontent with the world as it is. You invite us to establish a vision of how the spaces in which we dwell might be better. And you show us how to do the familiar in fresh and exciting ways.

You have encouraged those of us who have been privileged to be in dialogue with you to break away from the dominance of prevailing mindsets. With you, we ask: Why don't we pay more attention to the arts in schooling? How do we make issues of justice, ethics, and morality central to conversations both in school and nonschool settings? How do we create minds that are willing to linger on tough issues and, with others, find possible answers that make life together more compelling, dynamic, and just?

I recall some years ago being at my dining room table with you and a group of women friends. Our original intent had been to consider alternative modes of inquiry growing out of philosophy, the arts, and literature. As we were in conversation, the question asked of you was this: How do you account for the impact you are having in so many areas? Your answer: "I have seen the darkness." Clearly you have, but how can you see the darkness without being immobilized by it? You help me constantly raise questions of mattering. Do what I do, think, and am make me a better person? Does who I am matter in the settings in which I find myself? Do I need to find new settings when the old ones seem to be outworn?

I share with you your love of cities, their messiness filled with immense possibilities. Cities lend themselves to conversation and diverse kinds of people, to moral and ethical reasoning, to artistic endeavors, and to new ways of thinking about people and their communities. You have done so much for New York City and the world, and I am sure those who gather around you will further your efforts.

As you continue your journey, Maxine, allow me to share certain of your gifts to me:

> Where some see scarcity within the human condition, you see opportunities for abundance.
>
> When some might hide in cloaks of loneliness, you create reasons for community.
>
> Where some see ugliness of the human spirit, you see instances of beauty, love, and compassion.
>
> When some fail to use their imaginative powers, you provide settings that invite expression of imagination.
>
> When some see themselves languishing in poverty, you invite them to see their potential for magnificence.
>
> When some might try to ignore their pain, you see the heightened sensitivities pain might bring.
>
> While some garner energy from light, you see creativity fueled by darkness.
>
> While some might seek a wealth of earthly possessions, you see riches in lingering in yearnings and longings.
>
> When some create lives filled with meaningless activities, you weave a life of meaningful splendor.
>
> While some may see education as primarily reasoned activity for the young, you see education for all as passionate inquiry into the human condition and the will to make and leave the world a better place.
>
> While some are content to use vacuous language, you use words that invite higher levels of perceiving and acting.
>
> When some see the world as it is, you see it as having possibilities for higher levels of ethical thought, poetic nuance, sensitive behavior, and loving action.

While some see life as opportunities for being served, you see life as opportunities for engagement with others in endeavors where all are serving and being served.

Thank you, Maxine, for sharing your life with me and so many others. I am the richer for knowing you.

> With deep affection and best wishes for peace and joy,
> —Louise Berman

Fully and Profoundly Engaged

DAVID FLINDERS

Dear Maxine,

While this letter was not written out of duty, my motives still include a deep sense of obligation. I am not a philosopher, and for that reason I am especially grateful for scholars like you who have been willing to engage those working across the broad spectrum of field. You have made philosophy less intimidating for outsiders like me—no small achievement, for the professional lives of educational researchers rest on the large ideas with which philosophers struggle.

My obligations are also personal, in the sense that my school experiences as a child, unfortunately, bore great resemblance to the way you described curriculum in 1971: "Curriculum, from the learner's standpoint, ordinarily represents little more than an arrangement of subjects, a structure of socially prescribed knowledge, or a complex system of meanings which may or may not fall within his grasp" (1971a, p. 253). Rarely did it fall within my grasp. But that, as they say, is another story.

My point is simply to underscore the debt we owe scholars of all types who have kept the possibilities of education alive. Particularly under the pressure of contemporary trends—the growing standardized testing frenzy and its objectification of school "quality"—we are indebted to writers who have given us a broader and more generous vision of learning. Of course, this debt is impossible to repay. At least, it is impossible to repay those who, like yourself, are most directly responsible for helping others understand education as a becoming, a way of sense-making, a way of seeing and hearing what would otherwise go unnoticed. On this count, my obligation is not to you or to other scholars or to the field at large, but to my students. It is an obligation to model for them the wide-awakeness and seeing anew that you and others have modeled for me.

Recently, I have been reading about "Lawn Chair Larry," the individual who probably inspired the recent Pixar film *Up*. I always believed Larry's story to be an urban myth, but apparently it wasn't. On July 2, 1982, Lawrence Walters departed from his home in San Pedro, California, lifted skyward by 45 helium-filled balloons tied to a patio chair. Reaching an altitude of 15,000 feet, Walters did not leave unprepared. He took with him a parachute, a pellet gun (to shoot out some of his balloons and thus initiate his descent), a CB radio, sandwiches, cold beer, and a camera. When asked why he had so risked life and limb, Walters simply replied, "A man can't just sit around." Walters's flight transgressed controlled airspace as his balloon drifted near the Long Beach Airport, and Larry was immediately arrested upon his return to earth. An official from the airport at the time is reported to have said: "We know he broke some part of the Federal Aviation Act, and as soon as we decide which part it is, some type of charge will be filed. If he had a pilot's license, we'd suspend that. But he doesn't."

I do not plan any balloon-cluster flights for myself, and I suspect that you are not considering this rather dangerous pastime, either. Still, Larry's exploit reminded me of how your incredible career has driven you to great, great heights. As I learned more about rogue ballooning, I also wondered how anyone could be lifted so freely into the clouds and not feel fully and profoundly engaged with life. That is how I think of you: fully and profoundly engaged.

Sincerely,
—David J. Flinders

The Miracle of Authorship as a Moment of Truth: A Letter to Maxine Greene

GLENN HUDAK

> When risks are taken, when people do indeed act in their freedom, a
> kind of miracle has taken place. Arendt reminds us that we ourselves
> are the authors of such miracles, because it is we who perform them—
> and we who have the capacity to establish a reality of our own.
> **—Maxine Greene, *The Dialectic of Freedom***

Dear Maxine,

What I'd like to highlight in your work is the importance of lived experience and its relation to truth, and the role literature, film, and popular culture play in helping us grasp the concreteness of our struggles to own our freedom. Let me begin by drawing from the film *Titanic* (Cameron, 1997).

Remember the scene in *Titanic* where 101-year-old Rose Dawson Calvert is shown a computer-generated re-creation of the sinking of the *Titanic*? After the viewing, Rose reflects, "That was a fine forensic analysis, Mr. Bodine, but the experience, well...it was something quite different." Mr. Bodine had put together a clear, concise account of the events that led up to the ship's sinking; he offers a crisp analysis of why those events occurred, and ultimately how all these causal factors led to the ship's unique sinking.

But Rose is nonplussed. However accurate and insightful the forensic analysis may be, it is not her experience, her "truth" of the sinking: the sheer panic that passengers and crew felt as the ship sank, the pain as loved ones were separated, and of course the ensuing death of her love, Jack Dawson. The film brings fact and fiction together to re-create Rose's (a fictional character) lived experience in all its richness. Mr. Bodine's earlier "fine forensic analysis" is necessary to our understanding of the sinking, but it is not sufficient to present us with the "truth" of the event. It is Rose's narration that cements understanding through lived experience, making it possible for us to emotionally engage with the "truth" about the sinking of *Titanic*.

What is one's lived experience? While the term is often used to describe the events of one's existential world, it is important to also note that "lived experience" embodies other, unconscious dimensions: *psychic structures that act as defense mechanisms which conceal painful events in our lives: "moments of truth."* Indeed, these moments of truth can be painful to face up to, we may prefer instead to turn away, to flee. What is this "truth" that I'm making reference to? In *The Dialectic of Freedom* (1988), Maxine, you quote the poet Muriel Rukeyser: "What would happen if one woman told the truth about her life? The world would split open" (p. 57). Indeed, when Rose Dawson tells her "truth," the world does split open, as we relive the trauma of the sinking with her. Here, the complete picture is difficult to process emotionally; the reexperiencing of loss is at once painful and entertaining. For the "truth" *unconcealed* is both disorienting and difficult to face, especially "truths" about one's life.

To "unconceal," you write, "is to create clearings, spaces in the midst of things where decisions can be made. It is to break through the masked and falsified, to reach toward what is also half-hidden or concealed. When a woman, when any human tries to tell the truth and act on it, there is no predicting what will happen" (p. 58). To break with "the masked and falsified," to unconceal the truth, is no easy matter, for confronting the "truth of the moment," lifting the mask of one's experience, acting on one's freedom, is both disorienting and painful. As Buddhist nun Pema Chodron (1997) observes, "When the bottom falls out and we can't find anything to grasp, it hurts a lot. We might have some romantic view of what [this] means, but when we are nailed with the truth, we suffer" (p. 7). Perhaps, then, in order to process the painful "truths" of our lives, we need the "falsehoods" that fiction provides to aid us in digesting the events confronting us; and here popular culture and literature provide just enough falsehood (that is, fiction) to allow us to reexperience these traumas at a safe distance.

The miracle of authorship, as I interpret it then, is that it provides creative space for imaginative engagements with the complex stories of our lives: our moments of truth that are painful and, as such, remain concealed or hidden from view. Authorship authorizes: It allows us to engage in the creative act of considering the world as if it were otherwise. Rose Dawson's story, in *Titanic*, makes Mr. Bodine and the rest of the crew fundamentally reconsider the events. After hearing Rose's version of the sinking, the salvage team captain, Brock, laments, "I never let it in." And what didn't he let in? What couldn't he hear and process emotionally?

Perhaps it's the human condition that we experience more emotionally in our lives than we can meaningfully digest, without pushing away from that which is painful to face. Authorship addresses the human condition, however, by allowing us to creatively explore and translate painful, perhaps oppressive, moments in our lives into fiction that embodies just enough truth to help us work through the full impact of what has and is happening to us. Authorship is the beginning of our journey to be what Lear (1999) refers to as "open minded": "the capacity to live nondefensively with the question of how to live" (p. 8).

Maxine, I believe that your work's essential lesson for the coming generations is its engaging articulation of the importance of lived experience, as we find it in literature and the arts. You convince us that the arts need a place in both our studies and the debates over education. Indeed, it is by taking our lives seriously, in the broadest sense, that we begin the pedagogical journey toward authorship and open-mindedness. As such, I want to let you know how much I appreciate your efforts as an *auth*or to open spaces for me, as a reader. You have helped me imagine new ways of thinking, being, and acting in the world, both personally and professionally.

Best,
—Glenn Hudak

Philosopher, Educator, Author, Friend

Linda Lambert

Dear Maxine,
    When I was a junior high principal in the early 1980s, you made a presentation in Santa Rosa, California. I was already excited by your writings,

which brilliantly folded literature and philosophy into the work of education. So you can imagine how delighted I was when I learned that you needed a ride back to San Francisco. A friendship began on that day that has lasted more than a quarter-century.

Over these many years, we've met at AERA, exchanged letters, and stolen time for short visits. I visited your classes at Columbia and understood how a small item in the morning paper could frame a searching discussion on social justice. Often, a seemingly small observation from you could focus my thinking about the tasks ahead. On the eve of my move to Egypt in 1989, we had dinner at a Chinese restaurant in San Francisco and you said to me: "Remember, Egypt has not experienced an Enlightenment." Realizing that I had a rare opportunity to affect the fundamental schemas of the younger generations in Egypt, I designed my work in those next years to focus on building students' understandings of self-directed learning and democratic instructional practices.

Then, in 1992, I brought my daughter April and 2-year-old granddaughter Chloe to your home in New York for tea. You were generous with advice to my daughter, then in her first years of teaching. April became the teacher we both can be proud of; Chloe, now 19, is at the University of Oregon preparing to become a teacher.

In 1995, when I wrote my first book, *The Constructivist Leader*, you composed the Foreword. You eloquently celebrated the democratization of leadership, realizing that the "constructivist leader" I envisioned is one who engages self and others in reciprocal, purposeful learning within a community. Such acts of leadership involve inquiry, reflection, dialogue, and action. You noted that this does not mean taking charge, directing, commanding, and subjugating others. Clearly, my conception of leadership was substantially borne of the ideas learned from you.

Coming of age in the 1950s in the Midwest, I could profoundly identify with your life as a pilgrim and a woman on a quest of becoming. Although we didn't experience the same historical moments or share the same ethnic identity, in many ways our life struggles paralleled each other. Your efforts to carve out a self from your identity as a Jewish woman and mother of two children, amidst the prejudices found in the professional world, inspired my own journey. I graduated from college in 1966, the same year that you were hired as the first female philosopher at Teachers College.

Over the following decades, your persistence and imagination have helped me understand the nature of my own quest for selfhood. From my perspective, two complementary paths played vital roles in your construction of the woman who is now recognized by many as the most important American educational philosopher since John Dewey. (I can almost feel your modest rebuttal of this label.) The first path was paved with an intentional and enlightened philosophy of being. The second path suggests how consciousness can be awakened in others. This awakening, or releasing of the imagination, defines learning in its most powerful forms.

Releasing the Imagination (1995b) has had the most important impact on me of all of your writings. Your belief that ideas worth learning have the capacity to awaken also laid the foundation for my latest book (with co-author Mary Gardner), *Women's Ways of Leading*. You've reminded us that we must awaken readers to the compelling need to build a just, compassionate, and meaningful democracy. To me, this is leadership, although I realize that you are reluctant to acknowledge yourself as a leader. Perhaps this is a result of your deep sense of humility.

To continue with your notion of being, I understand that the attitude of wide-awakeness develops and contributes to the choice of actions that lead to self-formation through a vision of constructing the self and the world. We share an understanding of one of the major goals of education: to nurture intellectual talents for the formation of our society into a more democratic, just, and caring place.

Further, you've argued that aesthetic experiences, such as the arts, lead to a defamiliarization of the ordinary, creating a metaphorical distance from the dailiness of life and enabling us to reframe our perceptions of the world. These sensitivities are essential in order for students and teachers to create meaning in their lives. Indeed, those who teach—as well as those who lead learning—ought to be "those who have learned the importance of becoming reflective enough to think about their own thinking and become conscious of their own consciousness" (Greene, 1995b, p. 65). Democracy, you've insisted, is a way of life, not just a form of government. It recognizes the capacity of everyone to choose, to act, to construct one's own life—to lead. The wonderful part about being a teacher, you once told me, is to liberate people to pursue their own hopes, their own freedoms. I hope that is what my own life has meant to others.

You have mentored me through your friendship, teaching, storytelling, aesthetic sensibilities, and writings. Your powerful words contain meaning, emotion, and music. I want you to know and remember, Maxine, that your combination of values, consciousness, passion, and imagination has informed my life, as it will others for generations to come. For this I am profoundly grateful. You often refer to me lovingly as "your Linda." And so I am.

With love,
—Linda Lambert

How Can an Educational Philosophy Withstand the Test of Practice?

Heidi Miller

It is clear to many of us by now that involvement with aesthetic questioning heightens awareness of what is demanded of us as listeners, as beholders. Such involvement heightens our consciousness of the mystery as well, as it discloses possibilities we could not have anticipated before.

—Maxine Greene, *Variations on a Blue Guitar*

Dear Maxine,

When I trained as a dance-teaching artist with Lincoln Center Institute, I was shown a video of a dance performance and asked, "What do you notice?" As a newcomer, that simple question spoke volumes to me of the philosophy driving the Institute's teaching practice. I understood in that moment, on a personal level, that the learner is held in high regard and plays a key role to themselves and others in a learning process. As a teaching artist-in-training, I also understood that, as an artist, I was valued for all I had discovered from a life spent investigating dance.

It's been 10 years since my training, and I have asked "What do you notice?" numerous times of a variety of audiences. The question is often difficult to answer, so unaccustomed are we to being asked, to someone listening.

But to explore, in practice, ideas about educating through the richness of the study of works of art, aesthetic experience, and the imagination, you have taught us to ask those unfamiliar, sometimes puzzling questions of ourselves and others, and to encourage others to pose their own questions. Entering a classroom, I have never felt as though I have to leave the philosophy at the door. Quite the opposite: I rely on it in a most practical sense—allowing the work of art and fellow learners in the room to guide me toward the next good open question. I am never lost, but simultaneously exhilarated and exhausted by leading a session asking questions I cannot know the answers to.

"What do you notice?" The question lingers in the room, creating a genuine importance of the moment in its simplicity and profundity. The participants and I reflect silently in our collective *not knowing*, that extraordinary instant of inquiry, where we are about to enter something, somewhere we could not have been before. Maxine, thank you for that experience.

With love and deep regard,
—Heidi Miller

Breaking Through the Crust

WENDY KOHLI

**To be sunk in habitual routines, to be merely passive is, we well
know, to miss an opportunity for awakening. But we as teachers take
the chances the young do when we try to enable them to defamiliarize their familiar situations—to take another look at them, to break
through the crust, to reflect on things as if they could be otherwise.**
—Maxine Greene, *Variations on a Blue Guitar*

Dear Maxine,

Since I first set foot in your apartment upon moving to New York in
1973, I have relied on you—whether you knew it or not—to keep me on a
path to "wide-awakeness." You were 55, and I was 23. As a small-town girl
with big-city visions, I drew on your cosmopolitanism to support my hoped-
for transformations and liberation. Through your embodied, interdisciplinary philosophy, I was able to imagine a life as a philosopher of education,
knowing that you, against great odds, had made it possible for our field
to be "otherwise." *Teacher as Stranger*, published in 1973, spoke to me in
multiple ways. It gave me a conceptual framework for "doing philosophy"
that resonated with my own strengths (and weaknesses). I savored the literary references amidst the existential philosophy and critical politics. And
it prompted me to experience more of you, in person. In my search for an
expanded world, I took your large lecture course in Social Philosophy and
your seminar in Existentialism. I had found my teacher. But, as you know all
too well, life choices make us who we are. And for personal reasons, I chose
to move away from the city and from you.

For many years I regretted the decision to go to Syracuse for my Ph.D.
and not study with you at TC. Yet, in retrospect, I think that our 36-year-
long friendship may not have been possible had I been your doctoral student. But we will never know, will we? What *is* certain is that I have been
able to learn from you, and with you, over these decades and continue to be
challenged by your capacity to avoid "habitual routines." Your energy and
stamina, your commitment to stay current, to read across many disciplines,
to engage with people from a variegated palette, was an invitation for me to
choose complexity and to embrace contradictions.

You live with your contradictions and complexity as humanly—and
as neurotically—as most of us do. And you aren't afraid to reveal them in

your public and private "quest" (Greene, 1988, p. xi). I think, for example, of your self-disclosures in the film *Exclusions and Awakenings: The Life of Maxine Greene* (Hancock, 2001). Through your story, we can grasp threads of your particular lived reality, while weaving them together to better understand a more general strand of Jewish, white, middle-class U.S. women's history. Yet even as you embodied some of the struggles of the women's movement, and digested the scholarship of feminism, you didn't *choose* an explicitly feminist path—at home or at work. You resisted that identity—in fact, you resisted any *one* identity or label. Your resistance to closure, to completeness, to being "finished," allowed (and perhaps forced) you to welcome multiplicity, heteroglossia, and becoming. This is poignantly conveyed in the film when you cross the street from the Guggenheim to your apartment and remind us that "you are . . . not yet." After more than 9 decades, you certainly are not finished.

You are still creating phenomenal educational situations for teachers, students, and artists—in a range of venues, from Lincoln Center to your apartment salons to the new small school that you co-founded, the High School of Arts, Imagination and Social Inquiry, in Manhattan. I marvel at your capacity to continue on, year after year, with your teaching, with your speaking, with your writing, with your responding to the incessant requests for some part of you.

Never embarrassed by the project of "teacher education" (Greene, 1995b, p. 1), you have ignited the intellect and imagination of generations of teachers and students, who in their unique ways have been able to summon up the courage to think "of things as if they could be otherwise" (Greene, 2001, p. 116). Many of them have taken the initiative to act on that courage in order to right the social injustices they confront. Your insistence on educating the *social* imagination requires us to embody the arts in and for our lived realities as we create new possibilities. At the same time, you caution against sentimentalizing the imagination, and warn us not to reduce the aesthetic experience to the technical or the measureable.

When we take up your challenge to think anew, to "defamiliarize . . . familiar situations," we are more apt to resist passivity and to pierce the "cotton-wool" of daily life (Greene, 1988, p. 2) that can keep us "sunk in [our] habitual routines." You have shown us "the potency of the arts" (Greene, 2001, pp. 196–197) and how they help us, as Dewey says, "'to break through the crust of conventionalized and routine consciousness'" (quoted in Greene, p. 197).

I continue to be moved to reflection, to action, to creativity, to transformation, by your presence in my life. If I could have one wish come true, it would be to turn back the clock 20 years so that I could have dozens more baked spaghetti and chicken suppers with you while catching up on gossip or watching *Charlie Rose*. Thank you from the bottom of my heart for your generosity, for your prodding, for your support, for your wit, and for your love.

—Wendy Kohli

An Anxiety of Influence

WILLIAM PINAR

Dear Maxine,

I read you before I heard you or met you. In graduate school I had been assigned to read that powerful piece you did for *Teachers College Record*'s classic 1971 issue "Curriculum: Interdisciplinary Insights." (I reprinted this essay, "*Curriculum and Consciousness*" [1971a], in my 1975 collection.) Your brilliant *Teacher as Stranger* followed. I watched for every one of your books thereafter, devouring each eagerly. For me, they were "breaking news"—not the parody CNN performs, not information parading as knowledge, but erudite events that would alter my understanding.

Once I'd heard you speak, your voice was audible whenever I read. Yours is a voice I have always associated with Paris and the Left Bank in the 1930s as much as with New York in our time. You often wore black, accentuating your black glasses, and that cigarette that dangling from your lips did nothing to mute the echo of Sartre in you.

There was always drama associated with your public appearances. Most of all, there was the public excitement generated by the audience at the prospect of hearing you, but also (as I learned when introducing you to the 1973 University of Rochester Curriculum Theory Conference) there was the private anxiety that you said you felt before commencing each public address. As I noticed your trembling hands grasping the lectern, I accepted this as a sign of your humility.

Was that anxiety, confided in private before the public, also an acknowledgment of the dissonance between these two domains? "Anxiety signals that the threat cannot be exteriorized, objectified," Joan Copjec (2004, p. 103) suggests, "that it is instead internal, brought on by an encounter with that limit which prevents one's coincidence with oneself." Such anxiety, then, would seem to mark the "creative tensionality" between what is and what is not yet, the very project of education you enacted through print, *en personne*.

The anxiety you associated with your public persona metamorphosed in private. What fun—how wicked!—you can be *entre nous*. Among the photographs between pages 144 and 145 in Quentin Bell's biography of his aunt Virginia Woolf, there is one of Ethel Smyth in shock over something wicked Virginia Woolf is telling her. The expression on Smyth's face conveys something of the surprise I felt every time you said something "scandalous" to me.

Speaking of surprise, do you remember the party Bill Doll and I gave during the 1994 AERA meeting, held in New Orleans? I was living just outside the Quarter in that ancient, elegant apartment. In the crowd, you and I met in the passage between the living room and kitchen. Having visited you at your home, I thought I remembered where it was. With you in front of me, I told whoever was standing next to us that you lived in a fabulous apartment on Third Avenue in Manhattan. You slapped me hard across the face, pointing that long finger at me as you corrected my error: "It's Fifth!"

Maybe 20 years before that night I enjoyed (with 7 to 10 others) a weekend with you somewhere in the woods up the Hudson. The conversation was meandering—as if there were no agenda (ah, those were the days!)—but you were, as always, mesmerizing. Quietly and (is it possible?) calmly you conveyed the urgency of what was at stake: nothing less than survival during a time of plague.

That 1973 book—*Teacher as Stranger*—haunts me still, reminding me to notice where I am, what time it is, and what is at stake. In her breathtaking *The Very Thought of Education*, Deborah Britzman juxtaposes your book with Kristeva's. After discussing her sense of being strangers to ourselves, Deborah notes that 35 years ago you named the teacher as stranger, as "an incomplete project" (quoted in Britzman, 2009, p. 30). Britzman continues, "The teacher has a choice to choose her past, to wake up, and to experiment." Then she quotes you: "The teacher who dares to do philosophy must be open to such a multiplicity of realities" (1973, p. 11). Embracing the unfamiliar, she becomes, in your fine phrase, "not yet," thereby engaging the "power of incompleteness" (Greene, 2001, p. 154).

It was Philip Wexler who approached me (it must have been 1997) with the idea of organizing a volume in honor of you, an invitation I accepted with enthusiasm and some trepidation. How could you be adequately honored? It was the scale, not the specificity, I was after when likening you to Susan Sontag. Bill Ayers and Janet Miller had recently done a book in your honor (to which I had contributed, associating you with Edward Said's intellectual). As if it were a competition, Bill took offense that I was editing one as well. I replied to his e-mail of irritation by noting that 10 books on Maxine Greene would be an insufficient number; 2 is only a good start. Many texts will be required if we are to acknowledge adequately your accomplishment, for not only your generation but also those that follow. Only Freire achieves the scale of your visibility among scholars and teachers worldwide.

As memorable as they are, these personal moments are supplements to the main thing: your significance intellectually. No one wrote as you did: with agitation, urgency, determination, and invoking that vast array of sources—literary, philosophical—to point us away (through the pedagogical encounter) from the plague. It is an encounter I enact still when I try to teach or write or study.

Last winter, it was my privilege and pleasure to write about your work again. I focused on the *Blue Guitar* collection. The book seemed perfect, containing lectures given at the Lincoln Center over a 20-year period, lectures addressed to teachers and concerning the main points of an aesthetic education. Your work is still the main thing, Maxine, from which, against which, and alongside which I experience my own aesthetic education.

With gratitude,
—Bill Pinar

Negotiating Freedom

SHAIREEN RASHEED

When Freedom is the question, it is always time to begin.
—Greene, *The Dialectic of Freedom*

Dear Maxine,

I can never forget that crisp autumn day, September 6, 1996, when I entered your class on literature that you were co-teaching with Rene Arcilla—my first class as a doctoral student at Teachers College. Yes, I had defected from pursuing a doctoral degree in pure philosophy and, armed with my master's in continental thought from the New School, I was ready to put my liberal philosophical education to pragmatic use. What awaited me was a life-changing experience. And, looking back, I realize that it was this specific gap—between theoretical and practical—that I was trying to bridge in all my years studying traditional philosophy. You started the class by talking about passion, literature, emotions, and what it means to be a human being. You insisted that we explore our existentialist possibilities, our own historical narratives, not just as students but also as teachers and, most importantly, as individuals continuously striving to re-create ourselves.

Fast forward to 9/11, when as a country we were trying to grapple with the horrors of what happened and was happening in the United States. It was during that time that I suddenly found myself grappling with questions about my own imposed identity, about what it meant to be a Muslim American. I was struggling with my own self-defined boundaries. Who was I? A doctoral student, a new mother, a wife, a feminist, a Muslim? It was your continuous search for meaning that consoled me in these times. I learned through your writing, and our many conversations, that we need to accept and even appreciate the fluidity of categories collapsing into one another. More importantly, we must continuously negotiate the fluidity of life's disciplines, cultures, and various self-identities.

This was the impetus for my own teaching pedagogy, contextualized in the Existentialist curriculum, one that embodies a student's right to examine his or her culture without being punished. You taught me that the purpose of any teaching must be to help students develop the intellectual and critical skills they need to become informed citizens. Through articulating my own obstacles, I developed my "curriculum of action"—the need to conceptualize the appropriation of new discourses as a process of learning new languages, languages that allow access not only to different ways of thinking, but also to the reconceptualization of problems themselves.

Now, some 8 years later, every time I walk into my first class of the semester, I am armed with the Existentialist question you presented to us in my first class at TC: "Who are you?" In the attempt to answer that question with my students, my teaching and their journey of self-reflection happens. For that and for forcing us to imagine alternatives to create our own Existentialist freedoms, I thank you!

—Shaireen Rasheed

Compassion in a Chaotic World

TERESA RISHEL

> Why love, if losing hurts so much? I have no answers anymore: only the life I have lived. The pain now is part of the happiness then. That's the deal.
>
> **—C. S. Lewis in B. Eastman, *Shadowlands***

Dear Maxine,

As I collected my thoughts for this letter, I felt humbled addressing you. With grace, with style, and with compassion, you have led a generation of educators toward a better understanding not only of their profession, but of themselves. You have given meaning to the power of reflection and have challenged commonplace ways of thinking, causing your audience to dig deeper, to feel more strongly and to excite a passion of renewal in spirit, thought, and action.

As with many of us, I will never forget the first time I saw you at AERA 2008 in New York. I was among the Division B folks gathered when you entered the room in a wheelchair. You looked up to greet your colleagues as the room roared with a huge round of applause. You smiled a smile of acceptance, understanding, and knowing. At that moment, the words of Maxine Greene became more real to me. And I started to think about your emphasis on what is important to learn.

Concerning the quintessential question of our profession, "What is worth learning or knowing?," your answer digs deeply, not only into questioning or assessing *who* we are as people or educators, but also the limitless possibilities of who we can become. In Pinar (1998), you stated that you wanted to awaken and move people "to see, to hear and to feel in often unexpected ways" (p. 70) through works of art.

Expanding your statement beyond the arts, we as educators can address what knowledge is deemed valuable and recognize our own propensity to be drawn into these "unexpected ways" of knowing through reflection. This openness to change and to grow allows us to ponder the value of what we teach and learn, but also opens us to explore what we didn't already recognize. When we accomplish this, we can more adequately address the needs of our students and come closer to knowing who they are.

You further our understanding when you suggest that failure to act after reflection is a mistake, asserting that *action* is the true form of change, not merely the knowing. To be free, you urge us to accept responsibility for our experience in the world (Pinar, 1998). Therefore, you ask us to attempt to understand human behaviors by developing an attitude of "wide-awakeness" in what is around us—to learn to discern that which we resist, that which challenges our ways of thinking, and that which we need to accept. In this case, you emphasize allowing our experiences, knowledge, and stories to intersect with those of our students to impact and enhance classroom life.

In "*Against Invisibility*" (1969), you use Ralph Ellison's 1952 novel *Invisible Man* to illustrate many of your points. Highlighting the idea of humanness, you describe how our interactions, actions, and reactions allow for open and honest dialogue, greater learning, and honoring individual differences. On the other hand, you point out how educators can exacerbate students' circumstances by ignoring or not addressing the "alienated or rebellious student" (p. 432). These students become adversaries (to the Establishment) because educators dismiss them for not fitting into a particular way of thinking and doing. You write that some students may feel as though they do not exist, and they therefore approach those attempting to oppress or demean them by retaliating through words or actions, described as "bumping people back" (Greene, 1969). In the following, Greene gives voice to the student's experience:

> You ache with the need to convince yourself that you do exist in the real world, that you're a part of all the sound and anguish and you strike out with your fists, you curse and you swear to make them recognize you. And, alas, it's seldom successful. (Greene, 1969, p. 433)

Your impact on my professional journey has been unique. Taking the above into consideration, and understanding your words through the lens of adolescent suicide, I find that your work and mine intersect. As a suicide researcher concerned with the emotional and social stresses burdening youth, I address how educators may either be a lifeline for students on the brink of self-harm, or make an already tenuous situation worse. Your term "alienated and rebellious student" translates, for me, into the student who is looking at life through a dark and narrow tunnel—one who is engaged in an internal struggle that may or may not be observable by others. These students may be rebellious, but they may also be very quiet, alienated by self-imposed choice or by educator judgment. "Bumping back" occurs when students feel unseen or unheard and describes the suicidal student, regardless of academic ability level, socioeconomic status, race, or sexual orientation. These students may bump back *or* remain in an alienated hell where their fists and cursing and swearing are not heard. And, as Ellison tells us, often they are not successful academically or socially.

Your wrote that these types of students lack the ability to "have enough trust to look beyond the 'now'" (Greene, 1969, p. 432). Because of this, you assert that teachers who *refuse to tamper or judge* "may be able to give the rebellious student the kind of respect and the kind of care the young person is so silently demanding" (p. 436). This is also regarded as a highly effective method of dealing with distressed youth, and especially those who are considering suicide.

However, before an educator can initiate these refusing *actions* (tampering with students' lives, judging them, making assumptions, etc.), they must develop wide-awakeness, listen carefully, make themselves available to students, and, mostly, be prepared to take action. The teacher must look for the underlying reasons behind a student's lack of participation or academic success. But for many, it is easier to chastise, record a zero in the grade book, or send the student to the office.

Your message brings to the forefront what it means to respect and care for our students. The life lesson you so eloquently address is that recognizing who our students are helps them transition beyond the now and possibly squelch their desire for self-harm.

You shared that in the face of adversity, Maxine, you had two choices: go to bed (and give up) or find something to do (Hoey, 2008). I relate on a deep and personal level in the loss of my son to suicide. Truly, these types of losses are what it means to be human, but it is in the moving forward and holding onto hope that we find meaning in our lives. Moreover, the knowledge gained from the experiences—as well as the exploration for greater understanding—is what allows us to dig deeper into the value of the learning. I thank you for your endless passion, commitment, and attention to our profession. I honor what you have given us to ponder and understand. I applaud your emphasis on *action*. And I continue to learn from you.

Respectfully and sincerely,

—Teresa J. Rishel

Flunking Retirement

BARBARA THAYER-BACON

Dear Maxine,

In my 1995 copy of *Releasing the Imagination* (1995b), on the page titled "The Author" (ix), I have penciled in your age at different stages of your life. As a woman who also went to graduate school after having children during my 20s, you were an inspiration to me. I earned my master's degree while teaching in a Montessori school (I was 33, same age as you), and got my Ph.D. when I was 37, just 2 years younger than you. I, too, chose my graduate courses around my children's school schedule. I knew that if you could begin your career in higher education in your early 40s and become successful, there was hope for me.

I was not assigned any work written by a woman in my undergraduate philosophy courses, and we read very few female writers in my graduate philosophy of education courses. I had to find that material on my own. When *Releasing the Imagination* was published in 1995, I was in my 4th year as an assistant professor and had only recently discovered your work. During those years, I started putting together my "dream team" of women philosophers of education I wished I had as teachers, all women whose work was contributing deeply to my own thinking. You were at the top of my list! At some point, I realized I could still have that wish, and thus began the development of sabbatical plans that came to fruition with a wonderful semester in New York City in 1998. I was a visiting scholar at Teachers College, working with you, Jane Roland Martin, and Nel Noddings—my dream team of teachers come true.

I have tried to find ways to thank all three of you for being the pioneers who led the way for so many of us, and took the direct blasts of resistance as a result. Because of your courage and stubborn persistence, life is a little easier for your followers. Now, like you, I am charged with serving as a mentor and friend to others trying to find their way into the academy and through the tenure process, and I write letters of support continually, just as you have done—including your letter for my tenure case, and the Foreword you wrote for my latest book. Thank you, Maxine, for being such a good role model and mentor.

If my math is correct, you were 82 that fall semester I was in NYC on sabbatical, and you told me it was your first semester of not teaching. You talked to me about how much you missed the classroom, and complained that you were flunking retirement. By the end of the semester, you decided to come back into the classroom. I could relate so much to that feeling, as I missed my elementary classroom deeply when I left to go to graduate school, and I still spend time in K–12 schools regularly, so that I don't forget what it is like to be a teacher, or lose touch with what children today are experiencing. I remember leaving New York thinking, *There is no hope for me to ever stop working, as none of my dream team of teachers has stopped, even though they have all retired.* I started preparing my family for the possibility that I will flunk retirement, too. You have taught me never to be done, to always be in process, to always be open to learning more.

You have also taught me to see *all* that is around me as possible sources for enlarging my thinking and helping me to become more wide-awake and aware. Through your powerful use of the arts as metaphor in your philosophical writing, as well as in your teaching, you have taught me to not be afraid to be playful, and to develop my own voice, in my classroom and in my writing. Whenever I come across writing of yours, I take away from it a big list of literature to read, and I have learned you are a hip source, open to all sorts of genres, including hip-hop music and comic books.

I was open to these lessons, and so in need of the affirmation they gave me, for I stepped back into graduate school after a decade of playing with children, at home and in my elementary Montessori classroom. Maria Montessori also paid close attention to aesthetics in her classroom, and taught me to value art. Those years were a wonderfully creative chapter in my life. As I struggled to find ways to continue to be a creative teacher in higher education, you stepped forward as a model for me. You gave me the courage to take the lessons I learned in my Montessori classroom and apply them to my teacher education classrooms. My students gave me affirmation of the powerful impact my teaching was having on their lives. Just when I think I can settle into my curriculum in my classroom, you push me on to renewed consciousness of possibility, as I continue to bring the arts more and more into my graduate classroom, and revel in the transformative results my students and I experience. What a thrill! Your work continues to stir us to imaginative action. I include much of your writing in my classroom curriculum, so you are not ever far away, and when I want to be inspired to be creative and brave and let my voice be heard, I start a project by reading something by you. I hear your voice in your writing, and I want people to hear mine in what I write as well. Thank you for that inspiration. In just being you, you have given me and so many others hope. You have opened up possibilities for us to find ways to contribute to the conversation, too.

With care and much love,
—Barbara

Channeling Maxine's Hillbilly Younger Brother

SHIRLEY STEINBERG

Dear Maxine,

It's hard to remember when I first heard your name, read your work. My guess is that it was during my master's program at the University of Lethbridge, and my second guess is that it was either or both of my mentors, David Smith and Julie Ellis, who introduced me to you.

Attending the Bergamo Conference in 1989, I met and immediately fell in love with my future husband, Joe Kincheloe. I remember that one of our first conversations revolved around your notions of motivating the young, and your visit to Shreveport, Louisiana, with Joe as your host. Somehow, Joe was able to bring you to visit his newly formed cohort of graduate students. He was just a young professor at the time, and I was impressed that he had the chutzpah to invite the legendary Professor Greene. Joe was never afraid to let people know he respected their work, and had no embarrassment in inviting you to his fledgling program. It was clear to me that Joe's respect for and secret "romance" with you boded well for a relationship with me—a Jewish, outspoken woman. Indeed, I am quite sure that his academic romances have always revolved around them, beginning with you, Madelaine Grumet, and Karel Rose. No wonder we fell in love, and what scholarly prototypes you all were for me.

A year or so after Joe and I married, we planned to visit New York, and he wanted to phone you. I told him that one just didn't call up Maxine Greene and say, "Hey, we're here." But he did, and you invited us to dinner at your amazing apartment on the Upper East Side. You cooked us chicken, and we talked all evening, telling stories. Joe's elongated Southern narratives and your stacatto New York accounts plastered me to the couch. I'm not sure who kept up with whom, but you both danced a *pas de deux* worthy of your beloved Lincoln Center. A part of Joe was always in awe of you, but his comfort trumped that awe, and he authentically respected, loved, and admired you. I told him that he was the redneck younger brother you never had, in a Dorothy-Parker-meets-hillbilly way. It was terrific. One of the funniest stories you told us that night in your apartment was of the time you visited Bill Pinar in Rochester. Bill's name had come up easily, as he and Joe had been collaborating on a graduate program at LSU. Your eyes widened as you recalled going to the University of Rochester and stopping over at Bill's home. You walked into that grand old home and were immediately bombarded by a visceral scream coming from the upstairs. Evidently, Bill's partner Denah was engaged in a therapy session with a client, and they were doing primal scream work. After you collected yourself from that cacophony, Bill came running over to you with his son, little Gabriel, in his arms (at that time, you recalled, Bill was in his Buddhist phase, with a shaved head and a somewhat Zen demeanor). He panted that he was late to class, thrust Gabriel at you, and flew out the door. You found yourself standing in the foyer, babe in arms, with primal screaming above. It was very apparent that the Pinar home had made a lasting impression on you.

Your ability to tell stories, to get to the point, yet elongate the very gut of the issue, is phenomenal. Not one for wasting words, you paint your canvas with thick, broad strokes, and follow with accent. Both Joe and I have always appreciated not only the content of your writing, but the style. You have brought us through the galleries of teaching, aesthetics, creativity, and philosophy. You have informed us, guided us, and entertained us, and set more than just a standard for us.

In the last few years, we have seen you from a distance, and warmly smile at your never-ending entourage. Many times, it has just been too hard to leap over the hordes and actually speak to you. It was easy to keep up with you through your capacity to best yourself each time you put pen to paper. As the accolades have streamed in these past years, both of us have laughed and enjoyed the comments you may have made about them. I know there is a wry sense of humor and self-effacement that must accompany these events/books/films.

Maxine, thank you for having us in your home. Thank you for your stories, your scholarship, your humor, and your contributions to our own work and our own stories. And thank you for allowing me to share with you a few precious slices of time in which my life and love blended with yours.

—Shirley Steinberg

Lived Imperfection

LYNDA STONE

Dear Maxine,

I am honored to be among the educators who are penning these letters, who share a debt to the role model you have been for so many. Thank you for your early, personal attention to me and my work. You have mattered a great deal to me.

I learned a central lesson from you regarding perfection. It is embedded in a mantra that I share with teaching candidates—excellent students at my elite university who believe that immediately they ought to be perfect teachers, since they are good students. The mantra is, "there is no perfect": no perfect instructional unit or lesson plan, no perfect relationship with a student or class group. Offering them this insight, hopefully, helps free them for the real work of teaching. Herein, I want to connect this insight about educational practice to issues of scholarly perfection. Of course I want to be "perfect" in what I write but know that I am not and cannot be. A first understanding of this came from you.

My earliest memories of our acquaintance take place at large academic conferences. Over several years, I came upon you getting ready to deliver major talks that I, of course, heard and thought were perfect. I would say hello as you were putting finishing touches on a presentation, seemingly dissatisfied with your own ideas, logic, illustrations. You would be working on a pile of pages, scratching out, adding in, almost lost in a process of thinking through. I would watch, enthralled. What I took away from these moments was something that has, over the years, tempered my own moments of dissatisfaction. Our work, whether it is the penning of a philosophical presentation or the planning and execution of a course session, is always unfinished, incomplete, imperfect. And that is how work should be.

The idea of imperfect work relates to that of imperfect philosophy. Although I am part of a scholarly generation that comes after yours, I believe we share three aspects of a belief in the value of imperfection. First, imperfection seems natural to the gendered, historical and contemporary, discordant lives of women. For me, as I think for you, life in the academy has never felt completely comfortable and secure, even as I am "senior" in our field, at my institution. Even as women's successes, especially in education, abound, there often seems no home for us. A relatively recent panel presentation by junior women professors confirmed, at least in my own context, that these feelings persist. While perfection need not be sought, surely comfort and contentment should be both sought and possible. This one lives with but especially for the sake of those who come after us. Perfection need not be sought, but comfort, even contentment should be.

Second, imperfection, rather than perfection, characterizes our overlapping philosophical training. Bottom lines and closed systems of thought have never made much sense, I think, to either of us. Roots in Existentialism, in pragmatism, in poststructuralism—these "non"-ism isms—are nonfoundational, nonessential, nonteleological. "There is no perfect" in theory. Holding these beliefs has meant that, led by you, many of us continue to push against, to counter tradition. There is no comfort here, but perhaps there will be inroads over time.

Third, countering tradition has meant incorporation of particular kinds of connections and components in our writing, especially as this relates to style. I think here of your writing about the arts, of a unique textual incorporation of references to literature and poetry, and of a logic all your own and by now instantly recognizable. From these influences, I see writing as an art form and philosophy as, itself, a form of literature. I am uncertain whether I can be said to have a "style," but I do know that form matters to me, that the aesthetic and the rhetorical shape what I write. I know that each and every word I choose and sentence I complete incorporate stylistic attention.

I want to be clear that imperfection is the natural state of things, of lives worth living that you have so well described. Even a dichotomy of perfect–imperfect seems misstated. Persons believing in the value of imperfection will attempt to undertake each endeavor "as best as one can at the moment." Teaching can be thus; writing can be thus.

One more point about perfection: Every person ought to experience some "near-perfect" moments. These are the highlights of which life-memories are made. They concern big things and small things. They are characterized by a drawing in, a cessation of what is termed cognition or intellection; we often live through them without recognizing their importance until later. Big moments might include a special trip, a bestowal of an honor, a set of letters such as this volume to celebrate you. Small moments might include a meaningful conversation with a student or a friend, a passage read with sudden insight, a painting immediately loved. For both you and I, I believe the latter also encompasses special times when we, as women academics, philosophers, and educators, evoke an idea just as it must be written. No other time holds such near-perfection. To you uniquely and as a representative of a generation, I am most grateful for what I have come to understand and experience as our lived imperfection.

—Lynda Stone

You Are Our Muse

LEONARD WAKS

**To provoke our students to break through the limits of the convention-
al and the taken for granted, we ourselves have to experience breaks
with what has been established in our own lives; we have to keep
arousing ourselves to begin again.**
                                           —Maxine Greene, *Releasing the Imagination*

Dear Maxine,

I recently read Ann Beattie's story "Mr. Nobody at All," a devilish
send-off built from self-serving eulogies at a fictional memorial service. And
you tell me celebrations of your life and work make you feel like you are
being eulogized, so I want to tread carefully.

Maxine, I first want to thank you for being a living philosopher of
education for our time. You often told me that analytical philosophers of
education "frighten" you. (I guess that can be taken several ways.) You
offer a counterpoint: a living "philosophy"—an inviting pathway to an
open future. You draw from your wide reading in literature and the arts to
make brilliant and startling and liberating juxtapositions. The analysts in
their day won a readership among their peers; you also won an audience
among educators and educated people looking for something new and alive,
the signs of the times. You are our sentinel.

Some analytic philosophers found you "alien" because you drew upon
Continental philosophy. But your work is squarely in the American Grain,
a continuation of the spirit of Emerson, Whitman, and Dewey, pointing to
a world of possibility and hope. Nothing in your philosophy is a matter of
words, though you use them so well; real philosophers and teachers, for
you, don't provide verbal lessons but models of freedom in living. Words
mean little unless backed by personal experiences: taking risks, "breaking
free" from self-limiting definitions, moving to the "not yet." You are our
model in freedom.

So I thank you for your own infinite capacity to reinvent yourself and,
in doing so, to reinvent the role of philosopher of education, to take new
risks, to discover new ways to invite others into the conversation: uncon-
ventional literate essays, public lectures, salons, a foundation...and who
knows what you have up your sleeve next? You always find new audiences,
or remain accessible so they can find you, and thus find words that speak
to their longings for something liberating, beyond their conventional selves.

I wonder at your uncanny ability to find yourself at the center of action. President of the American Educational Studies Association and the Dewey Society—well, perhaps those honors were to be expected for your achievements. But AERA? I remember what AERA was like in the 1960s: dusty, intellectually empty, a death trap. Talk about being "frightened": I took a few whiffs and beat a hasty retreat. Yet you, along with Elliot Eisner and Phil Jackson and a few others, kept plugging along, taking risks, stepping out of line, bringing the humanities into educational scholarship, and breathing fresh life into what appeared to be a corpse. You had faith that under the dust real people were longing and searching for a way to make a contribution to life. And what a difference you made. You are our knight and champion.

I also want to thank you for being my friend. You supported my work when I was young and lacked self-confidence. Out of the blue, a letter would come from Maxine Greene saying what a wonderful and important article I had written. When we crossed paths at meetings you always called me aside to offer words of friendship and praise. Once, when you heard me speak, you said, with a backwards glance at Emerson, "*You* never disappoint!" And in time I learned that you gave these priceless gifts to other young philosophers, encouraging them to be fully themselves. Perhaps other senior scholars give these inspiring gifts so generously, but I never caught wind of it. You are our muse.

Thank you for being present, for always being ready to come and speak to so many different audiences at so many events, for never holding yourself back. When I was organizing the National Technological Literacy Conferences in the 1980s I invited you twice and you came both times, though characteristically insisting you knew nothing about technology or even about what technological literacy meant. And you found just the right words to wake up our participants—engineers, scientists, professors, and activists. We heard talks from the presidents of IBM and Intel, directors of the National Science Foundation and Office of Technology Assessment, congressmen and senators, and even technology critics like Ivan Illich and Jeremy Rifkin. Many of our participants told me that for them you were the most important speaker at those meetings.

I hope you forgive me for telling this story: I recently prepared a book of intellectual self-portraits of leading philosophers of education. You were not included, and reviewers have been unanimous in pointing to this as a serious defect. How were they to know that I had personally almost begged you for a contribution? You said you had already traced out your intellectual life in several essays and in a good documentary film. And then you added that, in any case, you never regarded yourself as a "leader" in the philosophy of education.

You are a leading philosopher of education; that cannot be questioned. So I had to ask myself: What could you have meant? Perhaps you meant that, unlike Israel Scheffler or Richard Peters, you didn't have a school of "followers." Perhaps you think that being a "leader" in this sense is a complete repudiation of your philosophy of "we are what we are not yet." Dewey says that culture is life leaving the past behind. Perhaps you think that reclaiming and privileging leading voices from the past undermines the free development of our field as it responds to new problems with new intellectual and cultural resources. I hope we can reflect together on these questions soon.

Finally, thank you, Maxine, for living your life as an open book, for welcoming me and so many others into your home, for being so forthright and guileless about your own feelings and doubts and sorrows, for not playing king of the heap. You are our friend.

—Leonard Waks

Chapter Three

Strangers, Others, and Friends

Expanding the Conversation

To take the stranger's vantage point on everyday reality is to look
inquiringly and wonderingly on the world in which one lives. It is like
returning home from a long stay in some other place. The homecomer
notices details and patterns in his environment he never saw before.
—Maxine Greene, *Teacher as Stranger*

*There are several letters in this section that continue the conversation initi-
ated in* Teacher as Stranger, *and in the other letters, the stranger's experience
is an implicit theme. Yet even as strangers we are not alone. This chapter also contains poignant glimpses into sustained friendships, collegiality,
and empathic connection with "others" in a way that reminds me of this
line from Gwendolyn Brooks: "We are each other's magnitude and bond"
(1998, p. 235).*

Down the Same Roads for Many a Year

ELLIOT EISNER

Dear Maxine:

Advancing years are supposed to provide perspective, a long view—or
at least a longer view than is usual in ordinary living. Do I have a long
view of you and your work? It seems to me that I do. In the first place, we
have been tramping down the same roads for many a year now. Our common direction is a function of a common, but not identical, array of values
concerning what the process of education is about, especially what needs

attention. Some of my grandest memories include interactions with you and Jack Getzells at the Hilton Hotel in Chicago many years ago. We had something of a debate going on up there on the stage, and it was a lot of fun! It also, at least I hope, provided a forum for the expression of our ideas.

In the direction that you have taken, which, as I say, is not all that diverse from my own, you emphasized the experiential or, as we say more recently, the qualitative side of our educational ledger. Your work, I think, has more mystery than mine. It is this mystery that attracts people because it provides them with a perspective that is all but absent in the technological orientation that has been dominating American education for well over 50 years. You have offered them another perspective, perhaps not as long-term but equally as important. And the troops responded. They responded, I believe, because pervading your writing and speechmaking is a source of inspiration that simply is extremely rare among those who speak for education. We are so bullied about by technocratic conceptions and bureaucratic regulations that your words to countless educators are an enormous relief.

Just what is it that is inspiring about your work? Let me suggest a few features that seem to me to be expressive of the inspirational tone that your language frequently reveals. First, you don't get tied down by the linguistic rules and regulations that are so characteristic of technocratic functions. You don't yield to conceptions that you believe counteract your most deeply cherished values. For example, the preoccupation with standards in American schools is not something that ranks high on your list of personal priorities. Your task, as I see it, is to remind students of education of what really matters, to awaken them to the unrealized potentialities that attentive experience makes possible. This is no small task, nor is it an unimportant one. Becoming wide-awake, as you say, is one of the fruits of a rich life. You have tried to awaken those who read and listen to your remarks to that kind of light. You have succeeded in more ways than I suspect you know.

A second feature of your speaking and writing is related to the magic of your expressive and poetic use of language. You have not been afraid to write about education using a language that is sometimes hard to nail down, but you're not interested in nailing down, you're more interested in opening up.

I believe that such features are of fundamental importance in any effort to significantly reshape schools. You have tried to introduce students to new seas on which to sail rather than old ports at which to dock. In providing this vision, you helped expand awareness of the possibilities in education, particularly those embracing a phenomenological perspective. Your major message for me is, "Wake up!" That signal is particularly important today. Students are known to watch two or three frames on a television set simultaneously. In the process, we consume our meal but never really taste it.

Maxine Greene is about helping students taste what is possible in the hope that they will like it and that they will pursue more delicate satisfactions in the future. I am happy to have been a part of our conversation.

Cordially,
—Elliot Eisner

Accompanying the Artists as They Choose What to See

Peter Appelbaum

Dear Maxine,

More than once you have told me it would be impossible to update *Teacher as Stranger* (1973) for a new edition, claiming that the book is too early 1970s in its outlook. Noting that all of the references to films and literature were particular to that historical period, you have dismissed my pleas to make the book more available to new generations of educators. I reread it at least once a year. Each return is as refreshing as my first time, back in 1985, when I was a new graduate student in education. Just this summer, in 2009, I have had the remarkable experience of your writing helping me to articulate my own ideas, to help me choose for myself, to do philosophy and build a world. "It is particularly difficult for the teacher to give up the conviction that he possesses some independent faculty enabling him to know, under all circumstances, what he ought to do" (Greene, 1973, p. 237)

Not only is the school itself being challenged; the teacher's legitimacy is now being questioned, along with the value of his subject matter and the methods he has been taught to use. He is asked to defend and justify beliefs he once could take for granted. He is asked to account for himself to diverse groups of people. It becomes increasingly evident that he cannot fall back on shared agreements or find his sanction in what is understood to be the moral law.

Now, as always, I find myself in the position of a stranger, my vantage point on everyday reality one of wonder and inquiry, as if I were returning home from a long stay in some other place, finding myself struggling against unthinking submergence in the prevailing social reality. Always estranged, engaged in extraordinarily reexperiencing the ordinary, in interpreting a reality forever new, I am alive. I lose that communicative gesture if I walk in the shadows of slogans and pieties repeated warmly but reassuringly. Fighting the plague. Cooking the feast, like incendiary Babette, the artist chef in the 1987 film *Babette's Feast*. "An artist is never poor," she said.

After close to 30 years of teaching, I accept that I cannot tell another person how to live. I knew this 30 years ago, as well as that I cannot demand that my students exercise their will and become in their own way "volunteers." But I have been spending about that many years setting up classroom situations that make it difficult to maintain "peace of mind," whether it be through engagement with the arts, contexts of crisis, or simply concrete questions by students of what standpoint they need to occupy. I had forgotten where my inchoate idea of a "taking action" curriculum had come from, until I again read the last chapter of your book, page 286, where you write about the tensions originating for the teacher who is truly concerned with stimulating such action rather than merely mechanical behavior. This is what I have spent the last 30 years working on: On my return home to Maxine Greene's *Teacher as Stranger*, with wonder and estrangement, I have been asking of the 1970s Maxine, "What do I do *with* that implicit threat of coercion in a classroom" by the teacher and the curriculum of the students? My current explorations continue to be inspired by a notion of the artist avoiding the mechanization of representations. For schools that accept uncritically their purpose as the development of automaticity of skills and procedural knowledge, a sort of counterartistry in the very mechanized representation espoused in *Teacher as Stranger*, this is often received as profoundly disturbing, disruptive, bewildering. I have been pursuing the notion, one I first encountered in our discussions of *Babette's Feast*, that incendiary artists "perform" rather than "illustrate" what they have to make of the world; maybe we didn't quite express it this way back then, but I believe now that this is a fundamental difference that educators can use as a lens to understand their work.

When the artists are young mathematicians, scientists, writers and historians, choosers and creators, and if I am their teacher, I *know* there is no final explanation of any particular experience with a work of art; and I know that no one can bring about appreciation or enjoyment in another, that I can only accompany the artists as they choose what to see. The word you used to make such a distinction, in 1973, was "significance." Today, one might employ "meaning" or "naming the world," or the exhortation to change one's life in imagination, to build the world in the never-ending wonder of what assumptions and idiosyncratic confusions will cause us to rebuild that same world in process, before there can ever be a feeling of completion. Thank you for setting me on this path of losing my sense of certainty to the demands of what I believe I know.

—Peter Appelbaum

Big Maxine and little maxine

Suzanne de Castell

Dearest Maxine,

"*There is Big Maxine...and there is little maxine...*" First, who is this addressed to? Thinking about writing to you after years out of touch swells, immediately and predictably, into an odd, familiar "Maxine-esque" sort of feeling. I am pretty sure that's what, or a good part of what, "love" means. So although I know in writing this letter into a book, I must be addressing Big Maxine, it is a letter intended for little maxine whom I could otherwise directly address, and it's little maxine that the rest of this is about. This is a letter composed of two things: fragments I remember and am grateful to acknowledge, addressed to whomever can get from them anything like what these fragments made possible in my own life, and, I am pretty sure, a belated love letter.

"*I will have no trouble remembering THAT name...*" It was Linda, my partner then, to whom I had just introduced you. And it was Linda, your daughter, whose memory you invoked and shared without an instant's hesitation, without the slightest flinch of that loss, inviting inside two daughter-aged "strangers," or nearly so. This attentiveness to thresholds, as strangers and familiars cross and converge, doorways where gatekeepers admit and deny entry, is what has to me seemed at the center of the intense joyful sparkiness of Maxine I love and feel so relieved by. And I want here to thank Maxine for that incredible relief—that other people, very famous, very good, very productive and creative people, also have trouble containing the amazement and delight (let's pass over the abyss for now, and defer the hell of other people) of living the world in ways that look in public so dangerously like madness. Is this what enables Big Maxine to leap across giant conceptual edifices in a single bound, this so-open, so-joyful, so-brave willingness to inhabit and act within the liminal, to work at thresholds and barricades? At any rate, I have never seen before or since in anyone that generosity of spirit, ease, and quickness to allow that one's most loved ones are like these strangers here—more and less like, but that's a further and deeper thing yet—and the ability to hold fast to insights as much as to share them, even if of course sometimes seeing in the most clear and uncompromising way how terribly, painfully in error someone might be. The incredible kindness...I have gratefully learned about whole new regions of ethics, both personal and professional, from watching, always raptly, always in admiration, how you have lived your very personally public life.

"I'm running away from the abyss..." Maxine, remember one year at a Philosophy of Education conference, a session where nobody was showing up, and you hauled up your elegant mid-length black (wasn't it always black back then?) skirt to show off no less elegant, fine black-stockinged legs, and stood just outside the doorway pointing and indicating and "enticing," you said, audience members? That's when I bought *Seduction*, hoping Baudrillard might help me theorize my way out of an entirely unprecedented, unlikely but undeniable desire. Couldn't touch it. I was shocked in the middle of one day with a realization of having dreamed of you, images that came quite, as they once said, unbidden and intruded themselves into pretty much everything. This was not just and maybe not even intellectual attraction—far, far too clearly etched and colored for that! What we roughly and too carelessly designate "passion" comes less often than we could wish. You were pretty obviously sick in those years—so how come we were doing maybe two sessions at AERA, and you were doing five (packed in between a couple of other conferences, to boot)? Why the red-eye flights to talk here or there, sometimes just at a friend's small gathering, a local conference? And so many things endlessly written, in bits, on single sheets or scraps of paper, envelopes, and napkins, all getting pulled together in one after another absolutely brilliant, always dizzying response or keynote or panel or meeting. Amazing, wonderful, powerful honesty and bravery were what I gratefully received from your flight from the abyss, back to Sartre, refusing "stuckness" while embracing "thrownness." But I assure you, it wasn't the lofty "life of the mind" kind of love it engendered for me, nor even the rather more embodied "spiritual" passions the prodigious feats and inexhaustible energies of "Big Maxine" ignited—no, indeed, it was the wiry, aging body of the little maxine driving all of this wonder, the (characteristically smudged, reapplied, smudged again) red lipstick, the invariably fly-away hair that I, as a then quite young would-be academic, was hopelessly enraptured with.

"Oh no! I am SO sorry! I'm so terribly awkward..." Maybe a decade later, AERA, New Orleans, and yet again I was astonished at the eagerness with which you accepted an invitation to dinner. Astonished, because after all, Maxine was so "Big," everyone wanted a bit of you, and yet every time we met, you always found a way to have a lunch or dinner together. I introduced you to my new partner, Mary B, who was understandably starstruck and nervous. No sooner had we poured very large glasses of red wine and started to eat than Mary reached out and caught the edge of one full glass with her shirt cuff, and over it tipped, spilling quantities of red wine

over the crisp white table linen. Before any breath could be caught, you launched into the most irrefutable account of how your carelessness had caused the spill and how sorry you were, as we all mopped up, and Mary and I exchanged glances silently assenting to this generous fabrication, sharing astonishment at the incredibly deep well of generosity out of which this one small-BIG kindness had been drawn.

It's too easy to say I, and "we," are all in awe, because being wonder-struck doesn't make for much real-world action, which is my understanding of y/our imperative. So this is what I have drawn very literally from you, not in books but in far simpler speakings. This is the shape of your edge from which those who will and dare can, in response, allow themselves to be reshaped. For years and years now all who know you have wondered, "Where do we see the next generation of Maxines, of those exemplary intellectuals who show 'ostensively,' by making themselves into 'object lessons,' literally embodying in daily being, life, and work the era's most urgent and dangerous agents and agencies of societal structuration, as well as their most glorious oppositional counterparts?" Methodologically, this enactment has, I know, looked to some folks like a species of madness. Early on, one philosophy of education colleague responded to my exhilaration after first hearing you speak, "Ah, Maxine...none of us can make any sense of what she is saying." Because, refusing the "discipline" even while embracing it, you have reconciled differences, conjoined opposites, crossed boundaries, braved contradictories, bridged chasms, and named unspeakables. You have inhabited doorways and barricades and thresholds...and prison windows.

Women in my day, we just didn't know what was possible. To choose a life with women wasn't anything we could imagine for ourselves. Maybe I was a coward—I just found ways to live inside the restrictions and expectations...but when I was a girl, I used to hide myself away and cut out paper dolls, and we would play for hours. That was the closest I could get...

Because it could make no sense to any other reader, the last can only be written to maxine, not Maxine. As one queer British philosopher accustomed to great chasms of silence once said, what you can't talk about, you must pretty much just shut up about, so I'll end this letter here. But not without one last quote, captured as you're leveraging *Flaubert's Parrot* to pry open a bit of postmodern theory:

The doctor asks how we can ever seize the past. He remembers that, when he was a medical student, some pranksters at a dance released into the hall a piglet smeared with grease. "It squirmed between legs, evaded capture, squealed a lot. People fell over trying to grasp it, and were made to look ridiculous in the process. The past often seems to behave like that piglet." (Greene, 1993c)

And so, given what we see happening today, does what we used to call "objective reality." It does occur to me, however, that there *was* an actual pig.

Paper dolls, or whatever it is for each of us... For me, I'm done "letter-writing," and it's long past time to make a phone call to maxine.

With love,

—Sz.

Burdening Aesthetics

Greg Dimitriadis

Dear Professor Greene,

I am honored, of course, to write to you today—to share with you my thoughts and reflections on your monumental body of work. I've returned to it many times over the years, particularly at times of personal transition. Like many, I was drawn early on to your work on the arts—and, in particular, the ways in which the arts can provide resources for re-visioning and imagining our quotidian circumstances. I am thinking, in particular, of its influence work I began in the late 1990s with Cameron McCarthy, around globalization, art, and the postcolonial imagination. Your writing on the aesthetic imagination allowed us to examine a range of artists and intellectuals from around the world, bringing their insights to bear on the proliferation of difference that has so marked our global condition and moment. When we wrote of "the work of art in the postcolonial imagination," it was in homage both to you and to Walter Benjamin. *Reading and Teaching the Postcolonial* was published in the summer of 2001. You provided the Preface—a singular honor.

Much has changed since then. We've lived through 9/11, George W. Bush's two terms as President, the invasion of Iraq, the election of Barack Obama, and the meltdown of global capitalism, among other events. If nothing else, the "work of the imagination" has proven to be more complex, dangerous, and unpredictable than I could have anticipated. Indeed, who can speak naively of the imagination after 9/11? Those who planned this atrocity lacked neither imaginative capacities nor the desire to remake the world. A few simple box cutters helped decimate the Twin Towers, effectively reordering the world political stage for years to come. The impulse to transcend one's circumstances can be dangerous indeed.

Of course, you already knew this. As I reread your work, as I return to essays such as *Teacher as Stranger* (1973), the deep, existential dread at the heart of your project is readily apparent. The work of the imagination has no guarantees. The aesthetic impulse is not necessarily a moral one. You reminded me of this again recently as I reread *Teacher as Stranger*. As you wrote, "Our responsibility, then, is immense, especially when we consider (for the existentialist) there are no predetermined values, no moral principles which determine in advance what is good. Alone and condemned to freedom, the individual *must* choose" (p. 279).

Like so much of our language, the term "freedom" has become debased—reduced in many cases to a commercial cliché. Echoing Sartre, you remind us that personal freedom is a tremendous burden. We are "condemned" to a state that provides us no alibis for our actions and effects in the world. We have an inescapable imperative to "author" our own lives.

As you underscore throughout your work, we can only understand the role of art and the imagination in this context. Art provides us the resources to expand our own emotional and intellectual palates. You remind us that this is the *beginning* of a struggle—not a simple answer to a question. Art is a resource to work toward a life lived in "good faith." You write, "Nothing is more difficult to be—and to ask others to be—in good faith" (p. 283). These are strong words—and I take nothing you say lightly. Brute empiricism and simple, willful transcendence—the two pillars of bad faith— remove us from the struggle to realize ourselves as authentic human beings, always carrying the burdens of living lives honestly. In bad faith, we refuse to become the "stranger" about which you write. We take up *a priori* roles. We take recourse in static belief systems. We allow ourselves to be swept along in the "everydayness" of the world around us. The aesthetic transactions you write about provide resources for living in good faith. But they demand much of us.

This seems to be the great challenge of our times. The new imageries unleashed by globalization have too often taken hold in inert belief systems—the "bad faith" about which you and Sartre have written. We see this in the rise of world fundamentalisms—Islamic, Christian, and otherwise—that have been the driving engine of world politics for the first part of the new century. These fundamentalisms do not lack imaginative impulses. Nor do they lack revolutionary zeal. Rather, such impulses are deeply wed to inert and unchanging belief systems—deterministic ones. As I reread your work, as I return to essays such as "Teacher as Stranger," I see these dangers anticipated. I can feel the tremendous possibilities you invest for us in art and the imagination emerging from the profound dangers of "bad faith," the dangers of deterministic pulls that would render us inert and inauthentic. I suppose every generation has to be reminded of these dangers.

Your metaphor of the "teacher as stranger" seems, again, an apt one. As the cultural, material, and social shifts and dislocations of the last decade continue to register, the temptation to fall back on comforting and familiar explanatory mechanisms is strong. Curriculum theory, cultural studies, critical pedagogy, and other schools of thought have provided some important tools for understanding the condition we find ourselves in today. But none seem wholly adequate to the task. You return me, rather, to this metaphor—the struggle to be a stranger in the world, to continually reacquaint myself with the world around me in new ways, to resist conscription in the intellectual and administrative routines of academic life, to face the world in good faith every day. Again, you pose this as a challenge, not an answer—and it's appropriately unsettling.

I recall assigning Carlos Torres's book to my class a few years back—*Education, Power, and Personal Biography: Dialogues with Critical Educators* (1998). Many of the most important scholars in education are included in the book, and my class loved it as a whole—in particular, they enjoyed seeing the authors we otherwise read in essay and book form reflect on their lives and work. They had an interesting response to your interview with Torres, however. Of all the figures in the book, they said, you were the only one who seemed to intimidate him! I confess not seeing this myself, but several of the students came to this conclusion independently and were insistent. I think they saw something in the dynamic that I missed—something vital and important about the challenge you continue pose for us all—something we miss at our collective risk.

Best,
—Greg Dimitriadis

The Uncanny Legend of Maxine Greene

NOREEN GARMAN

> Language alone protects us from the scariness of things with no names.
> Language alone is meditation.
> —Toni Morrison, Nobel Prize acceptance speech

Dear Maxine,

I suspect by now that these letters have exhausted every superlative that exists about your inspirational life. How lucky we are, Maxine, to have the opportunity to struggle for ways to name the source of our thankfulness. (Naming, after all, has been a leitmotif in your work.) These voices of colleagues give testimony of your stature; our insights here come directly from your lyrical and profound ideas. Your life's work has given rise to what

Michelle Fine has called you, *a social movement with thousands of grand-children*. However, as you've read in the letters, there also exists a *Maxine lore*, stories that many of us hold about our cherished encounters with you. I offer one of these here. And over the years my story has grown to legendary status. I'm glad I now have the opportunity to share it with you.

"*The Uncanny Legend of Maxine Greene*" is the story I've told my doctoral students for several years as they prepare for their first academic conference presentation. They are looking for good advice. Their papers have been carefully crafted and revised several times. They struggle to hone a summary, worried that the significance of their work will be lost in the brevity of relentless conference sessions. They imagine how they might encourage the audience to discuss their key points. Maxine, they've taken to heart your words about the "making and remaking of public space, a space of dialogue and possibility." A few years ago Jo Victoria, one of the novice presenters, was especially influenced by your challenge. She worked diligently to imagine how she might enact your words: "The aim is to find (or create) an authentic public space, that is, one in which diverse human beings can appear before one another as, to quote Hannah Arendt, 'the best they know how to be.' Such a space requires the provision of opportunities for the articulation of multiple perspectives in multiple idioms, out of which something common can be brought into being" (*The Dialectic of Freedom*, 1988, p. xi).

As you know, Maxine, it's a privilege to witness the passion and com-mitment that novice academics give to their scholarship. Presenting at a con-ference is their induction into the world of the academy. It's the opportunity to bring their ideas to an audience that chose to come and hear them. They worry about those in the group who might challenge their work. They try to anticipate how to respond. Mostly, they hope they'll be able to engender a genuine dialogue, even as they concentrate on their image as conference presenter. Those of us who are old and jaded about conference presenta-tions know the vagaries that face the anxious novice. (Paper presentations are often combined with others, and there's little time for audience discus-sion. Ironically, for her paper, Jo Victoria was given a single slot at 8 A.M. on Sunday morning, where one person and myself showed up.) So as my students prepare to leave for their first conference presentations, I tell them the following story, "The Uncanny Legend of Maxine Greene."

In the early 1980s I was active in the Northeastern Educational Research Association. NERA was one of the regional affiliates of AERA. At that time the fall conference was held in Ellenville, New York, at one of the venues, a slightly seedy former Borscht Belt hotel. Actually, I loved going to the Catskills in the glorious time of autumn leaves—probably one rea-son I remained a contributing member for 4 years. (NERA members were primarily measurement and evaluation researchers, and I was having a difficult time speaking the legitimate language of educational research.)

Traditionally, at each conference, the NERA board issued invitations to two nationally known scholars, one to give the keynote address and the other to provide a session on the state of the literature related to a topic of interest to the membership. In 1980 Robert Glazer was invited as the keynoter. I was delighted to see that Maxine Greene had also been invited to give the state-of-the-art session on aesthetic education. When I read her 1973 *Teacher as Stranger*, she had named what was troubling me.

She introduced me to a rich language and perspective that I couldn't find in the mainstream research of that time. Her book began by reminding us that the commonly accepted purpose of education is the effort of a community to re-create itself with the rise of each new generation and to perpetuate itself in historic time. But her astounding questions challenged educators: "If the community is clearly unjust and inequitable, should not the educator be concerned primarily with social change? Why transmit a heritage conceived to be sterile or 'sick?' Why keep a declining culture alive?" (p. 4). Bravo! I loved it!

I knew that Maxine Greene would be the Stranger as she spoke about aesthetic education, inviting us to take a different vantage point on everyday reality—to look inquiringly and wonderingly on the world in which we live—to enter the multiple provinces of meaning that create perspectives. "To enter these perspectives," she would say to us, "(be they those identified with the arts, the social sciences, the natural sciences), the learner must break with the taken-for-granted, what some call the 'natural attitude,' and look through the lenses of various ways of knowing, seeing and feeling in a conscious endeavor to impose different orders upon experience" (later published in *Variations on a Blue Guitar*, 2001, p. 5). I could hardly wait for the day of her presentation.

Friday morning came, and a half-hour before the presentation, I headed for the assigned room. I thought I'd better get there early for a good seat. I took out my tablet for notes, knowing I could never capture the resonance of her language. And, at the designated time, four other people showed up for her session. I couldn't believe it . . . *Five people to hear the magnificent ideas of Maxine Greene? How could this be?*

Maxine Greene was dauntless. She treated us as if the five of us were the most important people in the world. She invited us into her intellectual world and then proceeded to create a common space and a mutual "tuning-in relationship." It was like being part of a musical experience that she would later name in *Variations on a Blue Guitar* (2001). In her book she likened the musical experience to the other experience that we were having then: "what can happen in situations . . . and in our classrooms when, by means of performance, an enactment, a reading, or an exhibition, a 'We' can emerge in vivid presence—something crucial to our lives" (p. 189). Here at NERA, in these temporal moments of "vivid presence," we had lived out an aesthetic experience.

So, one message to you, as first-time presenters on your way to perform your first reading—you may find a sparse group of people at your session. But if, in her résumé, Maxine Greene can have a conference presentation with five people in attendance, so, too, can anybody. It has nothing to do with numbers . . . it has to do with those *who came*, hoping to bring something into being with you. For that moment in time, as with Maxine, they are the most important people in the world.

It should be noted that in 1989, nine years later, Maxine was invited back to NERA for the keynote address. I wasn't there, but the report from the program chair in a recent e-mail to me indicated that "she was an amazing lady."

I'm not sure, Maxine, how you feel about being a legend in your own time. Legends are meant to reveal a moral definition about people and events that lifts the stories above the constraints of average human lives. And, indeed, you are an academic legend, one that has a universality that makes it worthy of repeating through the generations of students.

Moreover, the Maxine lore, full of cherished memories, is alive and in abundant supply. The memories are certainly a significant part of my repertoire, especially when I think about how I've confronted the lesser side of my own actions. Some of my fondest memories and personal awareness happened in the mid-1980s when I was part of a teacher renewal initiative at Teachers College. Fran Schoonmaker Bolin brought a group of us together each summer to engage in exciting ideas and activities with teachers, and you were part of it. After a morning session we would sit around a big lunch table with graduate teaching assistants and discuss the day's encounters. (In those years Bill Ayers was one of the grad students at the table.) As I watched you in conversation with those students, it was again clear how you treated their ideas with affirmation, not always agreeing but always extending, with humility, the insights that emerged. Again, Maxine, those moments of vivid presence made us all feel significant. Even as we were contentious, we mattered. I watched you, awakened to those around you, and I realized how many times I really didn't hear others. Too often I was focused on reshaping my own ideas in my head for further argument. It's a normative ego filter that still surfaces periodically to interfere with my fully hearing and appreciating the other. Then I try to recall how your words and your bearing became my touchstone. I think of those summers around the table and try harder to open my hearing and my heart to the possibilities that are "not yet."

Please know, Maxine, how much you are loved.

—Noreen Garman

Learning Quality and Becoming Human

JAMES GIARELLI

**Man is a creature who makes pictures of himself, and then comes to
resemble the picture.**
                                   —Iris Murdoch, "Metaphysics and Ethics"

My Dear Maxine:

Sorry I've been out of touch. You always taught us how important it
is to express ourselves, but always forgave us when we lost courage or suc-
cumbed to the bad faith of imagining that we had good reasons for doing
something other than that which was true and right. Well, you forgave us
for a while, but we knew you weren't happy. I always took this not as disap-
proval, but as a kind of active caring—a kind of Freirean "love." It wasn't
just a vague, sentimental feeling; it was always pointed toward liberation.

"We" is a funny word here. When I first started teaching the philosophy
of education more than 35 years ago, I taught your books. At that time,
it was probably *Teacher as Stranger* (1973), then *Landscapes of Learning*
(1978). I still teach your books in 2009: *The Dialectic of Freedom* (1988),
Variations on a Blue Guitar (2001), and others. I did this originally because
I had some idea that I was supposed to "cover the material," and you were
certainly part of the material. But I was never quite sure how to fit your work
into the boxes of the syllabus. Existentialist? Sure, but every Existentialist
worth his or her salt had written that they were not one. Feminist? Of course,
but there's no identity lurking anywhere in your ontological basement. Public
philosopher? You bet, but you always told us to worry about the false and
often dangerous consequences of talk from "the center." Maybe my whole
idea, *the* whole idea, of "boxes" was wrong, and instead we should think
about dialogues. But "dialogue," unfortunately, has itself become a hack-
neyed phrase, nowhere near Dewey's conception of Dialogues as expressions
of a "dramatic, restless, co-operatively inquiring Plato" (Greene, 1973, p. 9).
Maybe "dialectical" was the right phrase (after all, it was the theme of one
of your books), but "dialectical" also is mired in mechanistic images. Maybe
"conversation"—but it's a slippery slope from conversation to the kinds of
postmodern elitism that ridicule serious public debate as casually as the analytic philosophers used to try to tell us that talk about most of the things that
mattered to people was philosophically meaningless.

Why am I worrying about these boxes, anyway? More important than
where you fit in some syllabus is what you've taught me in person, *as a*

person, over all these years. I think we first met at a party at Henry Giroux's apartment, when he and I were both at Boston University. I rambled about some things I was working on at the time on moral education and you sent me encouragement and papers you were doing about Carol Gilligan's work, which I hardly knew. After every conversation, you wrote me, told me I was thinking about things that mattered, even if it wasn't true, and suggested sources and alternative pathways to explore. We talked about the journal *The Social Frontier*, and you wrote me about liberalism.

At one point, you asked me to teach a course on social philosophy in the AEGIS program at Teachers College. These adult educators who came every summer to study at TC were expecting a "capstone" course with Maxine Greene and got me instead. At my request, you suggested I should make "an effort to study the critical tradition in its various forms and to look at the difference between a 'polis' and what Marx would call a society. Focus on themes of reflectiveness, articulateness, ideology and mystification. Suggested sources: Marx, Harriet Arnow's *The Dollmaker*, Habermas, Dewey, Freire, Arendt, Apple, Giroux, *Habits of the Heart*, the Nizan novel, *Antoine Bloye...*" It was pretty intimidating, but you told me to go my own way, and I did and learned a lot in the several years I taught the course.

Later, you had a lot to do with me being asked to teach a couple of classes at TC while the philosophy of education program was in transition while I was still working full-time at Rutgers. I wasn't quite sure where I was all the time, but you wrote me to convince me that this was not a bad thing. Your letters are full of this kind of stuff: "I am mad, insatiable, and full of denials, but it gives me energy," "I am flunking retirement badly," "I'm feisty enough to fan continuing outrage at administration and to struggle for ways to keep hope as well as resistance alive."

Every single part of this history educated me about what Dewey called "becoming human." Little by little, you taught me how to make some sense of what I do as a philosopher and educator. A few years ago, I had a chance to write some of this down for a session at the American Educational Studies Association conference. I said,

> Maxine taught us that reflection was not about correspondence or even coherence, but rather was about the rereading of texts from our own perspectival vantage points and that the world was a contested, delirious text that was always being written and newly read.

In Bill Pinar's book, *The Passionate Mind of Maxine Greene*, I wrote, "The work of Maxine Greene stands out as the most original and compelling response to [the problematic relationship of the school and the conscious quest for a public education] in the latter half of the twentieth century" (Giarelli, 1998, p. 174). I think the most engaging and danger-ous educational conversation is about "quality." Dewey taught us, and you showed us, that the aesthetic was not about theories of beauty, but rather experiences of quality. You taught us that the aesthetic was not a response to a what, who, or how question, but an *event*, a response to a "when" ques-tion. When is quality? That's why your books are not about "art" in any of the ways it is defined in schools or universities. You taught us that art is a quality of an encounter, a special kind of relationship. The aesthetic is a particular kind, maybe the most significant kind, of freedom.

You wrote me once, "I do not want to be treated as a guru, a leftover, priestess, old woman...But to be remembered as a friend." Okay. You're not a "doyenne," as someone once called you, and I won't call you a guru or anything of the sort. But you are my teacher, *our* teacher, and you are my friend. Thank you, my friend.

Love,
—Jim Giarelli

The Dialectical Diva

CHRIS HIGGINS

Dear Maxine,
The first thing I heard when I got to Teachers College was that you had retired. Gullible as I was, I spent my 1st year or so in the doctoral program believing such a thing to be not only possible, but true. Later, I would come to know and love just how unretiring you are in every sense of the word.

I think it was midway through my 2nd year when René Arcilla, the department chair, suddenly pulled me aside and, with a look that said we were both in trouble, told me, "Maxine wants to know why you haven't been to see her yet." Imagine my surprise. You were supposed to be retired, after all, and as far as I knew, you were completely unaware of my existence. But, as I later learned, you don't miss much, especially when it comes to people and the interpersonal. Like Socrates, you love gossip and can sniff out fresh interlocutors from a mile away. Like Arendt, you love natality. Each year after that, you would ask me: Who are the *new* students? Are they any good?

I am sure you don't remember that first meeting, but I won't forget it. You were the queen and I had been summoned for an audience. Except you were the strangest queen I had ever imagined. As it turned out, you had us cast largely against type. I was to play the role of the Ivy League Elite and of the Discipline of Philosophy, even though I was a novice and you were the William F. Russell Professor Emerita of the Foundations of Education at an Ivy League school. But you had axes to grind, as I found out later, hearing how you had been initially placed in quarantine in English Education/ *Teachers College Record* while it was determined whether your work really counted as philosophy.

I will never forget you remarking midway through our conversation: "I feel like Yale itself is sitting on the other side of the desk judging me." You had a mischievous look, that look of yours that says: While the angst I am sharing is real, I enjoy people and ideas and the sharing of real things like angst so much that I actually feel pretty happy talking about my angst.

Now, most people wouldn't say something like that, but of course you're not like most people. For one thing, you've taught us that no real person actually fits the category of "most people," but that it remains a powerful rhetorical construction, a shelter where many of us hide, from others and from ourselves.

Whether we are talking about "most people" or most people, you do stand out. We could roughly divide the human lot into two groups: those who are full of themselves and those who have lost themselves, those of the inflated egos and those of the deflated hopes. You are much too complicated for a contrast like that. You're a dialectical diva: a dynamic combination of active refusals of both of these extremes.

Take the first type. Bores are not interested in others and so they don't listen. You are just the opposite of that. I have always loved how annoyed you look when you have to ask someone to repeat something. "Whaaat?!?" you bark. You don't like to miss a single word. Now consider the other side of the coin. Too many of us, as Emerson put it, "but half express ourselves, and are ashamed of that divine idea which each of us represents" (Emerson, 1982, p. 267). Again, you are just the opposite of such "hollow men." You are full of interesting projects, yearnings, ideas, and, yes (if I may borrow your signature syntax for a moment), regrets and insecurities, too. Never full of yourself, you display a rare fullness of self.

You have always been the best argument for the Existentialism you have advocated. You would quote Thoreau, saying that he had "never yet met a man who was quite awake" (in Greene, 1978, p. 42), and we would think: great quote, but he never met Maxine. A real person in process—a person who has never lost touch with her "shapes of childhood," an academic who cares about almost everything else more than her CV—such a person inspires us to wake up, too.

There is no fullness of self, no dynamism like yours, without contradictions, and so we love these, too. One of the wonderful ironies about you, Maxine, is how much you hate groupies and how good you are at attracting

them! We are grateful that you haven't tried to weed out the various con-
flicting strands of the human condition and become . . . a potted plant.

Instead of a coherent project and a unified self—the potted plant—
Thoreau discovers himself to be more like:

> A bunch of violets without their roots,
> And sorrel intermixed,
> Encircled by a wisp of straw
> Once coiled about their shoots,
> The law By which I'm fixed.
>   (1947, p. 228)

Like Thoreau, you realize that it is empty to celebrate our green and
growing edges without also acknowledging the ways in which we wither.
You have always had the courage to face the fact that the Law of the Self
turns out to be as unbearably light as a wisp of straw.

Even when it is unseasonably bitter—at the "End of March" as Elizabeth Bishop would have it—with a "rackety, icy, offshore wind," you have
opted to take the "walk on that long beach" (1976, pp. 179–180). Like
Bishop's narrator, you may have wanted to take shelter in your "crypto-
dream-house," to sip your "*grog à l'américaine*" by the fire, "to retire and
do nothing." But because you have never mistaken imagination for fantasy,
you have seen that "many things about this place are dubious," and that "of
course the house was boarded up."

So, a strange first meeting . . . and I was hooked. Soon I was your TA
and working on those conferences. Watching you teach was important for
me. Because I had found much of "liberal education" to be preprofessional,
it was ironic, if somehow fitting, that I should find you and René, such
remarkable liberal artists, tucked away in a professional school. The things
you tell about, Maxine, are wonderful, but as we both know, in writing
and teaching it is the *showing* that counts. And that is what is so impressive
about your teaching. You show your students how one might (should, must)
combine concerns for the arts, education, and social justice, not abstractly,
but in a lived life. And you do what exemplary teachers do: show their students why freedom matters, what freedom might be freedom for, embodying
what William Arrowsmith calls "a ripeness of self" (1971, p. 12).

Recently, in a master class on Plato, Jonathan Lear was asked by one of
the students whether Plato's Socrates was more of a portrait of the man who
actually lived or a fictional creation, and whether this even mattered (2008).
He said something surprising, something I found moving. He said that he
thought that it was a faithful portrait and that indeed the question mattered
a great deal. To know that a Socrates, someone who conducted himself

more or less as Plato reports, once lived—that there had been at least one Socrates—was a source of hope for him. To know that an ideal you hold has been and can be instantiated in this world is of the utmost importance.

And you, Maxine, are living proof of several of the things I care most about. In the midst of education talk, which as you know so often tends toward kitsch, there you are refusing that simplification and sweetening of reality that stunt us.

In the midst of theory talk, which so often chases novelty rather than plumbing towards originality (to borrow George Steiner's [1989, p. 27] distinction), which opts for disembodied statements rather than true Deweyan expressions, there you are mining the deep veins and finding fresh and fleshy ways to embody the ideas you discover.

Most importantly, in a world that is always growing old, "superannuated" (1958, p. 193), as Arendt puts it, there you are providing us such a remarkable example of a person who has stayed in touch with her natality.

It is because it was so crucial to find you, to find these things in you, that I am sure we will never lose you.

Love,
—Chris

An Interview That Never Really Began: An Afterword to Maxine Greene

CLYDE COREIL

Dear Maxine,

The first time I met you, my hope was to garner enough of your views on imagination for one of the articles in a book I edited in 2008 called *Imagination, Cognition and Language Acquisition: A Unified Approach to Theory and Practice*. The interview was included in the volume, and for some of the readers, it is the first section they turned to in the text. However, what I share with you in this letter are my inner musings during what I call an interview that never happened.

I have found that sometimes the contact one makes with a person deepens into a long-term friendship, partly on the basis of carefully meted-out, shared confidences. Thinking back on it, I certainly didn't recognize what went between us as confidences—and they weren't. What they did constitute was the welcome background where confidences can be brought to the foreground more or less without pain precisely because the other person is in essence a stranger.

We began talking about the internal and external passage of time. "It's curious how our bodies register time with the accuracy of trees," I said. I told you of a recent incident.

"One day, I saw a good-looking girl sitting on the bus—so good-looking that I had to catch my breath. The bus jolted and when I looked back, she was gone. Then she was right before me. I tried to think of something James Bond–like to say, foolish for a sixty-four-year-old man, but she beat me to it: 'Would you like a seat?' She was doing what her Hispanic parents had taught her to do: offer her place to a much older gentleman who seemed about to fall on his face.

"'Thank you very kindly,' I said in a consciously stilted phrase and voice, 'but I'm getting off at the next stop.' 'I was crushed,'" I revealed to you.

"Age often plays tricks on your mind," you said. "You never stop changing, whether you like it or not." I was quiet, and you almost stunned me with bywords of passing wisdom, punctuated by references to authors.

I did not get to the questions I had jotted down in preparation for the interview that had, I realized, already started. I forgot about them. That list, like the apprehension I felt, had disappeared like the puff of smoke I thought I saw captured in a striking photo of you that I had mistaken for Barbara Stanwyck.

I wanted to stretch my legs while you took a brief call. I was drawn into the photo. The background seems now to have been some barricade or other, and you were dragging on a cigarette and deep in conversation. The police were probably nearby. Possibly someone who looked one hell of a lot like James Dean had just brought you yet another cup of coffee.

It is most unlikely that any of that was in the photo. I had just tried to follow you down the nooks and crannies of your comments on the imagination, and now my imagination had probably stated up its engine. I was glad my tape recorder was running, because while all of your arguments made perfect sense, attempting to reconstruct them was something like having teeth pulled by a dentist who kept asking you really interesting but tough questions about Hawthorne and Melville.

I imagine that if there is anything real that happened during that interview, it was in your making me think of imagination and my crooked life more deeply than I had ever been made to do before. I do believe that that is likely one of the most valuable gifts ever given to me.

I felt for a moment that I was being addressed, talked to; and it seemed that no one had ever done that before. Probably they had and I was off drifting somewhere. I was always disappearing behind a corner or a closing door. Yet at that moment in my counterinterview, I was positive that the imagination is very close indeed to whatever is of lasting and real value in the constantly evaporating mist that is at the heart of the human soul.

The comparative value of the imagination in a life full of the troubled leaves of spring—that might have been one of the things I had planned to ask you. But we never got around to it or any of the other questions I had jotted down.

I thank you for helping to make me aware of my own imagination. It's not much, but still it's the greatest gift I was given when I joined the vast multitudes in this grand party of past, present, and future human beings. I realized that sitting with me there on that dreary afternoon was the person who had doubtlessly spent countless such afternoons trolling assiduously in heavy seas with hopes of reaching really focused readers such as I would never be.

When the time promised for the interview that never began was over, I was frightened because I could remember so little that you and I had talked about. In my list of questions were Foucault, Arendt, and Brecht. I could have prepared references to Milton and Beelzebub and Luther's hammer for all the difference it made.

I was further saddened when I saw that the long tape I had put in my recorder had run out. But it made little difference. I knew it would have contained nothing of T.S. Eliot or Wallace Stevens. Instead, when I rewound the tape, I would find the incident of the girl who had offered me her place on the bus. Likely, I had wasted the entire interview on nonsense that was far too embarrassing to tell anyone about. Yet I had told you without the least hesitation.

It was not anything like an interview or even, it now seems, a conversation. Yet I appreciate deeply whatever it was. I thank you for those singular moments, Maxine. And I would like to think of this collection of letters as a truly grand party for someone who has that most glorious and charismatic of gifts—a large and kind and peaceful soul graced with deeply empathetic listening ears.

Sincerely and with much respect,
—Clyde Coreil

One of the Conditions of Happiness

CRAIG KRIDEL

One of the conditions of happiness is the opportunity of a calling, a career which somehow is congenial to one's own temperament.
—John Dewey, "In Response"

Dear Maxine,

I am enjoying the irony of preparing what typically is a private statement when, in fact, I know that my comments will enter a public realm. For one who has articulated and defined public–private space with such care, I find myself somewhat baffled as I write not just to you but to others. We have exchanged hundreds of letters through the years and, as you know, my correspondence is regular and at times lengthy; yet, why am I even saying this to you? You are well aware of our letters and the nature of our friendship. Our exchanges will always remain private. However, now I move into this public sphere, speaking not really to you but to many, and seeking, as always, to be sincere rather than sentimental and thankful rather than precious and pretentious.

My comments will not take the form of personal stories and anecdotes; as a biographer, I have little patience with that type of autobiographical narrative. Rather, I express to you my thankfulness for being able to share a true calling, work that brings happiness and torment as we stand in the world not merely as academics but living lives as educators moving into troubling times. You have always portrayed your existential angst with imagination and, as frustrating as we find the moral collapse of the university, you have reminded me that living a life of the mind and having a calling of action remains a privilege and honor and, for us, is indeed congenial to our own temperament. From our time together, I will always remember first the laughter and true glee of conversation, often recounting flourishes and forays into the arts. But I will never forget our inevitable return to the field of education and the call for engagement, praxis, agency, and action in universities and schools.

Writing this letter of appreciation proved an occasion not to reminisce but, instead, to reread. I find that your significant works are not just those well-known publications that frequent everyone's bibliography except your own. (You certainly are not a self-referential author!) Nor is your scholarship solely within the realm of social imagination, blue guitars, and the arts, as some more recent readers may think. I have delighted in what have become private spaces—those somewhat fugitive publications from the 1960s and 1970s that seem to carry even more impact and insight with every passing decade. While you mutter about the dated aspects of *The Public School and the Private Vision* (1965) and *Teacher as Stranger* (1973) the writing speaks to all. Every autumn as I prepare for the beginning of another academic year, I reread *Liberal Education and the Newcomer* (1979) and am reminded of the significance of a liberating general education and the importance of knowledge to enable the young to enter many worlds and realms. The essay allows me to choose, for another year, to be a teacher.

Yet, within the context of your call for wide-awakeness, new beginnings, and searches for meaning, knowledge remains important. Some works of social commentary, educational critique, literature, art, dance, and music appear "better"—more resonant, more troubling, more perplexing, basically so much more engaging and so substantially complex—than others. *Liberal Education and the Newcomer* reminds me that a teacher guides and takes "responsibility for creating situations in which young persons will be enabled to connect what they are learning to the search" (Greene, 1979, p. 636). My role as teacher, similar to your role as friend, becomes not a cavalier acceptance of all experiences or an unconditional approval of all thoughts and opinions. Welcoming a newcomer and introducing individuals to new communities is to know that some works and some ideas are indeed so much more sensible than others. And while I feel great unease in making such a public statement, you have given me courage to attempt to discriminate between "the better" from "the good" and the truly complex, seminal works from the "great books."

I believe this is where another aspect of your congenial temperament comes to the forefront in unique ways: the importance of thoughtful criticism. You graciously accept praise, but you seek insightful critique. And I continue to be astonished not just with the insight of *Teacher as Stranger* but with your rather harsh analysis of that work, written 26 years later, for the Museum of Education's "Books of the Century" exhibition and catalogue (1999). You surpass all others' critiques of your own book (including the lovely quip by one reviewer, as you make the point of underscoring, who, in questioning your "superfluity of quotations," maintained that searching "for my referents was like picking up hubcaps on the Indianapolis Speedway"). Rather, your criticism, harsh as it is, becomes a fitting epilogue, bringing out new insights wrapped among your barbs and critical analysis. For one who is so admired, it seems as if you learn more from critique than from accolades. Shouldn't we all?

I will continue sending my letters, Maxine, meant only for you. I remain joyous with this wonderful calling of teacher and educator that causes us such torment and angst. And I will continue to try to make a difference in this odd land known as South Carolina, and will smile as I near the museum each day to see a seven-foot portrait of you, next to the portraits of Septima Clark and J. A. DeLaine, "inquiringly and wonderingly" gazing down on me and others as we seek to engage the world.

Life, light, love,
—Craig

24/7

WILLIAM AYERS

Dear Maxine,

I'm wandering along an open road tonight, wobbly and a bit unhinged, wondering where I'll be by morning, writing you now under a sea of stars.

You're on my mind 24/7—I love you, you know—and here's a simple sampling of love letters from this day. I've got one for every hour, followed by a week's worth of questions:

1. Your eyes, why not? Laughing eyes, and worried, too. Wonderful eyes, burning bright, aware, alert, day and night.
2. The sense beneath every conversation: you're just waking up, at this very moment—this morning's news! That cabdriver's comment! The piece on the war in the New Yorker! Rachel Maddow! The show at the Public! Bill T. Jones! Rashid Khalidi on *Charlie Rose*! Brecht!—and you're breaking loose. You're speaking to me (I know it's a narcissistic illusion, but I allow myself, why not?) as if I'm just waking up, too, and in our first waking moments I must pay urgent attention, gather whatever courage I can, and prepare to break loose as well.
3. You offer me a bowl of soup and a bed for the night—me, the natural narcissism again, why not?—but you offer a bite and a bed for the night to many others, including the homeless man on Fifth Avenue one night in a snowstorm (puts my hopeful invitation in perspective!). His aggressive rejection: "What do you want from me, lady?"
4. Your crazy question after that lecture: Was it okay? It was, yes, it was surely okay. It was only words, after all—let's not make more of it than it was—conceived and constructed and spoken by you for perhaps an hour, a bit more, in a crowded room, a stuffy place at the start. And yet people who heard you were gasping throughout, some weeping, some laughing and reaching out to touch another's hand. The air sizzled and crackled, until, as you would have it, fresh and startling winds began to blow through the room. No one left quite the same, not even you. It was okay. Why do you ask such a crazy question?
5. That one persistent rule: to reach. And your dazzling embodiment of the practice, trying again and again to speak beyond barriers and without bounds.
6. Those exaggerations, the excesses—all the little efforts and grand gestures, I think, designed to clear the air of humdrum, ho-hum, and all the tedious repetition and buzz.
7. The admonition to create—right here and right now, in this community or in this school or on this corner—a place to do philosophy, and a bit of the possible world we might want to inhabit.
8. Your inner rhythm: Wake up! Be astonished! Act! Doubt! (REPEAT!)
9. Storming the barricades, especially your own.
10. Reminding us again what it means to be alive and in dialogue with others, unfinished and situated, in motion and struggling to expand

the public square as a place of balance and decency, human dignity and possibility.

11. Your sense that we are all necessarily blind to our own blind spots, anesthetized, sleepy, and in need of occasional jolts and shocks into new awarenesses.

12. Your contradictions and conflicts, your reversals, your dialectics.

13. Another world—not necessarily a better world, possibly much worse, but another world nonetheless—is inevitable: Imagine a possible world you'd like to live in.

14. All the echoes: Arendt and Camus and DuBois, for example; Addams and King and Horton; Ginsberg, Shelly, Hughes; and Brooks. Orwell. Morrison. Saramago. DeLillo. Woolf. That wild, unruly cacophony.

15. Your invitations: to try once to construct a classroom on a base of fearless and relentless inquiry, for example. You throw every established and received bit of wisdom, common sense, and dogma open for examination, interrogation, and rethinking.

16. Your impatience with gurus of every stripe, and with anyone who would pin you, like a beautiful butterfly, to that particular board.

17. Your invitations: to change the world, for example, or to change the people who will change the world.

18. Embracing the rebels again and again, and glimpsing the ghost of Dewey behind the barricades.

19. Imagining a classroom where all the messages, implicit and explicit, are built on the idea that we are swirling through history, alive and acute, that nothing is guaranteed, and that we are each a work in progress and an artist in residence, swimming shakily toward an uncertain shore.

20. That elaborate and painful-looking tattoo you inspired on the inside of my student's small wrist: "I am ... not yet."

21. Your endless invitations: to act out the possibility that school, for example, far from being a preparation for life, is indeed life itself.

22. Your open meditation concerning the fear of imagination, the fear of choice and free will, that characterizes the people who are drunk on power. Your words to the men of facts without ethics, or to those cynics who can tell you the price of everything but the value of nothing. Your Dickensian, dystopic description of the degradation that marks the classroom as slave galley, where the teacher's central task is to beat the drum mindlessly: "When thou shalt fill each jar brim full by-and-by, dost thou think that thou wilt always kill the robber *Fancy* lurking within—or sometimes only maim him and distort him!"(Dickens, 1885, p. 7)

23. Your self-designated task to follow the town crier through the streets as he puts the people to sleep with his constant "All's well," and to

contradict that soothing lie: "All is certainly not well," you say, lighting altogether different lamps for the night.

24. Your invitations: to dive into the wreckage, for example.

Now, questions:

1. What does it mean to be human in the 21st century?
2. How can teachers who feel shackled, bound and gagged, develop a pedagogy of alert engagement with and activism for humanity—practice that tries to tell the truth, tries to stand against violence and war and exploitation and oppression, tries to act in fairness and balance and peace, and tries to enact the power of love that does justice?
3. How can we look at the world of children—the sufferings, the accomplishments, the perspectives, the concerns—and develop an awareness, sometimes joyous but just as often painful, of all that we find; how do we account for every person, each entangled and propelled, and sometimes made mute, by large social forces, each with a wild and vast inner life—a spirit, a mind, a future?
4. How can we forge ourselves into artisans of a new humanity?
5. What are our wildest dreams?
6. What are *you* planning to do now?
7. What should I do with the rest of my life?

—William Ayers

The Slow Fuse of the Gradual Instant

REBECCA LUCE-KAPLER

Just as the earth invisibly prepares its cataclysms, so history is the gradual instant.

—Anne Michaels, *Fugitive Pieces*

Dear Maxine,

The other day I revisited "The Slow Fuse of Aesthetic Practice," a chapter I wrote over 10 years ago about your work (Luce-Kapler, 1998). That reading was a revelation. While I thought I remembered the result of some lovely days of reading your essays and the literature of Virginia Woolf, Toni Morrison, and Elizabeth Bishop, I was surprised to see how the influences I identified a decade ago continue to shape my thinking. With the distance of time came insight, and I realized that I had intuitively identified the seeds of your work that would become an impetus for mine. Anne Michaels (1996) writes about how history is the gradual instant, how things continue to move and are at work even without our awareness. So, too, your work has continued to deepen its rivulets in my research and writing. It truly is a slow fuse that has been lit—one that continues to burn long and bright.

I began the chapter with the words "if imagination is the spark that ignites the possible, then aesthetic experience is imagination's tinder box" (Luce-Kapler, 1998, p. 148). I was responding to your call for aesthetic practice that meant developing conscious participation with a deep noticing of what can be discovered. This idea of deep noticing reminds me of Jane Gallop's (2000) call for the "close reading" of texts as an ethical practice. We need to slow down, she suggests, and pay attention to the words, the syntax, the punctuation, rather than predetermining what will be found— just as you call on us "to attend to shapes, patterns, sounds, rhythms, figures of speech, contours, and lines" (Greene, 1995b, p. 125).

The close attention of your aesthetic practice influenced my study of Canadian painter Emily Carr. I learned to open myself to what was present and listen for the resonances in her writing and art, knowing that "if I can make present the shapes and structures of a perceived work...I believe my own past will appear in altered ways" (Greene, 1995b, pp. 77–78). I learned the rhythm of close and extended attention with the objects of art, and from that grew a collection of poetry (Luce-Kapler, 2003) and an ongoing interest in interpreting the lives of women, closely studying their aesthetic practices and art: Margaret Bourke-White, Geraldine Moodie, and Kate Chopin, among others.

The fascination with aesthetic practice—in my case writing—also became the focus of my academic research. I was drawn to what you call experiencing the *as if*. The rich *as if* hypothetical worlds (our own or those of others' creations) reconfigure experience and make it less familiar and repetitive so that we can become conscious of "what is not yet, of what might, unpredictably, still be experienced" (Greene, 1995, p. 62).

Through close attention to what was before me—a research transcript, a painting, a glorious shagbark hickory outside my window—I saw the opening of possibilities and understood how to see anew.

In the chapter, while I focused on your writing about aesthetic practice through close readings of literature, I gave more subtle nods to your considerations of consciousness. We have an obligation as teachers, you believe, "to heighten the consciousness of whoever [we] teach by urging them to read and look and make their own interpretations of what they see" (1995b, p. 35). And it is through my teaching of aesthetic practice and close attention that I have come to understand your thinking that "human consciousness...is always situated; and the situated person, inevitably engaged with others, reaches out and grasps the phenomena surrounding him/her from a particular vantage point and against a particular background consciousness" (Greene, 1988, p. 21).

In particular, I have been reading about how literary theorists are finding interesting insights in the work of neuroscience and consciousness. For instance, theorist and novelist David Lodge is fascinated by how writers are committed to exploring the nature of consciousness through the minds of characters, or how they represent life through the qualia of poetry. Lodge describes qualia as the "specific nature of our subjective experience of the world" (2002, p. 8): this morning's freshly ground coffee; the sweet white cherries; the sound of water hitting the shower door. The challenge of qualia, of course, is exchanging that experience with others. How can I possibly share with you my subjective experience of the gray curls of hickory bark with the startling blue lake behind it? Perhaps you would say that it is "wide-awakeness" that is needed where "consciousness throws itself outward, *toward* the world. It is intentional; it is always *of* something: a phenomenon, another person, an object or event in the world" (Greene, 1973, p. 162).

As a poet, then, I am interested in how this intentionality of consciousness, and this desire to know others means that I struggle with qualia as I try to deepen my understanding through aesthetic practice.

Maxine, it seems that your slow fuse is a rhizome. It reaches throughout my work and then stretches outward and touches that of my students, appearing in their essays, theses, and dissertations. Their writing is colored by the theme of discovering the possible, of finding the spaces for generative understanding, of noticing and practicing deeply. And it is the brightness of that fuse that is the light of hope in the ongoing work of teaching and learning.

We have so much to thank you for.

With warm regards,
—Rebecca

A Conversation over Time

LORRAINE KASPRISIN

How can one act on one's commitment and at once set others free to be?
—Maxine Greene, *Teacher as Stranger*

Dear Maxine,

I have come to think that writing is never merely a moment in time and place, or a chapter in a book, but rather a conversation over time. I remember when I first reflected upon this. Over a decade ago, I was invited to present the commencement address at my university. Struggling to find a way to go beyond the formulaic style of writing that predominates at such occasions, I began to reflect upon what a commencement address is and what it is supposed to do.

I thought back to my own commencement at the City College of New York. It was 1963, and the speaker was Dr. Martin Luther King Jr., just before the historic March on Washington. I could still remember Dr. King's words that afternoon and the indelible mark they left on my consciousness. I told my young audience that in many ways, Dr. King's presence was also here in this auditorium today. He was here in the influence he had on my life and the topics I had chosen to discuss that morning. Rather than an event in time and space, I treated the commencement address as a conversation that occurred through time—from Dr. King's words to me at my graduation, filtered through my life's experiences over the years, then to the graduates, as they embarked on their own journey and continued the conversation with their generation.

As I thought about that experience, I realized that this letter also had to be a conversation over time with another person who has so affected my life's experience. In 1968, I began my doctoral studies in the philosophy of education at Teachers College, Columbia University. I had already taught in New York and was on a quest for the deeper meaning of what you often describe as our "fundamental project."

Do you remember those turbulent years? The college buildings were often in the process of being "liberated," a euphemism for taking over a building and blocking all entrance and egress to it, and city police would be on campus in the midst of demonstrations and marches against a war in a far-off part of the world. It was the midst of the civil rights and women's movements. Your classes, indeed all the classes dealing with the philosophical and social conditions of education at Columbia, were the most popular classes on campus in those days. (How do we explain their disappearance and marginalization today?) Everyone seemed to be searching for meaning, for institutions that were more responsive to human needs, for a community that reflected its nation's democratic ideals, and for a deeper purpose to our lives.

My own individual quest for the meaning of my life's purpose as a teacher was caught up in a much larger cultural search for a more just and humane world. As my teacher and mentor, your life and your teachings were the forks in the road that allowed me to find my way. In your book *Teacher as Stranger*, which was published during those years, you said that the most crucial question confronting the self-conscious teacher is: "How *can* one act on one's commitment and at once set others free to be?" (Greene, 1973, preface). I left Columbia with that question and tried to engender it in my own students, who were in the process of choosing their own "fundamental projects," as they defined their teaching lives.

The same disquietude and tension that I always found in your teaching and books was the cognitive dissonance I sought to induce in the students I was to teach at my university over the next 30 years. I would often start the year's class with a quote from *Teacher as Stranger*:

> To take a stranger's vantage point on everyday reality is to look inquiringly and wonderingly on the world in which one lives. It is like returning home from a long stay in some other place. The homecomer notices details and patterns in his environment he never saw before. He finds that he has to think about local rituals and customs to make sense of them once more. For a time he feels quite separate from the person who is wholly at home in his ingroup and takes the familiar world for granted.... The homecomer may have been such a person. (Greene, 1973, p. 268)

It was the kind of wisdom that goes all the way back to Socrates (another fork in my road), who would challenge his students to realize that what they thought they knew, they really didn't know at all. Socrates often reminded his students that it wasn't in knowing the answers himself that he would infect others, but rather that he was infected with the very questions and perplexity himself. Sharing this perplexity together, he would then invite the students to join him on the quest for new answers—teacher and student together—as they embarked on this journey we call education, for only then can we think anew about what is possible.

After teaching generations of teachers and prospective teachers, I found that this authentic teaching and learning experience with new teachers, and hopefully with their students, is growing more difficult to undertake in the classroom alone. The cultural ethos in education today is creating a language that makes it more and more difficult to think outside of a prescribed mode of thought. It is, as Wittgenstein would say, as if we were bewitched by language. The growing focus on a corporatized language of accountability and standards, with its technocratic underpinnings, is creating a conceptual change in our thinking by unconsciously adopting language and assumptions that make it increasingly difficult to view human beings in the intentional, purposive language of human agency. The language will no longer permit it because it carries with it its own hidden commitments.

At this moment in our conversation, Maxine, I think we need to engage with that cultural ethos in which our teachers' and students' language is embedded. And so, in the twilight of my own career, I established the new *Journal of Educational Controversy: An Interdisciplinary Journal of Ideas*. As our mission statement says, we hope "to clarify the public debate [about education] and deepen an understanding of its moral significance," and maybe, in the process, affect our choices and actions. Our purpose is to engage scholars as public intellectuals in a conversation with the general public. And, of course, the first issue in 2006 was dedicated to you. In the dedication, I wrote that you remind "us that we must bring more to the pages of our journal than analytical reasoning if we indeed want to embrace the uncertainties, tensions, and controversies of our time in ways that maintain our humanity and avoid falling into simplistic answers that give us a comfortable but illusionary certainty" (Greene, 2006, online).

In the upcoming winter 2010 issue of the journal, we will focus solely on your life's work. The issue follows and further develops a theme we published in the winter of 2008 on "Schooling as if Democracy Matters." In that issue, we tried to get readers to think about what we mean by a democratic community in the time of the Patriot Act, NSA surveillance, extraordinary rendition, preemptive wars, enemy combatants—all likely to involve violations of civil rights and liberties and a curtain of government secrecy. We asked: What story do we tell our young about who we are, who we have been, and who we are becoming? How do we educate children about their identity in this global world? What sense are they to make of the "imperial" democracy they are inheriting? What are the implications of these forces for the education of the young on the foundations of our democracy and our collective identity?

Our upcoming issue on the arts expands our thinking about this topic by exploring the role of the arts in creating the social imagination necessary for sustaining democratic life. In posing the controversy for this issue, we started with something you wrote for the establishing of your foundation and followed up with a question. You wrote:

> My vision, in launching this Foundation, is to generate inquiry, imagination, and the creation of art works by diverse people. It has to do so with a sense of the deficiencies in our world and a desire to repair, wherever possible. Justice, equality, freedom these are as important to us as the arts, and we believe they can infuse each other, perhaps making some difference at a troubled time. (Greene, 2007b, online)

We then asked our authors to go beyond our narrow thinking that sees the occasional class in civic education as sufficient for preparing a public capable of sustaining the life of a democracy. We reminded them of your call for social imagination and the important role that the arts—visual art, music, performance art, and literature—can play in such an education and invited them to explore the many dimensions of such an education. Their responses are a continuation of the conversation you started and a continuation of my attempt to bring the conversation beyond the classroom and into the public forum.

Maxine, in the years ahead, I hope this letter (and the journal you inspired) will continue the conversation that began back in 1968 at Teachers

College with you and before that with my commencement speaker, the Rev. Dr Martin Luther King Jr. Thank you for being a part of each stage of my life.

Peace,
—Lorraine

A Gifted Teacher

MARTHA MCKENNA

Dear Maxine,

The year was 1973. You had just completed *Teacher as Stranger*, and I was to complete my study at Teachers College with your course *The Arts and American Education*. I can recall vividly the day in which a hundred of us entered a large lecture hall for your opening class. Although the room was crowded, you seemed to be speaking to each one of us individually, engaging us in a conversation through the questions you posed. You began the class, as you always did, by reflecting on what you had heard that day on National Public Radio, had read in the *New York Times*, and had recently seen on Broadway. You awakened us to what was happening in the world around us that related to our work that day in class, connecting our readings with lived experiences.

The Arts and American Education was an extraordinary course, introducing us to the public school movement by contrasting the work of educational reformers with that of artists and writers from the Transcendentalist movement through the 20th century. The central text for the course was your work *The Public School and the Private Vision: A Search for America in Education and Literature*, in which you contrasted the assurance and hope of school reformers with the darker perceptions of American writers and artists. You interwove education, philosophy, and the arts in the text and in our classes, pointing out the often opposing views of the American experience. You always included active engagement with works of art, whether a poem, work of literature, painting, or musical composition, to provide yet another perspective for our readings in each class. You recognized the power of the arts to move us to new levels of understanding of ourselves and the world around us. You asked more questions than you provided answers, encouraging us to seek our own truths. You taught us that education is situated in lived experiences, and you worked tirelessly to move us beyond receiving knowledge to constructing knowledge through active engagement with the readings and assignments of the course. You modeled best practice, encouraging aesthetic engagement as part of each class, teaching us how to engage our students just as you engaged us.

All of the students in *The Arts and American Education* recognized what an extraordinary opportunity it was to engage with you, for you modeled in each class the teacher that you encouraged us to become in *Teacher as Stranger*. You practiced the pedagogy that you wrote about, teaching us how "to take a stranger's vantage point on everyday reality . . . to look inquiringly and wonderingly on the world in which one lives" (Greene, 1973, p. 267). No longer could we be passive learners, for you challenged us to enter into each learning experience "wide-awake" to the possibility of new understandings of ourselves and our world. You shared with us the responsibility for constructing our learning experiences, whether engaging with you in the classroom or with the writers and artists in the literature and art or history and philosophy texts that you assigned. You taught us how to do philosophy, engaging us in discussions, giving value to our perspectives, questioning our assumptions, and challenging our ideas. Throughout the course I observed a master teacher at work, an experience that would transform my life and my teaching. What was to have been the last course in a master's program became the first in the doctoral program that we would design together.

Twenty-five years have passed since I completed my doctoral study with you, yet you are ever my teacher. Whether it is rereading your works, which I assign to every teacher I teach, or attending one of your lectures at Lincoln Center, or spending precious time with you at your home on Fifth Avenue, I continue to learn from you and grow as an educator, philosopher, and artist. I most treasure the precious learning on the weekends that I spent in your home in the spring of 2001, where our discussions of your work *Teacher as Stranger* eventually turned into your questions about my teaching, questions that would result in the book *Teaching for Aesthetic Experience: The Art of Learning*. You reminded me during these discussions of my obligation to write about the work I do, to become more self-conscious about my role in the sense-making process of aesthetic education, to "do philosophy," as you describe it in *Teacher as Stranger*, "to develop a fundamental project, to go beyond the situations one confronts and refuse reality as given in the name of a reality to be produced" (Greene, 1973, p. 7).

My last class with you was on a sunny Saturday in May 2002, when you invited the chapter authors of *Teaching for Aesthetic Experience* to your home to discuss our common purpose. The authors traveled across North America to join you for a discussion of our shared work, a discussion that would become the last chapter, "A Gathering of Voices," in our book. This group of mostly strangers had in common that each was an artist/educator teaching for aesthetic experience and each was your student, through engagement in either your classes or your writings. As we gathered around you to discuss unique approaches to teaching for aesthetic experience, once again I saw a master teacher at work. You challenged us to do philosophy, asking probing questions about what we teach, how we teach, and why we teach for aesthetic experience. You helped us to look as strangers, inquiringly and wonderingly, at our various teaching practices so that we might become aware of new possibilities for constructing our work with our students, our subjects, and our world.

You are truly a gifted teacher, drawing upon your lived experience and a rich variety of resources to challenge your students to examine our thinking and become "wide-awake" to the opportunities that surround us. More importantly, you have provided us with an example of a life dedicated to learning—about philosophy, about education, about art—that inspires us to continually seek new knowledge and meaning in our own lives.

—Martha McKenna

An Unabashed Confession of Love

HERB KOHL

Dearest Maxine,

I'm not in the habit of writing love letters, but I'm sure my wife, Judy, will forgive me this one, since love always comes to my mind when I think of you. Forgive my awkwardness and fumbling, but I know this love I feel is not Platonic, nor an instantiation of Spinoza's "intellectual love of god." It's not Buddhist, Christian, Judaic, or Hindu love. So what is the phenomenology of this exquisite feeling?

What first comes to my mind is that every time we come into contact, whether in person or over the phone, all parts of my mind and soul awaken simultaneously. I find myself in a very special place, which evokes feelings similar to the way I feel walking by the ocean or reading or writing something that opens me to new dimensions of my own thinking and wondering. Even the smallest conversation is a voyage, since you are always fully awake and fully sensitive, to the point of being sensuous. I imagine John Dewey sitting on your right shoulder and all the artists you celebrate, work with, and write about sitting on the left one, weighing your body and mind down to the imaginative, liberatory left. I remember moments when Dewey, one of your lovers, rises so strongly in you that your shoulders become balanced, your ideas and thoughts measured, and your sense of humor wicked. When we talk or are together I feel the love of the wildflower or weed for a wise, passionate, and permissive gardener.

Joan Miró's work affects me the way you do. Miró described the way in which he worked in terms that remind me of the way in which you continue to bring forth the most unexpected genius in educators, who thought so much less of themselves before they encountered you—in your classroom, but most fully in your living room, where you created the only educational Enlightenment salon in recent U.S. educational history. Miró talks of his work this way:

> I think of my studio as a vegetable garden. Here, there are artichokes. Over there, potatoes. The leaves have to be cut so the vegetables can grow. At a certain moment, you must prune. I work like a gardener or a wine grower. Everything takes time. My vocabulary of forms, for example, did not come to me all at once. It formulated itself almost in spite of me.
>
> Things follow their natural course. They grow, they ripen. You have to graft. You have to water, as you do for lettuce. Things ripen in my mind. In addition, I always work on a great many things at once. And even in different areas: painting, etching, lithography, sculpture, ceramics. The medium and the instrument I am using dictate my technique, which is a way of giving life to a thing. . . . my painting can be considered humorous and even lighthearted, even though I am tragic. (Miró & Rowell, 1992, p. 250)

I believe your students and friends are to you what Miró's paintings were to him. You do not control them or force them in any direction, but prepare the soil and provide the nutrients to allow them to grow as beautifully as they are capable of. And, being an existentialist, when they have achieved that wonderful state, you push more, show them that there are always more choices; there are always more ways to grow, and ways to challenge the world and make it a more decent place.

At this stage of my life, and at this stage of your life, the tragic dimension is central to my love for you. I'm 72, and you are in your 90s, and we both see the end of our time approaching, you more distinctly than me. And we both know how much is left to do and how difficult it is to turn the world upside down and achieve what Rimbaud prophetically called the Splendid City on the Hill.

Pablo Neruda (1971) spoke of the journey to this city in his Nobel Prize acceptance speech:

> All paths lead to the same goal: to convey to others what we are. And we must pass through solitude and difficulty, isolation and silence in order to reach forth to the enchanted place where we can dance our clumsy dance and sing our sorrowful song—but in this dance or in this song there are fulfilled the

most ancient rites of our conscience in the awareness of being human and of believing in a common destiny . . . It is today exactly one hundred years since an unhappy and brilliant poet, the most awesome of all despairing souls, wrote down this prophecy: "In the dawn, armed with a burning patience, we shall enter the splendid Cities." I believe in this prophecy of Rimbaud, the Visionary. I come from a dark region, from a land separated from all others by the steep contours of its geography. I was the most forlorn of poets and my poetry was provincial, oppressed and rainy. But always I had put my trust in man. I never lost hope. It is perhaps because of this that I have reached as far as I now have with my poetry and also with my banner. Lastly, I wish to say to the people of good will, to the workers, to the poets, that the whole future has been expressed in this line by Rimbaud: only with a *burning patience* can we conquer the splendid City which will give light, justice and dignity to all mankind. In this way the song will not have been sung in vain. (pp. 58–61)

You and I come from another dark, though not remote, region of the earth: New York City. And situated there are the same troubling problems of oppression, alienation, and, the greatest demon of all, ignorance that Neruda describes; and the same need for poetry, the arts, and theater—that is, for voice, expression, and dialogue. We are both fighters in the war against ignorance, as are many of our comrades: Myles, Paulo, Dewey, and more recently Bill Ayers, Michelle Fine, and Norm Fruchter. Of course, there are many others, but you are at the wise, cynical, funny, compassionate, accepting, and demanding center of all our efforts. It seems as if there is no affliction that you cannot integrate and transform into your artistic vision of the social imagination as a major force for revolutionary thought and action. Your physical struggles in the last few years have enhanced your work, informed your insights, and provided a model to us of the life force itself.

This is an unabashed confession of love. I know it will be returned because you always return the gift of love with whatever you teach and say.

—Herb

Being and Becoming

MAUREEN MILETTA

Dear Maxine,

Writing to you for this project is a challenge that I have accepted with trepidation, as I know that I can never find the words to describe our relationship. I think most of your friends and students probably search for adequate language as we try to describe your impact on our lives and on our work, the inspiration you provide, the devotion we feel. We think we are among the most fortunate because we call you friend.

I was sitting outside Lawrence Cremin's office during registration at Teachers College in 1962 and struck up a conversation with Amy Knox. She suggested I take a course with you, and even offered to introduce me to you, as your office was just down the hall. That meeting changed my life, just as similar meetings with you have changed the lives of thousands of your devoted students.

I know you remember the lunches you and I and Amy shared. We would hole up in your office, armed with a bottle of Mateus, planning to write dissertations that would transform the world of teacher education. We recounted special teaching successes and failures. Mostly, we'd gossip.

Then we had large dinner parties, and you cooked spaghetti with lots of mozzarella. We'd wear long skirts and sit shoeless around the coffee table while we devoured your secretly seasoned chicken, which everyone adored because it fell so delicately off the bone. When you discovered that I loved potatoes au gratin and leg of lamb, you faithfully cooked them for me for years. Our husbands also grew to respect and admire each other, so we four could spend many evenings together.

I have warm memories of the AERA meeting in New York when you were president. You had the deluxe duplex in the Sheraton, and we all hung out there throughout the conference. You ran a boardinghouse! Ann Lieberman and Mary Ann Raywid slept there almost every night, I think.

Then there was that little mishap on the Merritt Parkway. We were returning to New York after meeting with our writing group when there was a sudden explosive sound. Acting instantly, you muscled a bucking monster of a car with a blowout from the left lane across to the grassy slope at 70 miles an hour! I was driving directly behind you, and I thought we were on our way to Paradise. How I underestimated your strength, your determination, your confidence. It was a magnificent feat!

Our relationship is special, I think, because it has always reflected the quotidian nature of our lives. We've shared triumphs and troubles, joys and sorrows as we've communicated by phone, even into the wee small hours. But you are loved, respected, admired, and emulated by all who know you. You've taught all your friends, colleagues, and students about that mix of hubris and modesty that fuels a constant thirst for perfection. We learned from you that it is the search for the possible, the opening of windows on new landscapes, the engagement with the arts, that makes teaching the most exciting of human endeavors. You've taught us how to be and to become. And we are eternally grateful, Maxine.

Love,

—Maureen Miletta

Academic Courage and Grace:
A Case Study from Maxine Greene

EUGENE PROVENZO

Dear Maxine,

I first meet you in 1980. I had been a professor at the University of Miami since 1976. I was very young, barely 30 years old. My wife, Asterie, and I were presenting papers at a conference on urban education at Teachers College sponsored by the Olin Foundation. You were one of two critics assigned to respond to our papers. The second critic was a distinguished higher education professor, now long retired.

I was still very new to the field, which had not been very supportive of me as a beginner. Very few people graduated in the Social Foundations of Education in the mid-1970s. There was a recession, and almost none of us were able to get jobs. While I was excited about working in the field and being active in conferences and other activities, I found groups focusing around my areas of interest such as the History of Education Society and the Philosophy of Education Society to be very cliquish.

Asterie and I knew almost no one at the conference. We had prepared innovative articles on the history of children's museums and the child labor photos of Lewis Hine. This was a decade before PowerPoint was introduced. We had carousels of approximately 80 slides for each presentation. The materials were put together with a great deal of care. The photographs we drew on for our papers were stunning historical artifacts. The piece on Hine, for example, included his wonderful immigrant photographs of people coming into Ellis Island, as well as his child labor photographs of mine and agricultural workers. The research not only demonstrated how Hine's photographs were shaped by his experience of being a teacher at the Ethical Culture School in New York City, but also explored how Hine conducted careful, field-based "ethnographies" of everything he had photographed. The piece on museums explored the origins of American children's museums—particularly the Brooklyn Children's Museum and the Educational Museum of the St. Louis Public Schools—and their role in urban education.

We had each quote included in the paper set in a transparent type set against a black background. When projected, they looked rather elegant— nothing special in terms of today's computer presentation systems, but for the late 1970s, clearly something special. We timed our presentations perfectly and jointly delivered each paper without a hitch. The article on Hine was eventually published in *Teachers College Record*. The museum piece saw the light of day in the *Missouri Historical Bulletin*, and as a detailed discussion in an academic monograph.

The unnamed critic who preceded you got up and started making a series of vague and essentially unkind comments about the papers. He was playing the role of an academic bully. He basically said we had done a lot of fancy technological footwork, but questioned what there was of substance in our work. One needs to remember that this was long before academia paid much attention to visual sources or "popular culture." After a while, it became clear that our critic had not only not read the papers he had received weeks before, but had also barely listened to our presentations.

As he rambled on, I could feel my wife tense up next to me. As relatively new researchers in the field, we had worked hard to make our presentations something special, and here was a senior scholar dismissing us for being "too slick." We were devastated, and a little too young to realize that the distinguished commentator was being irresponsible. We waited nervously as you made your way slowly and gracefully up to the podium to do your critique.

You took a moment to begin, hesitating at first as you lit a cigarette and took an enormous drag. Then, holding the cigarette with your hand to the side (a gesture I would describe as a "Greenian" rhetorical flourish) and posing like an elegant fashion model in *Vogue*, you scanned the audience like a hawk eying its prey. Finally, you fixed your stare on the first critic and said something to this effect: "I think these young people did a wonderful presentation, their research is important, and Professor _____ missed something special by not having read or listened to their work."

I can't remember what else you said; that was enough. A hush spread across the entire audience of nearly 200 people that I will never forget. You finished by leading the audience in a quiet round of applause.

Over the years, I have occasionally been unfairly treated by colleagues. I have suffered damning critiques from people who have not bothered to read or listen to what I have said. In suffering the kinds of occasional disappointments that are perhaps part of many normal academic careers, I have always thought back to the image of you sucking in the smoke of your cigarette, and generously giving two very young scholars credit and encouragement for their work.

I thank you for your insights as a scholar, which have made me a better and more thoughtful teacher and researcher. I thank you for your humanity, which has enriched my life, and provided me with a model for how I wish to act and be perceived, especially in my interactions with students and younger scholars.

All the best,
—Eugene Provenzo
P. S. Asterie thanks you, too.

With Relentless Possibility

William Schubert

Keep asking, and keep wondering. It will keep you alive.
                              —Maxine Greene, *Variations on a Blue Guitar*

Dear Maxine,

I am so glad to express my appreciation to you for your influence and inspiration. Although communication between us has lessened over the past decade, you doubtless know that I am frequently updated regarding your exemplary contributions through our good friends Bill Ayers, Craig Kridel, and Janet Miller. Your influence on my work and career continues to be greater than you may realize, despite the fact that your capacity to realize is immense.

The Public School and the Private Vision (Greene, 1965), along with the larger corpus of your work, continue to help me realize that literature reviews should include actual literature! You powerfully give permission to me, and to so many, to craft educational insights upon novels, stories, poems, plays, and films. The literary, as your work shows so poignantly, is saturated with educational perception. I encourage my students to reflect on works of literature, or any kind of artistic creations, that have profound influences on their outlooks, envisioning these as curricula and authors or artists as curriculum developers or teachers. I recall a conversation with you in which you said you would like to write another rendition of *The Public School and the Private Vision*. That would be wonderful.

Existential Encounters for Teachers (Greene, 1967) is one of my very favorites, though I have not found a copy for my library. (I did find one in Ming Fang He's office.) I can sit for hours pondering the quotes and your commentaries. They probe deeply into the soul of meaning and the angst, mystery, and possibility in the contradictions of the human condition.

I see *Teacher as Stranger* (Greene, 1973) as a seedbed of messages that you deeply convey in subsequent work: being *perspectival*, seeing things as they might be otherwise, and making the strange familiar and the familiar strange.

Your essays in *Landscapes of Learning* (Greene, 1978) coalesce around the message of which you continuously remind me: Be *wide-awake* in every encounter. This is a valuable life challenge, indeed.

In *The Dialectic of Freedom* (Greene, 1988) I find the inspiration, courage, and challenge to engage in the construction of public spaces—new landscapes for education that seek whatever is just and good in each situation.

Releasing the Imagination (Greene, 1995b) takes me back to my years as an elementary school teacher, when I claimed that my principal resource for teaching and learning was the interplay of philosophy and imagination as I engaged with children. Still, today, these are my most ardent tools as I work with graduate students. I delve into new realms of philosophy, particularly when embodied in literature and the arts, and emerge inspired anew to join with students and colleagues to imaginatively consider ideas—not ideas for their own sake; rather, ideas in the stream of action.

In *Variations on a Blue Guitar* (Greene, 2002), ideas in the stream of life flow within the children, students, and teachers who have been illuminated through programs from Lincoln Center—they have been nourished by your aesthetic awareness, an imaginative artistry politicized in a search for public spaces and greater justice.

Clearly, the outlook of your *passionate mind*, illustrated by your comment "I am not yet," is deeply appreciated by many privileged to feel your influence. It will long continue to be *a light in dark times* (Ayers & Miller, 1998) for me and for many.

In your work and in your lived and shared experience, you dynamically blend the literary, the artistic, the phenomenological, the critical, the existential, the pragmatic, the postmodern, and so much more in a palette of imaginative thought and action that challenges us to cultivate diverse and novel possibilities. This configuration of literatures enables the tragic to be experienced, reimagined, and transformed in turmoil with the hopeful. For me, your work balances John Dewey's faith in the solubility of human dilemmas and the integration of dualisms with the insolubility of our existential predicament and the inevitable need to live with contradiction as depicted by Albert Camus. Like Walt Whitman, admirably, you show how to be large enough to embrace both at once.

I have experienced you as a kind and empathic person who has reached out to me since the beginning of my career. Many senior scholars are so immersed in their work that they take no time to recognize or encourage emergent scholars. Not you. I have a file of letters of encouragement and memories of thoughtful moments. Your generous letters have meant so much—they give impetus to continue my work, from a note on an article I did in *Educational Researcher* in 1980 to comments on my bibliographical essays, synoptic texts, and forays into the arts.

Etched in my memory, too, is the personal kindness you expressed in preparing a dinner for my family in your beautiful home after I was offered a professorship at Teachers College in 1988—your gifts of an Ernie (from *Sesame Street*) puppet for 1-year-old Henry and a *Ghostbusters* video for

5-year-old Heidi were experienced amidst an improvised game of paper-wad catch between Henry and your husband, Jack, as you, Ann, and I conversed about matters educational and artistic.

Moreover, the comments you bestow here and there at conferences carry a world of meaning, as do phone conversations and, more recently, e-mails and even a blog—showing how you have moved into cyberspace. More recently, your work has inspired my attempt to understand imaginative, utopian qualities in the work of John Dewey alongside innumerable other philosophical and literary sources (Schubert, 2009). As Ming Fang and I pursue life and education together, we have begun a book series that we call *Landscapes of Education*, the purpose of which is to foster intercultural, indigenous, imaginative, and artistic understandings of education. Surely, in no small way this is nurtured by seeds you have planted, especially with your alliterative titular phrase, *Landscapes of Learning* (Greene, 1978).

Your contributions continue to grow. I see this in my students and those of many others. For over 30 years I have led students to your work. Your inestimable influence resists summarization, because it is ongoing. You challenge us to seek landscapes of increased perspective, to see things as they might be otherwise, to make the familiar strange and the strange familiar, to study and value insights from the arts and literature, to ask questions of worth within a quest for social justice, to strive to create public spaces, to hope amid tragic contexts, to reimagine the public school and the private vision, to keep existential questions alive, to make the strange familiar and the familiar strange, to be increasingly wide-awake, to expose the colonial and tyrannical, to find faces of meaning in the Other, to embrace the dialectic of freedom, to release the imagination, to see the arts as both political and aesthetic, to awaken to the inhumanity of exclusion, to overcome, to know that we (too) *are not yet*, to strive to embody, expand, and enact multiple interpretations. What a legacy, what a worthwhile contribution—still evolving, with relentless possibility!

With enduring gratitude and affection,
—Bill Schubert

On the "Verge" of Possibility

Molly Quinn

If I were to wish for anything I should not wish for wealth and power, but for the passionate sense of what can be, for the eye, which, ever

young and ardent, sees the possible. Pleasure disappoints, possibility
never. And what wine is so sparkling, what so fragrant, what so intoxicating as possibility?

—Søren Kierkegaard, *Either/Or,*
—R. Zander & B. Zander, *The Art of Possibility*

Dear Maxine,

If I were to wish for anything, I should wish for those eyes of yours, ever
ardent and young, which have so persistently and keenly kept the possible in
view. From such vision has emerged not only a fierce "passion for the possible" (Greene, 2008a) but also an unfaltering *praxis* of the possible—and
fearless commitment to cultivating both in a precarious world through the
project of education. Herein you have illuminated how the imagination, and
a consciousness of possibility, is integral to the human struggle for freedom,
and "our historical vocation of humanization" (Freire, 1970/1995).

In my every encounter with you, I have been simultaneously humbled,
reproved, encouraged, provoked, uplifted, and emboldened in my own consciousness about the affirmation of the possible. Like you, I am a perpetual
seeker, laboring to transcend the limits of the given toward glimpses of the
"other-wise" (Greene, 1988); unlike you, I am often the embodiment of
angst, grasping for meaning and despairing before my own impoverished
imagination and agency. So it is not surprising that I should have been
powerfully drawn to you and your work. Writing from the shadows, then,
knowing you most perhaps through your writings, lectures, and the students
we share, I pen this letter gladly: for you have time and time again restored
me to vision and voice, awakening me anew to possibility in general, and to
my own possibilities specifically.

Far from timid in facing human vulnerability, "unanswerability,"
you have also ever affirmed those "on the verge"; even with such notable
renown, you live and work and embrace life there: possibility—for freedom
and fellowship, healing and humanization—best gleaned from the edge, at
the threshold, with particular attentiveness to human suffering. For this, I
thank you.

I confess: I can't remember when first I met you or your work. I recall
reading Dewey (1922/1964a, 1964b) on human conduct and freedom in my
early studies—that is, about countering "cabined and cramped existences,"
communities closed by "pathologies of goodness," and constraints on consciousness and choice in demands to carry out the will of others. His words
seemed to perfectly describe my past experience in a spiritual community
"gone oppressive." He helped me name my history, but you gave freedom
itself a name for me, and helped me begin my own quest—offering me
insight into the questions that pursued and continue to pursue me. Dewey's

work soon led me to your treasured *Dialectic of Freedom* (Greene, 1988), a text to which I often find myself returning, as it both cultivates and feeds some deep hunger of my soul.

A "shadow artist" (Cameron, 1992) as well, ever thirsting for the arts, I remember attending an AERA lecture where you indicted educational practice for its abnegation of the possible in allegiance to the predictable, and incited us to counter so much "anesthetic" by affirming the aesthetic. Such criticism is related to "a lack of poetry in our encounters with others, our inability to do more than flatten the complexity of the human condition" (Apple, n.d.) Thus lives your hope (which has gratefully become mine): for education "to recall some lost spontaneity, some forgotten hunger for becoming different, becoming new.... to remind people what it means to be alive among others..." (Greene, 1988, p. xii).

Years later, struggling to recover the lost and forgotten in my own life and work, the very week after I thought I had "quit academia"—having resigned a tenured position to pursue an as-yet-unknown course—I found myself in your apartment, with our friend Gene Diaz, watching a video of you that she and others had created, and conversing. I mostly remember how hospitably you received me, and honored my—to many, "on-the-verge"-of-another-kind (i.e., madness, nervous breakdown)—quest. I also remember leaving, reflecting upon both the video and our conversation, thinking: "That's what I thought being an academic would mean. Why couldn't I be like Maxine, living courage and conviction as she does?" Facing the uncertain journey before me, little did I know then that a year later I would be joining the faculty at Teachers College, where I would get to see you a lot more.

Still, I have largely remained in the shadows, on the floor in the corner of your apartment—eagerly taking in the stimulating conversations of your salons, whether participants discussed a wonderful book like *The History of Love* by Nicole Krauss or some Living Room theater performance paying tribute to you as the "wild hair" that inspires the new.

I have gleaned the fruit of other less-than-direct encounters with you, too, via the papers of and conversations with our mutual students, and in delicious engagement with your work in my own classes. This is why I relish giving voice here to the power of your visionary presence in my life, and to my gratitude. Even herein you have challenged my floor-corner comfort, calling me from those shadows more than once. Remember the time you laughed at me when I tried to introduce myself to you *yet again*? "Molly," you said, "I know you."

My issues with academic life may not all be resolved, or personal confrontations with "the void" dissolved. Yet I am ever encouraged by the vision of life, and education, you endorse and embody: that which "brings together the need for wide-awakeness with the hunger for community" (p. 23)—one wherein individuals are recognized for "speaking as *who* and not *what* they are" (1993a, p. 13). Affirming the "incomplete" and "discontented," you have always addressed me as who I am, summoning me also, in my life and work, to speak from the place of who I am.

Last year, struggling again with my academic voice, and vision, I attended your lectures at TC, for your 90th birthday and the AAACS conference. I heard you critique an education system that feeds on a hunger for final solutions and fails to nourish the stories of students and teachers—their existential engagements in and with the world and one another—or to acknowledge the life meanings that flourish in the dialogic telling of such stories. I heard you call for teachers who are awake to the inexplicabilities of their experience and aware in a world marked much by violence to work to create for children a space wherein trust is possible, as well as the capacity for outrage. Such teachers must work as healers of our "plague of indifference" (2008b). I saw, too, a vision of the "space of dialogue and possibility" (1988, p. xi) of which you dream: Education, herein, might consist in the very creation of a place "where persons attend to one another with interest, regard and care; there is a place for the appearance of freedom, the achievement of freedom by people in search of themselves" (p. xi).

Filling my world yet again with poetry, you moved me, too, to fresh ways of seeing and being with my work, compelling me to bring more of myself—even my own poetry—to it. Further, you renewed in me a fading commitment to my own "aesthetics of existence," the inspiration to sketch fresh flowers over the morning coffee, and pen poetic musings on the subway commute home. A full-fledged member of Michelle Fine's MOMA2 (Museum of Maxine's Adorings), I continue a search profoundly and gratefully inspired by yours. With lighter heart, I look forward to many more fragrant, sparkling, intoxicating encounters with you—the one who with such constancy "calls upon our passion rather than our fear. . . . the relentless architect of the possibility that human beings can be" (Zander & Zander, 2000, p. 163). I know (and am thankful) that each such meeting, whether from the shadows or not, is bound ever to awaken me anew to possibility, and to being more fully "alive among others," "on the verge" of possibility.

Looking forward, until, with love,
—Molly

Eleven Kind Words

WILLIAM REYNOLDS

I am suggesting that, for too many individuals in modern society, there is a feeling of being dominated and that feelings of powerlessness are almost inescapable. I am also suggesting that such feelings can to a large degree be overcome through conscious endeavor on the part of individuals to keep themselves awake, to think about their condition in the world, to inquire into the forces that appear to dominate them, to interpret the experiences they are having day to day.
                                           —M. Greene, *Landscapes of Learning*

Dear Maxine,

I was introduced to your work when I was a graduate student at the University of Rochester in the early 1980s. I was taking curriculum theory courses with William Pinar, and *Landscapes of Learning* was required reading. I still remember the impact your concept of wide-awakeness had on my thinking. Your knowledge and use of literature were inspiring. I related to this literary orientation because at the time I was teaching high school English in upstate New York and had been an English major as both an undergraduate and a master's student. Your literary allusions, such as this one, spoke to me:

> Instead, the metaphors, the worlds, offered by certain modern novels may release the imaginations of some of those who read them. If that occurs, those readers may be moved to think afresh and in their own terms about such matters as rigor and the new curriculum, about the possibilities of releasing the young to become different—to go beyond where they are. (Greene, 1995b, p. 173)

I was also reading the phenomenologists at the time, and your work clarified many of the ideas with which I had been struggling. In fact, your concept of wide-awakeness made its way into my dissertation.

Now I have been teaching at the university level for over 20 years, and I have consistently used your texts in my classes at the undergraduate and graduate levels. This fall my undergraduates will be reading *Variations on a Blue Guitar*. Over the years, my many students have had great affection for your work. I have also shown the video *Exclusions and Awakenings: The Life of Maxine Greene* (Hancock, 2001) to my students just before they read your texts. They find your life an inspiration. Women students in my classes particularly appreciate your life and voice. They find an affinity with such statements as, "I connect this, for example, with women who, after years of having their understandings dismissed, are now affirming that their experience is as significant as men's" (Greene, 1995b, p. 22).

But these reminiscences are not the primary reason for this letter. I am writing a letter about kind words. I mean, in particular, a few words of encouragement I remember from 15 years ago—words that you said to me at a party in 1994 that have stayed with me to this very day. It was a beautiful spring night in New Orleans, and the events of the day at the American Educational Research Association meeting were over. We were all gathered for the meetings in New Orleans. William Pinar was hosting a party at his home, a gorgeous place with rooms that overlooked a gardened courtyard. On this evening, the courtyard was buzzing with the voices of curriculum scholars and graduate students in curriculum studies—men and women devoted to the future of education. There were conversational groups scattered throughout the courtyard and house talking to old friends and new acquaintances. The words drifted over the music, words about curriculum, phenomenology, autobiography, and all matters of intellectual endeavors. It reminded me of a scene from the film *Reds* (Beatty, 1981), in which the radical intellectuals of the early 1900s discuss the future of the revolution.

I was chatting with a group of my graduate students from Oklahoma State University. When I turned to notice the entrance to the courtyard, I saw that you had arrived. I had read your works, of course, but had never met you. I decided I would introduce myself and my students. Since we happened to be standing close to the entrance, I could approach you before you were swamped with people. I walked up and introduced us. I noticed you were looking at me and thinking. After the introductions, there was a pause, and then you looked straight at me and pointed your finger at me and said words that echo in my memory. Here is how I remember it: You said as you gently waved your finger, "Yes, I know your work, and your writing keeps getting better." Then you walked on to meet and talk with other people. I will never forget those 11 words. Not only did they encourage me, but you said them in front of my graduate students. Maxine Greene actually knew my work. Those types of kind words stay with us. "I have said that I regarded words as the quintessence of things," writes Sartre (1981, pp. 141–142). I agree.

In the 15 years since that party, I have read your written words, and I have had my students read them. Your words have inspired them. My doctoral students (including Robert Lake, the editor of this volume) have used your words and works in their dissertations. And although I have managed to say hello at conferences, I have never had the opportunity to thank you for those 11 words. I hope that these 1,000 words can convey my gratitude.

—William Reynolds

The Day Maxine May Have Bombed

GEORGE WILLIS

> [I]t is the preoccupation with this [interior human] existence that makes possible the explorations of the more accessible portions of interior life. The more we take anything for granted, the less we think about it. And if a thing happens to be something of paramount importance, we may never get around to it or take the trouble to understand it. This would be a serious mistake, as anyone who has tried to explain existentialism to a class of students discovers. There are always those who cannot understand why one should spend the time thinking about the interior life (so "self-centered") for normal persons, like themselves, do not have to do so.
>
> —Ralph Harper, *The Existential Experience*

Dear Maxine,

As I write this letter of remembrance and thanks, I'm in my 39th year as a professor of education at the University of Rhode Island, and I have a lot to thank you for, both professionally and personally. I came to URI in 1971 after completing my doctorate at Johns Hopkins University. My interest in existentialism extended back to my undergraduate days, and at Hopkins I had met Ralph Harper, who at the time was a lecturer in the humanities and, as you know, the person sometimes credited with bringing Existentialism from Europe to the United States.

I read all half-dozen or so of Harper's books and considered doing my dissertation on him, but I was persuaded that a dissertation on Existentialism was "too risky," and so I chose a more prosaic topic.

So, Maxine, my first big thank-you is for writing *Teacher as Stranger: Educational Philosophy for the Modern Age* (1973), which is still my favorite among all your books. In my opinion, it is a wonderful example of how Existentialism and Deweyan pragmatism can be combined. It remains central to my basic philosophical position.

Furthermore, your "Stranger" reminds me of what some theologians call the "Other," that which challenges us to put aside old assumptions and to learn new things, to become something that we have not been before. The Other constantly beckons us in new directions, which can be exhilarating, but which also has a frightening, even terrifying, side. If we give up all that we have been before, we may be shattered, unable to put ourselves together again. And so we live in hope and trust that what we become will be better than what we have been and will leave us whole. Thank you for bringing us this message in all your talks, writings, and support for the arts in schools.

My other thanks to you are of a more personal nature. No doubt you remember that during my years at URI, you have visited the campus three times for speaking engagements. The first was in 1980, for a class on the *bildungsroman* that I was team-teaching with a comparative literature professor. The second was in 1988, for URI's Honors Colloquium, the centerpiece of a program limited to students with high grade point averages, and for which I was that year's director. The third visit was in 1994, for an endowed lectureship with which I had nothing to do. (Note that by 1994 you were sufficiently well known by URI in general so that your invitation required no lobbying by me.) For the first two of these visits you stayed in my home. Many thanks for these opportunities for my wife and daughters to get to know you. Thanks, also, for pitching in on the dishwashing and drying, something we were hoping you wouldn't do, but we could find no way to stop you! Thanks, too, for the charming books on art and creativity you gave my two daughters. By far my biggest personal thanks of all comes from 1988, the year you conquered a very serious illness and have since gone on for many more years of giving the world your vision and voice. Thank you. I'm sure I speak for many others.

Now, the first and third of your visits to URI went well, as expected; however, the second visit (for the Honors Colloquium of 1988) was much more problematic. The HC was organized so that each weekly guest speaker gave a public lecture one evening. The following morning, each then attended the HC class to talk further with the students and to answer questions about the speaker's own work. Furthermore, I had placed on file copies of all the speakers' dossiers and urged the students to familiarize themselves sufficiently with each dossier prior to the lectures so that the speakers could, in person, help students develop their own research projects within the speakers' areas of interest. Not a bad way to organize the course, I thought, to give students the opportunity to work directly with or at least to get some advice from some of the most knowledgeable people around. The HC students would be highly motivated, I thought.

I admit I was pretty disappointed with how the morning class went. Most of the students remained nonresponsive throughout, and it was obvious that few had spent any time with your dossier or had otherwise prepared themselves for the conversation we hoped would ensue that morning.

So, Maxine, as you may recall, the conversation was mostly between ourselves, with very little student involvement.

Later that day, as I was driving you to the railroad station for the train to take you back to New York, you said, "I bombed. I think I bombed," and I assured you that you had not, although perhaps a bit too hastily. In any case, we both had plenty to think about.

Now, someone who had observed the nonresponsive class that morning might indeed have reached the conclusion that you had bombed, but, of course, much more was going on than met the eye. A later speaker, one of our best-known and most highly respected colleagues, in fact, also felt that he had bombed and said so. Later still, after the HC had ended, I took some heat from its board of directors because several students complained that I had not sufficiently informed them of what to do to obtain an "A" on their research projects or in the course as a whole. So, who had actually bombed, if anyone? You, for the way you invoked existential themes, or I, for not preparing the students adequately for their encounter with you as the Stranger?

Also, many of the students expected the 1988 HC to be run as the previous year's HC had been (by a different director), in a decidedly un-Strangerly, feel-good manner. When this expectation was not to be met, the principal motivation of some became simply to defend their GPAs—hardly the kind of motivation I'd had in mind.

So, why this little story? First, to let you know that whether or not you think you bombed at URI in 1988, there are many ideas and a lot of evidence to consider before settling on that conclusion, much of it unknown to you. For instance: Rhode Island is an extremely insular state in both geography and attitude, and a large proportion of URI students are from families in which no member has had any previous experience with higher education. For instance, I surely bombed in my very first days at URI when asked to describe a good essay. In responding I used the word "cogent," whereupon another student, with a very cross look on her face and a decided edge in her voice, immediately told me, "You know, you shouldn't use words like that because this isn't an Ivy League school." I don't think I've ever quite gotten over that one.

Second, I've headed this letter with a quotation from Ralph Harper that reminds us all how hard it is not to bomb when talking with students about the interior life. While at URI, I've had many golden days and many golden classes, but I've also bombed over and over again. I suspect that's the way it is with most of us. There are both the rewards and the risks of trying.

Third, in this light, I wish to give you one final thank you, for being so undaunted, so utterly fearless in the trying. Whether you ever did or did not bomb is a question that quickly fades from relevance in the face of your example, from which so many have learned so much. But before I ramble on too long, let me close with what I hope is a bit of levity. Besides, Maxine, it might provide you with additional evidence about how you did in your 1988 visit to Rhode Island, and it might even help you decide whether you ever care to visit Rhode Island again. It is the opening paragraph of a newspaper article summarizing an academic study of the relative psychological and social health of the 50 states. Written by a staff writer who seems to know Rhode Island all too well, it appeared in the *Providence Journal* on July 13, 2009, under the headline "It's Just as You Suspected: Rhode Island's Got Issues":

> If researchers who studied the psychological profiles of the states are right, Rhode Island could benefit from an attitude adjustment—sooner rather than later. The study found us to be the second most neurotic state, and the sixth most disagreeable. (Miller, 2009, pp. A1 and A4)

And maybe that means Rhode Island is one of the hardest places in which not to bomb. After 39 years, I like to remind myself of that each time I try.

With warmest regards,
—George Willis

Our Imaginarium

GLORIA LADSON-BILLINGS

Dear Maxine,

It is both an honor and intimidating to write this letter. Of course it is an honor, because it places me alongside a pantheon of scholars who have taken the time to extol one of the real shining lights of our field. But it is also intimidating to try to put into words the meaning and significance of Maxine Greene for generations of scholars and practitioners.

Although I have known about you, Maxine, since my graduate school years at Stanford University, my up-close and personal experience with you began when you, along with 10 other academic women (including me), agreed to participate in a project initiated by Ana Neumann and Penelope Peterson entitled *Learning from Our Lives: Women, Research, and Autobiography in Education* (1997). The authors asked us to write about how our public lives intersect with, influence, and complicate our personal lives. I recall writing a rather angry chapter entitled "for colored girls who have considered suicide when the academy is not enough." I used that chapter to express the frustration I felt trying to negotiate the academy as a Black woman. One of the tasks that Ana and Penny set for us was to read and share one another's chapters. My anger seemed strangely out of place as I read the chapter that traced your journey. It was astounding to learn that you were turned down from positions and told to go home and raise a family. The academy never even considered your brilliance—you were a woman and there was no need for you to think that you could take a "man's place."

What struck me about your chapter is that there was not an ounce of bitterness in your struggle. Instead, you wrote beautifully about the value of persistence and struggle. These are the two qualities I have finally learned to appreciate and attempted to cultivate in my own life. You took that challenge as a way to build a powerful testimony to your intellect and passion for philosophy and aesthetics. This testimony would distinguish you from a generation of efficiency theorists who could only see education as a utilitarian enterprise designed to slot people into designated places in the society. You, on the other hand, saw education as a form of liberation that could help us break out of narrowly constructed roles of race, class, or gender.

Maxine, you dared to insert imagination into education—not just as a word, but also as a conceptual framework for thinking differently about what we can do in schools and classrooms. The very same imaginations that students engage *before* they encounter school, you urged us to engage as a part of school. Your brilliance pushed us to blur the borders between art and science, high and popular culture, sacred and profane. You moved us deftly from the imagined to the real and back again and opened new avenues of cognition and affective learning.

My other very personal encounter with you came as a part of the symposium series you instituted at Teachers College. I recall a December Saturday when an eclectic set of scholars, students, and activists came together to share their work. It was here that I first met Luis Garden Acosta and learned of the wonderful work of El Puente Center for Peace and Justice. I marveled at the work of the young people as they described the way their commitment to hip-hop helped them produce artistic and politically powerful intellectual experiences that allowed them to stay connected and engaged to school. I found it nothing short of ironic that you served as the catalyst for this revelation—the Black woman from West Philadelphia learns about organic street culture from the White woman philosopher from New York.

Maxine, you have always been the epitome of grace—something that is in short supply in the academy. Instead of focusing on careerism and academic politics, you seemingly have remained above the fray and helped each succeeding generation keep its eye on the proverbial prize. You helped me to realize that our work is always bigger than our jobs. Your focus on imagination seems to have evaporated in today's education discourse. We are inundated with discussion of "standards," "assessments," and "accountability."

But what of the imagination? What great work in any field was ever accomplished without paying major attention to the imagination? Many years ago, when I was a graduate student at Stanford University, I took an anthropology course with the late Robert Textor. Although his fieldwork was based in Indonesia, Bob was best known as a "futurist." He constantly pushed us to use imagination in our work. In fact, for one class Bob took us over to the Engineering School to spend time in what they called the "Imaginarium." It looked like a geodesic dome, and we entered it in groups of eight. Once inside, we lay down on a flat, carpeted floor that somehow created the illusion that we were floating and allowed our senses to be stimulated through sights, sounds, smells, and motion. It was a strange experience, and I was curious as to why the Engineering School decided to build it. The director of the Imaginarium told me that a large number of their students were international students from Asia, and most were perfectly competent to handle the technical tasks of engineering. However, few if any were putting their imaginations to work in order to solve engineering tasks. The Imaginarium was built to help the students begin to free themselves from conventional and stale thinking.

Maxine, in many ways you are our Imaginarium. When we read your books and articles, listen to your speeches, or just sit and share a cup of coffee with you, we have the opportunity to have our minds stimulated. You ask us about possibility and promise. You challenge us to see what might be, rather than wallow in what is. You dare to have educators engage aesthetic sensibilities. Your work provides us with an aesthetic grammar that extends beyond the pedestrian notions of what should happen in schools and classrooms. Your work elevates teaching to art (or at least to craft) that is rarely predictable and routine. Instead, you have taught us that teaching involves that perfect synergy of yesterday, today, and tomorrow. Your work gives us hope and challenge—a hope for a future and the challenge to make that future. Like great educational philosophers before you—John Dewey, Paulo Freire, Benjamin Mays—you spend less time worrying about what is wrong and draw our attention to the world of possibility that lies before us. We are so much richer for who you are and what you do.

Warmly,
—Gloria Ladson-Billings

Chapter Four

Blue Guitar Lessons

The Arts and Keeping
Wide-Awake in the World

I have recalled Dewey's view that the opposite of "aesthetic" is "anesthetic". Anesthesia for me implies a numbness, an emotional incapac-
ity, and this can immobilize, prevent people from questioning, from
meeting the challenges of being in and naming and (perhaps) trans-
forming the world.

—Maxine Greene, *Variations on a Blue Guitar*

*If Wallace Stevens had lived longer, he would probably be surprised to learn
that his poem "The Man with the Blue Guitar" has become a prominent
signifier for imagination and metaphor in aesthetic education. Lack of space
does not permit us to quote the entire poem here, but thoughtful repeated
readings of it in connection with the influence of Greene's scholarship continue to awaken possibility and personal meaning: blue guitar lessons. The
letter writers in this section share the impact that Maxine Greene's render-
ings of aesthetic education have made on their own lives and careers as
teachers, mentors, and artists.*

What If?

CATHRYN WILLIAMS

There is the effort to invent a situation in which there can be spaces
for doing, spaces for attending, spaces for becoming. And spaces for

---

action. I think of Hannah Arendt, making the point that action, in
contrast to behavior, means taking an initiative, beginning, setting
something in motion.

—**Maxine Greene**, *Variations on a Blue Guitar*

Dear Maxine,

What if my life as a dancer and choreographer had not led me to be
curious about working with children with whom I might share my love of
dance? What if that path had not led me to the Lincoln Center Institute?
What if I had not met you? What would my life now be like? It is hard to
imagine.

I might not have learned about creating spaces...

for wonder...

for joy...

for excitement...

for mystery...

for not knowing and for knowing...

and for wondering...

What if?

For the past 28 years, through listening to your words during your
lectures each Summer Session at Lincoln Center Institute; by making space
in my own thoughts to reflect on those words now captured in *Variations
on a Blue Guitar*; and through your friendship, I have benefited from the
companionship of at least one adult who has shared, inspired, challenged,
and opened up new spaces for me to discover.

My nervous sense of awe and wonder upon meeting you in those first
years was calmed by learning that you were curious about me as well, and
that a dialogue could begin...

With space

And spaces between

For words and for no words

Maxine, what if? . . .

these pages could hold in them my dance for you? What if we imagine my hands thanking you, the tilt of my head and my glance over my shoulder as I run to leap in the space, moving, moving forward, ever toward what we are not yet.

W

        H

              A

                    T

                                  I

                                          F

                                                    With love,

                                                  —Cathy

Keeping Wide-Awake

JACQUELINE ANCESS

When you go to a museum, don't leave your self home.
                    —Maxine Greene, unpublished lecture

Dear Maxine,
    There are thousands of school practitioners across the country whose spiritual mother you are, including me. You became my spiritual mother at our first encounter at the very first Lincoln Center Institute in the early 1970s. At the time, I was a New York City Board of Education administrator in a South Bronx public middle school. On the advice of a colleague, who told me that I "had to hear you" because you "were right up my alley," I attended one of your Lincoln Center Institute lectures, and I discovered that, indeed, you were "right up my alley." For some time, I had been

puzzling over the mysteries of reading that seemed to thwart the learning of the perfectly bright, normal students attending the schools at which I had been working. Although you talked then as you do now, not exactly about reading, but about engagement with the arts and the world, what I heard spoke to my struggles to understand my students' encounters with the written word. Almost 40 years later, I can remember vividly that what you had to say was what I needed to hear, and there was instant recognition. Aha! In the 40 years that have passed, you and your ideas continue to powerfully influence my worldview and ways of being.

In those early, magical Lincoln Center Institute days—when we sang and danced to *Appalachian Spring*, saw Aaron Copeland conduct it, shook hands with Martha Graham after it, watched as Margo Fonteyn and Rudolph Nureyev nearly crashed into each other during a dress rehearsal of *Romeo and Juliet*, stood alone before Rembrandt's self-portrait at the Metropolitan Museum of Art because it was Monday and the museum was closed to the public, danced with original members of Pilobolus, saw *Da* and *The Elephant Man* on Broadway, listened to the Emerson String Quartet, and heard Jan DeGaetani sing—about 50 of us school practitioners (from Scarsdale to the South Bronx), known as Maxine's Mafia, sat on your living room floor during the winter weeks and read Elisabeth Bishop's *Abaphora*, mesmerized by its unforgettable imagery, analyzed Wallace Stevens's black birds in 13 (and more) ways and wrote our own poems, or took excursions such as the one to see the Cézanne exhibit at MOMA. Summer after summer and year after year, we partook in your salons. Back in our schools, we collaborated with those talented Lincoln Center artists to engage our students in *aesthetic education*, the framework of which was your ideas about imagination, possibility, and encounters with the arts and the world.

As you know, somewhere along the way, another Maxine Mafioso, Marsha Lipsitz, and I had this crazy idea to start a school centered on your ideas about aesthetic education and the Lincoln Center Institute program. So joyful were our encounters with you and the Lincoln Center Institute, and such a reaffirmation of our resistance to the compliance-driven NYC public education bureaucracy was this Lincoln Center–Maxine experience, that we hungered to make it the core of our everyday work. And in 1981, when starting new schools was a very strange and rare occurrence, we started a school: Manhattan East, Center for Arts and Academics. Manhattan East was, and 26 years later remains, a New York City public middle school in East Harlem. As you recall, you were a member of the first board of directors. You climbed the five flights of steep stairs in our 100-year-old building to visit our school, review students' art portfolios, and attend art shows.

I think others would agree that our school is an extraordinary accomplishment and a tribute to your ideas of both artistic and social imagination.

As you may recall, the arts are a core component of the curriculum. All of the students take an aesthetics education class, in which Marsha and Lincoln Center artists (and sometimes I) engage them in those wonderful experiences we have had in the summers and at your salons in the winters. They experience the sounds of Shakespeare's language by creating and performing symphonies out of the words from his plays.

They write scenes analogous to dramatic conflicts. After watching professional actors perform their scenes as well as Shakespeare's, they discuss the nuances and meanings different line readings could produce. They attend productions of Shakespeare's plays and then debate the quality of the productions!

Under the tutelage of the talented Phyllis Tashlik, our students read as well as wrote and published memoirs, poems, plays, and novellas! Their interpretations of works they read take some of them into other means of expression, including dance, art, and drama. Over and over, the forewords in their publications thank Phyllis for helping them "find [their] voice." They write, perform in, and produce original operas. Everyone takes Marsha's studio art class, and even those who aren't naturally talented find the artist within. There is no students who cannot draw, paint, or sculpt. As a school, we create spaces and venues to make students' work public: the Renaissance Fair, the Beatnik Café, and the annual art show and Family Dinner.

Based on a shared vision, parents, educators, and children collaborate to create an academically and socially successful, racially, ethnically, and economically integrated middle school in East Harlem. Twenty-six years after its creation, in an educational climate much less hospitable to the initial vision that originally flourished, Manhattan East survives as a racially and socioeconomically integrated school, one of the only ones in New York City, now with a jazz band that tours the country, still drawing students from across the city, and still with very active parents who protect the value of racial and socioeconomic integration, as well as the arts, and who still very effectively practice resistance to the omnipresent demands for bureaucratic compliance. This is a legacy that would never have occurred if the power of your imagination had not been the occasion for Marsha and me to literally encounter each other at the Lincoln Center Institute.

Even though I do different work in education now, your voice is never far from my center, and when we get together you still say things that I need to hear. I am so delighted to always rediscover that you are still "right up my alley!"

Love,
—Jackie

Agradecida

GENE DIAZ

Let me fill you with the inner music of roses, their fragrant prayers.
—R. Dunlop, "From Canto"

Dear Maxine,

When people admire a flowering plant in the country of Colombia, they use the expression "*que agradecido.*" It means that the flowers are lovely, but the words mean, literally, that the plant is grateful. A plant that is grateful brings forth flowers; it blooms as an expression of its gratitude. And so I offer you visions of flowers in fullest appreciation for all that you have given to me, to my students, and to so many others. I bloom with gratitude.

The pastel gardens of Monet shimmer with shades of rose, lavender, and jade in gratitude for your strong voice that calls for including aesthetic experiences in education. Each large, saturated sensuous jack-in-the-pulpit of Georgia O'Keeffe shouts its thanks loudly for your writings and lectures that recognize the richness of many different facets and perspectives and challenge us to consider the world otherwise. Robert Mapplethorpe's soft black-and-white petals exude their gratitude in subtle whispers for your reflections on those who are marginal, excluded, unseen in schools. The sunflowers of Van Gogh and Faith Ringgold dance their gratitude across the page for your enthusiastic questioning of how and what we teach and learn, and your constant insistence that we imagine (and make!) education more poetic, more lyrical, more just and humane. Tiffany's lovely lilies, their glittering sparkle illuminating your gaze in the Met, wash you with a glow of gratitude for your steadfast commitment and enduring belief in beauty and the possibilities that we must imagine in our teaching and in our lives. And, of course, the generous bouquets adorning the tables in so many Dutch paintings sing thanks in raucous chorus for the wisdom in your words and the generous spirit of your teaching.

Flowers have long been a feast for the hungry eyes of artists, with their rich and varied textures, their joyous palette of colors, and their graceful shapes. Because you live among artists, museums, and galleries, you find art everywhere. You live in a world that offers gratitude to you constantly. Please let the flowers that you see around you, in pots and vases, in streets and gardens, in museums, galleries, and books, remind you that our gratitude and appreciation are as deep and rich as their colors, as sincere as their gently curving petals, and as enduring as their fragrance in our memories.

Like you, flowers are always becoming, always changing, and then... they shape the seeds of the future.

With great admiration and love,
—Gene Diaz

Maxine and the Furry Blue Guitar

BERNARDINE DOHRN

Maxine likes children. Not children in the abstract; not their imagined innocence. She talks to the child in front of her as fully human, perhaps just a bit more open to surprise, to juxtaposition. She meets our first grand-daughter with an unlikely and perfect gift. Riding the crosstown bus to visit the wise woman of words, D was engaged in naming the familiar fauna of Central Park. She was interested in the doorman and the elevator glide. Entering the apartment, she teetered between the windows looking down at the park, and the slightly scary old woman in a wheelchair. Maxine dis-armed her with a large, well-wrapped package. Tearing through the ribbon and paper, D found a long, floppy, neon-blue, long-haired stuffed guitar. The shiny blue fur had the quality of a shag rug. It was the campy fur on the guitar that twisted it from sentiment to playful. The shaggy, fake fleece reminded me of the dining-room walls at Graceland, covered in a similar long-haired fur.

The two-year-old was tickled: she liked its familiar quality as a "stuffie," and experimented with it as an air–musical instrument. It would join her animal jumble on the shelf in her room. She didn't know about Maxine's essay on curriculum or the Wallace Stevens poem that inspired it. She didn't think of Picasso's skeletal man wrapped around a guitar. She had only the beginning inklings of the blues. She cradled it, stroked it. Maxine twinkled. D remembered the blue guitar the next time we visited Maxine. They were improvising their independent relationship. They recognized each other.

Two decades before, Maxine had sent a similarly apt gift to our son, D's papa, then an early adolescent. It was a quality brown leather nail grooming case, filled with perfect tools for cutting and shaping, tending and buffing. It was an adult present, jarring and fitting. How did she know how to please and nudge our teenage boy into feeling sophisticated? Into even looking at his nails and hands as things to groom? He connected with that present and with Maxine with a depth that was more than passing good manners. He paid attention; he felt quietly jolted and recognized.

Maxine, with your glorious radiance and brainy connections, you are a glamorous presence, a rock star who exceeds her advance billing. We count on you to be a thoughtful commentator on the latest news; the homeless person on the bench across from her house; the books and articles she just read, film, theater, and painting. And to meditate and ruminate on the ethical life, our desire to look away, to deny our own implicated responsibility, to settle for the lesser evil.

I think her continuing connection to children is a revelation. She stretches every day to be capable of love and justice.

—Bernadine Dohrn

Attention to Wonder

Kieran Egan

Dear Maxine,

How wonderful it has been to have someone consistently drawing educators' attention to wonder. In an educational world that has been dominated for some time by rather dreary notions of what it means to be educated, the importance of a strong and eloquent voice saying with clarity and precision why those notions are dreary and inadequate is perhaps of greater value than even you recognize. Your voice has given hope and buoyancy to uncountable people involved in daily educational work, and your insistence that the imagination and a sense of wonder are at the heart of what it means to be educated continues to give heart to so many.

Wordsworth (1893/1940) wrote that the imagination is "reason in her most exalted mood" ("The Prelude," book XIV, line 192). One of the many values of your work with the arts, and the promotion of greater imaginative activity in general in the lives of schoolchildren, is your resistance to sentimental notions of wonder and imaginative engagement. As a result, teachers have been encouraged to recognize that there is no war between developing critical intelligence and the development of the imagination. You have also helped us to recognize that all knowledge grows out of human hopes, fears, and passions. Imaginative engagement with knowledge comes from learning in the context of the hopes, fears, and passions from which it has grown or in which it finds a living meaning. That is, in the everyday classroom you have constantly persuaded teachers to bring into every subject the richness of human experience that is patently there but too often suppressed by tired educational schemes.

You have helped many become more awake to human possibilities, and that's to be expected from someone who is herself so wide-awake. You have helped so many follow you in recognizing that even in the hardest conditions we can find beauty and hope. Not a bad legacy, eh?

With thanks and best wishes,
—Kieran Egan

From Critical Awareness to Wide-Awakeness

JAMES HENDERSON

> **There are works of art.... They are works deliberately created to move people to critical awareness, to a sense of moral agency, and to a conscious engagement with the world. As I see it, they ought—under the rubric of the "arts and humanities"—to be central to any curriculum that is constructed today.**
>
> **—Maxine Greene, "Toward Wide-Awakeness"**

Dear Maxine,

I want to tell a story of how your scholarship has been an invaluable inspiration to me. My story begins with Tyler's (1949) dominant curriculum problem-solving "rationale" with its literal, efficient approach to the integration of educational purpose, learning experience, instructional organization, and comprehensive evaluation, and with Kliebard's (1970/1992) critique of this rationale, which he concludes as follows: "The field of curriculum... must recognize the Tyler rationale for what it is: Ralph Tyler's version of how a curriculum should be developed—not *the* universal model of curriculum development" (p. 164).

In 1986, I began work on an alternative to Tyler's rationale that would be informed by the "reconceptualization" of curriculum studies (Pinar, 1975). I applauded efforts to rethink curriculum from an "understanding" rather than a "development" perspective. However, I didn't want to "throw the baby out with the bathwater," so I proceeded from the perspective of integrating curriculum understanding *and* development.

I have been consistently working on this project for the past 23 years, and, Maxine, you have inspired my efforts. As a doctoral student, I strongly felt that "critical" inquiry, in all of its "Western" manifestations, had value but was limited. Accordingly, as part of my doctoral socialization, I joined an

"Eastern" meditation community. My decision was based on the observation that critical awareness doesn't equate with expansive "mindfulness." To use one of your key concepts, *critically aware* people are not necessarily *wide-awake* (Greene, 1977). In our current era, academic understanding is often too narrowly specialized and disconnected. However, Maxine, your scholarship is broadly conceived and deeply embodied. Your critical concerns about "fairness" are balanced with deep insights into human flourishing (Greene, 1988).

I personally experienced your inspired consciousness on two separate occasions. A key moment in my efforts to advance a Tyler rationale alternative was the publication of the first edition of *Transformative Curriculum Leadership* in 1995, which I co-authored with Richard Hawthorne. You wrote one of the text's Forewords, which you composed with your characteristic generosity to young scholars. I had an opportunity to experience your affirming and supportive kindness in a more tangible, monetary fashion 2 years later when I was invited to introduce you in Burlington, Vermont. You gave a keynote address, inaugurating a new John Dewey Project on Progressive Education, which Kathleen Kesson had established at the University of Vermont. Immediately after your inspirational speech, Kathleen approached you with a check for your speaker's fee. You told her to keep the money and use it to support her John Dewey Project. I was truly amazed and humbled by your generous gesture, and it was a very tangible demonstration of how your deeds match your words.

I have now published three co-authored editions of *Transformative Curriculum Leadership*, the third edition co-authored with Rosemary Gornik, a school-based curriculum leader. Recently, Rosie and I have begun creating a Web site (http://www.ehhs.kent.edu/cli) that introduces and illustrates our notion of curriculum leadership.

Maxine, as Rosie and I have worked on the development of this Web site, we have realized that our "creative alternative to the Tyler rationale" is, actually, a qualitative deepening of Tyler's rationale based on your notion of "wide-awakeness." Using behaviorist language and a reductionist logic consistent with educational engineering and instructional management, Tyler asks curriculum workers to be attentive to matters of purpose, experience, organization, and evaluation as they proceed with their curriculum problem-solving. Our Web site invites and encourages educators to engage recursively in cycles of purposing, experiencing, organizing, and evaluating while practicing a fourfold disciplined mindfulness:

- Their *purposing* would be informed and refined by being mindful to moral imagination.
- Their *experiencing* would be informed and refined by being mindful to transactional aesthetics.

- Their *organizing* would be informed and refined by being mindful to deliberative artistry.
- Their *evaluating* would be informed and refined by being mindful to ethical fidelity.

The Web site provides numerous illustrations and explanations of this mindful problem-solving.

Maxine, this fourfold mindfulness represents key qualitative dimensions of your notion of wide-awakeness. In fact, we could readily provide quotations from your published works on each mindfulness concept. Instead, I will conclude by referring to the quotation from your work that I selected to open my thank-you letter. As we work on our Web site, we do want to encourage a critical awareness of the limitations of reductionist management strategies. We are inviting educators to approach their curriculum problem-solving as the "supreme" art in societies with democratic ideals (Dewey, 1897/2004). We believe that education is an art that inspires "moral agency" and "conscious engagement," and we feel honored to be part of such a professional calling. Thank you, Maxine, for the ways in which you have inspired and awakened us to this profound artistic challenge.

We are most grateful,
—Jim Henderson

Summer at the Park with Maxine

ROGER DELL

Dear Maxine,

As the July sun irradiated Central Park outside your window, I seriously wondered how I could concentrate on the task at hand. I was in the living room of your Fifth Avenue apartment, squatting on the floor with a dozen or more other participants in a 2003 Lincoln Center Institute Summer Session workshop. We were to read and discuss and travel through W.G. Sebald's *Austerlitz*, and you were to be our Pied Piper. Before long, however, and for the entire 5 days afterward, the throng on Fifth Avenue and the merriment of a summer's Central Park only flickered occasionally in the distance, as you guided us through Sebald's post–World War II Europe.

As I had experienced before and was to experience after, you always focused on the work of art—in this case the novel—no matter what hermeneutic lens you employed to pry out meaning. You moved easily from one lens to the next, and throughout the process, the text—the genius of Sebald's words and thoughts—remained inviolate. Over the 5 days, you helped us to see the novel in new ways and encouraged, nay, insisted that we bring our own insights to the task. A true work of art is always infinitely complex. And over 5 days within that glowing summer in New York, we who camped out on your living room floor experienced that exquisite complexity, thanks to you.

Today, half a decade later, I have been lately thinking about how your critical work ("critical" in both senses of the word) is needed more than ever. Yes, these downturns in funding for the arts are cyclical, and yes, now we are being whiplashed due to the implosion of the world economy, and yes, things will get better. Still, when major American universities are advising undergraduates not to take humanities courses, when students in the humanities are switching majors in droves, and when humanities teaching positions are frightfully light on the ground, it does seem as if we are at a watershed.

A good dose of Maxine Greene is desperately needed. How else, other than through an experiential approach to great art with the guidance of an enlightened teacher, are the young to envision a truly creative alternative to this current state of affairs. How are they to become what they are not yet?

I remember you saying that we must "have regard for what young people want." And, I would add, we have to put young people in a position to discover what they want. You said it more poetically, and now, alas and alack, I can only paraphrase it here: In order for new spaces to be opened up, one must create a magic circle around oneself. Years ago, driving to Boston on Route 2, I turned on NPR and heard an elderly gentleman say something like, "We didn't have the arts in the school I taught in, no music, dance, acting or painting. So, we didn't know that we had Ella Fitzgerald in our school. And because we didn't have music, dance, acting and painting, we didn't know what other Ella Fitzgeralds we had in our school."

I got goose bumps when I heard this, and I got goose bumps writing about it. True, some young people and some adults will succeed regardless of the odds, like Ella. For the vast majority, however, without exposure, without access, without opportunities in school or at home, and without a Pied Piper such as you, how can we expect the youth to know that they need a magic circle to romp within, discovering their own passions within and among the arts? With the economic crisis and the boundless distractions that bombard young people, your philosophy is critical today, as, indeed, it has always been critical. Thank God that through your unique teaching, writing, and public speaking there is now a small army of cultural warriors across the land who are making a real difference in the lives of students. And those students, moved and inspired as they are, magic circles intact, will make changes that we can only dream about.

I say your work is unique because even though there are tens of thousands of people working in the arts in America—creating, educating, analyzing, criticizing, selling, buying—one rarely hears the term "social justice" in all the accompanying chatter. Why is that? Many works of art have a social issue as subject matter. If one truly believed that art was infinitely complex, at some point one would see that art and social justice impinge upon each other. I think it is a problem of shortsightedness.

You, on the other hand, have always seen the direct correlation between the arts and social justice. If some disdain the discussion of the arts and their instrumentality in other areas of endeavor—historical, religious, economic, psychological, and, to the point here, societal—they had better check their eyeglass prescriptions. When I look around, I see our best private schools building new practice rooms onto their performing arts facilities, new additions to their campus museums, and new studio spaces for their visual arts programs. And I say, "Hooray! Well done! Now let's have the same for our public schools." Ultimately, we will not have equity without full access to all the arts for all the children.

In the above, I rambled and digressed, and now I am hoping not to make too fine a point of what I must say: We need you. We need your clear and tempered voice. We need your pitch-perfect metaphors and analogies. And we need to hear about what you are experiencing in your many circles, your many spaces of creative thinking and feeling.

Maxine, what do you say...?

With the highest regard and love,
—Roger Dell

The Point of Release

JOHN HOLYOKE

The daily warmth we experience, my father said, is not transmitted by
the sun to Earth but is what Earth does in response to Sun.
—John Cage, *M: Writings*

Dear Maxine,

The impulse to start with hemming and shuffling is strong. I can't convincingly write about how your ideas have shaped the formative chapters of my life, as others here surely will, only because I didn't have the luck of knowing you long enough, having met you in print and in person only in the past 10 years.

What I want to put forward is smaller in scope and scale than these other revelations. I can't compete with some of my formidable company for gravitas, and I won't gear up for elegy, or set my sights above the poignant and genuine testimonials of altered lives that are equally certain to populate this collection. I come forward here rapping on a single analogy like the little drummer boy of pop apocrypha.

I'll get this out of the way: What impresses me most about your work is how it works to scale. The largest strokes of thought work on the mind as powerfully as the smallest turns of phrase. I love the dynamic in-betweenness of your method of thinking and the rousing excitement in your written voice. It works like a particle collider. Allusions and concepts are sequenced in tightly linked progressions and ideas are fired through them at each other: down through three Toni Morrison novels flies Dickenson's "long slow fuse," right at the otherwising blue guitar.

My fondest encounters with you have been in person at the reading salons you have hosted over the years. And I think it is there that I've come to be influenced in ways that will be with me the longest. Sitting across from you on this cushion or that stool, I've watched you lift a passage from the text at hand and wind it with some observation about the current political moment or a take from a recent journal, working it into a coil. And then, after the thought is shaken and stirred, comes a moment when you throw it out to the room, lifting your hands from it, letting it go.

Often there is some moment, as the thing you've released bounds around the room, when you stop for a while as everyone else goes after it. In that moment, most of us, myself included, are often too busy climbing over one another's words to notice you, sitting back a bit to revel in what you've wrought.

John Cage came to Wesleyan when I was there for a sort of festival celebrating his work. He was quite old then. I attended a concert that, like most of his concerts, was conceived through some gamelike structure. An array of tape loops of many sizes, ranging between ridiculous extremes (something like 1 inch to 100 yards), almost impossible to play, were carefully laid out or coiled next to a long table of old reel-to-reel players. Cage moved slowly out on stage, amidst a squad of graduate students. The piece proceeded, with tape loops stretching out in every direction across the audience, students scrambling around trying to find new ways to steady a music stand in an auditorium seat, in an aisle, on a banister. What if we take the top off? Got any sandbags? Audience members held up their arms to support a sagging strand of tape; others vacated seats to get out of the way. Some of the tapes spooled slowly along across the room like gondola wires.

There he sat, amidst it all, bent over a bit in his swiveling chair. Not doing anything paticular, just listening, watching, looking around at what he had wrought. And two things struck me: That this was the first time (and remains the only time) I had seen genuine, unaffected audience participation.

But the more important revelation was this: Cage was radiating a certain, simple *glee* from his wizened, puffy eyes. "This guy knows how to live a life," I thought, in the most covetous way. It was the first time I thought in any kind of goal-oriented way about my later years. I thought to myself that whatever was to come of my life, whether it be as dashingly artistic as Cage's or something with more of a matte finish, when it ultimately wound down, I wanted to have his eyes. I wanted to have that glimmer and glow.

The concert proceeded interminably, like it hadn't any intention of ending. Some people walked out; some stayed. Eventually, everyone began milling about. I strode right up to John Cage in the midst of the concert (and why not? It no longer felt like a concert, but more like a cross between a lab experiment and Mardi Gras) and thanked him. He nodded, in a casual, kindly way, having no need for my thanks for himself, but welcoming it and reflecting it back.

You have that glimmer, Maxine, that easy glowing-out to the world. Throughout the past decade that I've known you, I've seen it. In reading groups, in the many discussions with teaching artists and educators around Lincoln Center, in the "question and answers" that come at the end, I see it. When the conversations you've coiled have sprung out as a galloping debate or a grand spray of ideas, at the moment when you've shaken up and released an idea, that glimmer is there. It must come, as I figure, from more than a good crop of clever thought or the satisfactions of accomplishment or wisdom or a life well lived in the humanist's or the romantic's sense of the phrase. It comes from some kind of balancing. Equipoise. And by "poise" and "balancing," I'm certain I don't mean balance between admirable qualities, nor just the graceful presentation of what fortune has given you. I'm thinking more about how one's philosophy disposes one to pitch things out into world. It's a matter of the point of release. For a pitcher (or anyone who relays any kind of ball somewhere), what the body does after the ball has left the hand has immediate impact on where and how the ball travels, even though the ball is already between the pitcher and the catcher when the pitcher's body is doing it.

I respect your intellect and your swashbuckling way with words.

I respond to your convictions, your powerful manner of reasoning. I make regular use of thoughts and ideas in ways that build my own. But I *aspire* to that glimmer. In this, I am your acolyte, and for this I'll give my final and heartfelt thanks.

—John Holyoke

Time with You

MADELEINE FUCHS HOLZER

It's in the imagination, with which you perceive this world, and the gestures with which you honor it.

—M. Oliver, "The Swan"

Dear Maxine,

How wonderful to have the opportunity to write a public thank you letter to you! How do I count the ways?

I remember a day sometime in the 1970s when I read a speech you gave to a group of school administrators at Lincoln Center Institute. It was called "On Passion and Reflection in Education." My husband was on our local school board and had heard you speak. I was in my 30s, not knowing where I would be headed professionally, and concerned that I knew no one in the world whose thought process was similar to mine. Marc came home from Lincoln Center and said, "This is what you have been looking for." And there you were, in black and white on the page. Your free associations whirled, your references dazzled, and you spoke about the things I valued in education—a passion for the work, a community of colleagues, and asking important questions that had no easy answers. Little did I know that 30 years later, I would find myself working at Lincoln Center Institute, trying to make your words sing for K–12 students as well as their educators.

There are more than a few moments in my professional growth that you have influenced since that first paper. There was my first visit to a seminar in your apartment when I was Director of Arts in Education at the New York State Council on the Arts. A group of teachers and staff members associated with the Educational Video Center sat on your sofas and the floor, talking and listening intently. Little did I know that this would be the first of many sessions where I would sit on that very floor, book and notes in hand, listening and asking questions. As I was leaving that day, you asked me if I had an art form that I practiced. I confessed that I was a poet. When you asked if you could see some poetry I had written, I felt as nervous as a 16-year-old. You read my poems and asked if I would do a reading at your apartment for one of your salons. You then published some of the poems along with ones written by David Gonzalez, who also had read in your salon that day. In so doing, you validated a part of myself, without even knowing.

Next came the many hours I spent poring over mimeographed copies of your speeches at LCI's Summer Session, to choose which ones would be included in *Variations on a Blue Guitar*, later published by Teachers College Press in 2002. I was commuting to work, and read your speeches on the train each day. Those 3 hours with your voice and your thoughts each day were a life-changing experience.

And then there were the many lunches and phone calls in which we discussed poetry, and you answered my questions relating to aesthetic education as it evolved at Lincoln Center Institute. I believe that, more than anything, it was these conversations that gave me the courage to write my own thoughts about aesthetic education and how it might evolve in schools.

At one point when I was fairly new at the Institute, I fell ill and could not work for several weeks. You called me almost every day. When I felt particularly low, you'd say, "Think about your work, Mady." I did, and I still do so each day. As you entered your 92nd year, you talked about the importance of "having a project." I understand fully what you meant. If I reach 91, I want to do so while working on my own "project"!

You have influenced thousands with your words. I have felt honored not only to spend time with those words, but also to have had time with you.

With a hug, and great love,
—Mady Holzer

Living in the Amber:
Conversations Between Red and Greene

PAULINE SAMESHIMA

> There is a crack, a crack in everything
> That's how the light gets in
>
> —Leonard Cohen, "Anthem"

Dear Maxine,
Thank you so much for the beautiful card you sent me after the 2008 American Association for Advancement of Curriculum Studies (AAACS)

conference. The black-and-white photo of the lily on the front is so close to how I imagine you—focused, sharp, crisp . . . the full range of black to white, like an Ansel Adams work, yet so delicate. Thank you.

I'm so sorry to hear that you are mostly homebound, but I still can't believe that you were in five AERA presentations right after AAACS! I'm glad for all your supportive friends and your "care ladies." Your presentation at AAACS was so moving. For some time after you spoke, I tried to express to others who were not there the way I felt sitting in that long, rectangular room. I felt your words literally, in the air, settling on me, and I had to try not to cry. Maybe your words were like pixie dust: magical. I cannot explain this physiological reaction to being in your presence. I wasn't feeling sad, and your topic wasn't poignant; it was simply an emotional response to the reconciliation of the dreams I have of you, hearing your voice, connecting your work, being near you, and talking with you.

Thank you for your response to my book, *Seeing Red: A Pedagogy of Parallax*. You wrote in your card that it was glowing and that when you reread it, it made you glow. You made my day by saying that. You said it was lovely and wise and sometimes bitter and that you were glad for it. This is so close to what I was trying to do. Bitter is a good word to describe Julia, the main character, who writes sent and unsent letters to the mentor she is in love with. *Betrayed, hurt,* and *bitter* are words we are so afraid to acknowledge—words so deeply ingrained with all the wonders of teaching. Thank you again for reading and responding to my work.

I just had a baby. She was born almost a month early, but she is healthy and perfect in all ways. She brings so much joy. I was thinking of you as I posted pictures on Facebook so my mum could download them. I was posting just the "good" pictures—when her face is angelic and beautiful. I recently looked back at the photos of my two older daughters and realized that the most precious baby pictures are the ones in which they are making funny faces—like the grimace of trying to get a burp out while asleep or the "oooh" lips that signal concentration on some bodily function. Again, you remind me of how we hide the full experience, and if we didn't, our joys could be even fuller. I mean, if I could weave the wounding of teaching into the triumphs, I could better feel the fullness of what I do. I often feel my teacher identity residing in the space of abjection.

In honor of your work, I'd like to share an adapted passage from the Preface of *Seeing Red*, because it is a rich reminder of how I have internalized your presence in my work. You've helped me live in the amber, in Julia Kristeva's (1982) "prosody," the emotional field connected to instincts that reside in the fissures of language, rather than the denotive meanings of words. It's the in-between that really matters: "I am sitting with you in my dream" (p. 205). I wrote:

> We sit at a small round metal table. The air is damp and grey but I do not feel the chill even though my hair keeps blowing across my cheek, irritatingly sticking to my lipstick, reminding me of my unsettledness even in joy. The cobblestone street makes the flimsy table wobble when you decisively tap your cigarette in a staccato movement on the glass ashtray centered on the table. We are smoking with gloved fingers, legs crossed, crimson lipstick stained on our filters, perfectly natural in another era, a different context. I see the smoke but cannot smell it and wonder if the haze in front of your eyes is just my own breath blurring my vision. I imagine your eyes are green but this is my fiction. We're sipping something thick and almost syrupy but it bites my throat with an echoing the way your words are electrifying my synapses—strangely fast, yet smooth and warm, gliding knowingness and recognition into my capillaries and spreading through my emptiness. I feel myself in the limen, teetering on the edge, uncomfortable in the brink but filled with desire to stay. I feel in love, engulfed in the anticipated moment of realization, in the love of desire to learn, knowing the space before me is all open. (Sameshima, 2007, pp. xxi–xxii)

In the Prologue for the *Journal of Educational Controversy*, you write a piece titled "From Jagged Landscapes to Possibility" (Greene, 2006):

> the crucial demand of our time is to attend, to pay heed. . . . To speak of dialogue is to suggest multiple relationships, multiple perspectives. There must be a connectedness among persons, each with a sense of agency, each with a project. And there must be a capacity to imagine, to think of things as if they could be otherwise. . . . Thoughtfulness, imagination, encounters with the arts and sciences from the grounds of lived life: this is the beginning and the opening to what might be. . . . There must be an ability to anticipate and accept incompleteness. Even when a controversy appears to be resolved, gaps and spaces remain, and the need for open questions. And where there is a space, a gap, there is the possibility of new choices, renewed reflection. (online)

I've been looking more closely at the fissures in language and in documented experience. I'm interested in what we don't acknowledge as teachers. I work with pre-service teachers, and they are so idealistic and "good." I know this is a good thing, but I also feel their resistance to noticing the cracks. I'm unsure how to approach the issue because I think the complexity of teaching is so vast, and at this early stage, even before their careers have started, how do I open this door carefully and supportively? I wonder if our high national attrition rates are connected to not acknowledging the fissures in the "good teacher" identity. It's almost as if "goodness" becomes the blinders we wear as we gallop to some arbitrary benchmark.

"Goodness" has surfaced in another team project I'm working on. We're looking at the experience of women and methamphetamine addiction and recovery. We've been interpreting the women's interview transcript texts through poetry, photography and other arts (see Sameshima, Vandermause, & Chalmers, 2009, and www.womenandmeth.com). In looking closely and thinking about commonalities across newly recovering addicts' interview transcripts, we've found significant connections between the idea of being a "good mother" and justifications for using and selling the drug. For example, one of the participants said she had to sell the drugs in order to support her children. In recovery, she stopped her addiction for her children. I can't help but wonder how our notions of "goodness" direct so much of how we appreciate our current joys and living in our present. Thank you for always reminding me to be awake.

In gratitude,
—Pauline

Questions, Anyone? Let's Hope So.

JULIE TEEL

> Try to love the questions, themselves, like locked rooms and like
> books written in a foreign language. Do not look now for the answers.
> They cannot now be given to you because you could not live them. It is
> a question of experiencing everything. At present you need to live the
> question.
>
> **—Rainer Maria Rilke, *Letters to a Young Poet***

Dear Maxine:

It is Friday, 5:20 A.M. I sit curled up in an overstuffed, olive green, $7 Goodwill-purchased chair, contemplating the shifting of the night shadows into the early-morning dawn. A steaming cup of Colombian coffee, my grandmother's quilt, and silence envelop me. In the lamplight's soft glow I reread words you have written—words that still evoke deep emotion. Tears fill my eyes. In the introduction to *The Dialectic of Freedom* (1988) you wrote:

This book arises out of a lifetime's preoccupation with quest, with pursuit. On the one hand, the quest has been deeply personal; that of a woman striving to affirm the feminine as wife, mother, and friend, while reaching, always reaching, beyond the limits imposed by the obligations of a woman's life. On the other hand, it has been in some sense deeply public as well... (p. xi)

When I began my graduate work in curriculum studies, almost 15 years ago, your writing was pivotal in my search for freedom. Your ideas led me to believe that teachers and professors ought to be able to take informed theoretical, philosophical, and political positions in the debates that ensue about curriculum and pedagogy, about learning, about the nature of truth, about what it means to be human, and about values. To be critical, for me, meant to be able to open up those ideas, to expose the relations of power in which they are enmeshed, and to articulate a response to those relations. It meant to be actively engaged in the practice of freedom (Dewey, 1969). You reminded me that "Teachers, like their students, have to learn to love the questions, as they come to realize there can be no final agreement, or answers, no final commensurability" (Greene, 1988, p. 134).

For me, it meant asking tough, often disruptive questions and changing the way I live my life. It meant putting existing assumptions about and interpretations of education into question. Raised in a working-class family in a small East Texas town, I learned early on to bite my tongue. The problem was, Maxine, that I realized that I was not going to have much of a tongue left if I did not find a way to explore the myriad questions I had about teaching, education, and pedagogy. And since I was viewed as "feminist," I figured I had better go find out what that meant. For the record, I still don't know. But the good news is that I was encouraged to think about the connection between marginalized discourses and my understanding of liberatory and democratic classroom practice, pedagogy, and research. You encouraged me to take the freedom to go the distance, to analyze the lived experience, and also to realize that every story has more than one reality. So, headlong, I plunged into the questions.

Is there such a thing as feminist pedagogy, and what is its relationship to other forms of liberatory pedagogy, such as critical pedagogy? These questions concerned the feminist scholars I studied. Ideas about feminist pedagogy seemed to swirl around notions of power and authority. The research on feminist pedagogies attempted to examine possibilities and limitations of deconstructing and reconstructing power relations in classrooms. I distinctly remember that as I was reading *The Dialectic of Freedom* (for the first time) I was enrolled in two very different graduate classes. One was in the School of Education and the other in Women's Studies. These classes were held in buildings about a quarter-mile apart from each other. They were weekly, 3-hour, back-to-back classes. As soon as the SoE class ended, I had to run at breakneck speed to arrive semi–on time to the Women's Studies class. As I was soon to learn, the distance between buildings was only the foreshadowing of the chasms between the questions each course raised.

In these classes, I experienced both pedagogy that perpetuated a regime of truth and a pedagogy that deconstructed notions of power and authority. One class's discourse silenced oppositional voices by referencing the selective traditions of "moral" education. Ironically, we were discussing dialogue, but our own dialogue was restricted to certain acceptable notions of morality that were consistent with an essentialist point of view. When oppositional voices, such as feminist perspectives of morality and pedagogical practices, were raised, they were rebuked with calls to provide more "uplifting" or "happy" feminism.

Surely, I thought, this demonstrated an authoritarian response to the "other" and an example of power operating in the classroom interaction. It was, to me, an attempt to shut down difference in the name of sameness.

The other class was in some ways as anxiety-producing as the first. It challenged the participants' conventional notions concerning feminism and society. The class's sustained critique was never reduced to one counter-hegemonic voice crying for utopic social visions of truth. This critique was accomplished via a challenge to practice various pedagogical positions. It offered both in its content and process a manner of feminist pedagogy. It attempted to speak across the differences rather than trying to meld differences into sameness. The challenge was to analyze the very nature of claims to *truth*.

Maxine, you have encouraged me to move beyond taking the status quo for granted. You have been a voice reminding and encouraging each of us to become more fully conscious: intellectually, emotionally, and spiritually. And so, in this early morning hour, I am reminded, once again, to move beyond this sleeplike state and become more fully awake—awake in the undertaking of raising my daughter, being a friend, learning more about how to help my students and their local community, and always reaching beyond that which limits me.

Friday morning, a cup of coffee, my grandmother's quilt, reflections of Maxine's *The Dialectic of Freedom*, and still loving the questions. Thank you, Maxine.

—Julie Teel

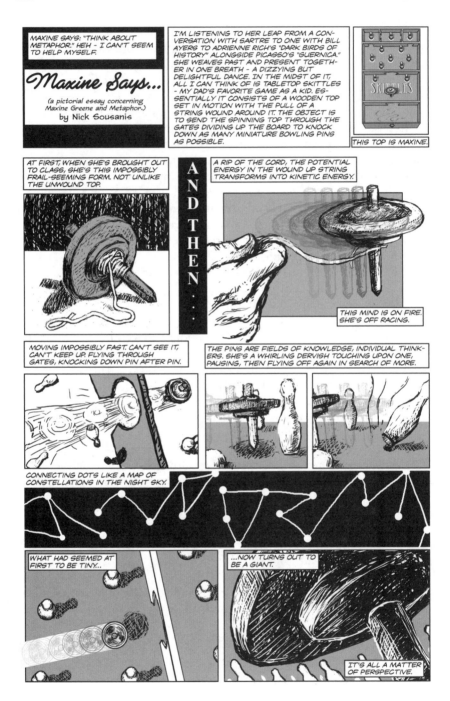

MAXINE SAYS: "THINK ABOUT METAPHOR." HEH - I CAN'T SEEM TO HELP MYSELF.

Maxine Says...

(a pictorial essay concerning Maxine Greene and Metaphor.)
by Nick Sousanis

I'M LISTENING TO HER LEAP FROM A CONVERSATION WITH SARTRE TO ONE WITH BILL AYERS TO ADRIENNE RICH'S "DARK BIRDS OF HISTORY" ALONGSIDE PICASSO'S "GUERNICA." SHE WEAVES PAST AND PRESENT TOGETHER IN ONE BREATH - A DIZZYING BUT DELIGHTFUL DANCE. IN THE MIDST OF IT, ALL I CAN THINK OF IS TABLETOP SKITTLES - MY DAD'S FAVORITE GAME AS A KID. ESSENTIALLY IT CONSISTS OF A WOODEN TOP SET IN MOTION WITH THE PULL OF A STRING WOUND AROUND IT. THE OBJECT IS TO SEND THE SPINNING TOP THROUGH THE GATES DIVIDING UP THE BOARD TO KNOCK DOWN AS MANY MINIATURE BOWLING PINS AS POSSIBLE.

THIS TOP IS MAXINE.

AT FIRST, WHEN SHE'S BROUGHT OUT TO CLASS, SHE'S THIS IMPOSSIBLY FRAIL-SEEMING FORM. NOT UNLIKE THE UNWOUND TOP.

AND THEN . . . .

A RIP OF THE CORD, THE POTENTIAL ENERGY IN THE WOUND UP STRING TRANSFORMS INTO KINETIC ENERGY.

THIS MIND IS ON FIRE. SHE'S OFF RACING.

MOVING IMPOSSIBLY FAST. CAN'T SEE IT, CAN'T KEEP UP. FLYING THROUGH GATES, KNOCKING DOWN PIN AFTER PIN.

THE PINS ARE FIELDS OF KNOWLEDGE, INDIVIDUAL THINKERS. SHE'S A WHIRLING DERVISH TOUCHING UPON ONE, PAUSING, THEN FLYING OFF AGAIN IN SEARCH OF MORE.

CONNECTING DOTS LIKE A MAP OF CONSTELLATIONS IN THE NIGHT SKY.

WHAT HAD SEEMED AT FIRST TO BE TINY...

...NOW TURNS OUT TO BE A GIANT.

IT'S ALL A MATTER OF PERSPECTIVE.

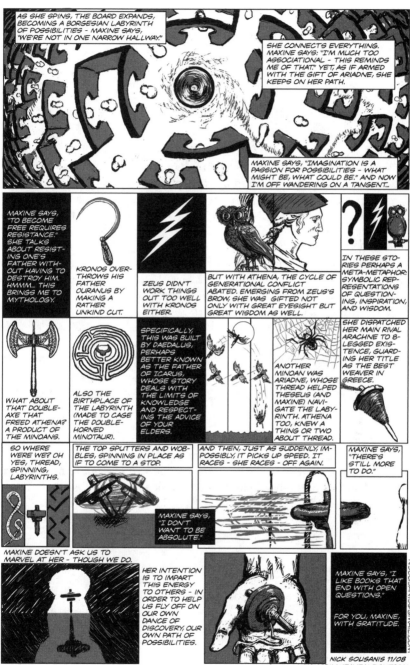

Awakening and Choosing

SUE STINSON

Dear Maxine,

What would I, what would the field of dance education, be like without the influence of Maxine Greene? Most likely, we would still be stuck in the romanticism of 1950s and 1960s creative dance for children, with its primary goal of expressing ideas and feelings through movement. Creativity and self-expression were noble goals then, as they are now. But you revealed even more possibilities for arts education. Your work helped me break through the comfort of what one colleague called "feel-good dancing"; feeling powerless in a troubled world, I found escape and solace in dancing and creating. Through your words, though, I came to realize that educators ought to do more than help young people experience the joy of dancing and making dances: we should bring them into consciousness of the larger world. After all, it is only through a change of consciousness that the world can be changed.

The first time I cited you in a publication was in a piece I initially presented at the Bergamo conference, on "Curriculum and the Morality of Aesthetics" (Stinson, 1985). You were one of the judges who selected my essay for the first James B. Macdonald Prize. Fresh from doctoral study, I was nervous presenting my paper, not knowing of the award it was to receive, and you were in the audience. I still recall my awe when you spoke to me afterward, affirming my uncertain beginnings as a scholar. A young mother at the time, I was especially moved when you shared how you had created your life as a scholar around the schedules of your children.

Your piece that I cited in that essay is one I *still* assign to my own students: "Towards Wide-Awakeness: An Argument for the Arts and Humanities in Education," from *Landscapes of Learning*. Every time I worry about assigning a 1978 publication to 21st-century students, I quickly realize that every dance educator needs to read these words:

> There are works of art, there are certain works in history, philosophy, and psychology, that were deliberately created to move people to critical awareness, to a sense of moral agency, and to a conscious engagement with the world. As I see it, they ought—under the rubric of the "arts and humanities"—to be central to any curriculum that is constructed today. (p. 162)

In the mid-1980s, before dance works had become readily available in electronic format, I had thought little about what kind of choreography ought to be central in curriculum. Your emphasis on perceiving art (as distinct from making and performing it) challenged me. You, as a New Yorker, had seen more art, and even more professional dance, than I would ever see. Your words, however, started me on a journey that has continued even since I last wrote about your influence in arts education (Stinson, 1998), preparing me for a collaboration with a colleague in dance history/performance studies over the past 5 years (Dils & Stinson, 2008). We developed a graduate course (Dils & Stinson, in press) in which students engage in a semester-long study of a carefully selected dance work, with assignments designed to enhance critical awareness, a sense of moral agency, and conscious engagement with the world. They eventually teach this work to *their* students, and then analyze and reflect on "what happens" in that experience, for learners and teachers. Among works we have used over the past 5 years are those by Alvin Ailey (*Revelations*), Bill T. Jones (*Still/Here*), Efva Lilja (*Movement as the Memory of the Body*), Victoria Marks (*Outside In*), and Jawole Willa Jo Zollar (*Walking with Pearl: Southern Diaries*). Although our students watch these works on DVD, I am certain that you have seen many of them live, and would find them good examples of the kinds of art that should be central in curriculum.

I couldn't have made this step without you. And every year, when suggesting "additional readings" for our students' reflection, I place one of your books into someone's hands. A recent student, who made good use of *Releasing the Imagination* (Greene, 1995b), explored how Victoria Marks's choreography for differently-abled bodies helped her and her high school students to *see*, as they considered embedded cultural images and meaning in the movement. She eventually realized,

> My interest is beyond students connecting with dance and facilitating this process. I also want to assist them in acknowledging their own perspectives so they can reach beyond what is familiar and find connections to dances that are outside of their usual realm. This desire is far deeper than the world of dance and connects deeply to my sense of how the world should work. We cannot function as a society without recognizing our own perspectives and attempting to expand our understanding through this perspective. This process must begin with me. (Ward-Hutchinson, 2009, p. 68)

This is only one example of how your work is still helping dance educators awaken a bit more, choose ourselves with more passion and insight, develop more courage to be. The conversation continues.

Sincerely,
—Sue Stinson

When Teaching Becomes Reaching

GRAEME SULLIVAN

Art offers life; it offers hope; it offers the prospect of discovery; it offers light.
                                    —Maxine Greene, *Releasing the Imagination*

Hello, Maxine,

I'm writing this letter from a lockup—a former jail—in Newcastle, north of my hometown, Sydney, Australia, the place where I used to live and teach, and the place where I first came across your writing on art and the social imagination in the 1980s. It seems right that I'm using words that echo your thoughts as I reflect on how my present and past experiences continue to be changed by what you say. But, as you know, it is the images created that leave a lasting impression, especially when personal skirmishes with the things around us trouble us enough to want to change them. As I look about me, I think of the importance you give to the individual voice in a local space and the capacity we have to see things as if they were otherwise.

My message comes from the comfort of an artist's residence a floor above 150-year-old prison cells kept in stark condition as a museum site. It is nicely ironic that this former police lockup now doubles as a creative space. It seems right that the paper art pieces of an artist you know well, Mary Sullivan, and my streetworks can come together within these walls. Originally built to contain what was disruptive, this space now helps the community create its own historical memory. Being invited into a place that opens up an imaginative space that is unavoidable requires creative action, and this carries with it the critical disruption necessary to keep us awake to how art educates.

I was reminded several times recently of the need to be invited into an artistic encounter by some prompt or quizzical itch that demands a response. You rightly see this as a responsibility of the educator for whom the arts embody the motives and means to make things happen in ways that are body-snapping and life-changing. Although others can open opportunities to art, the need to pause and reflect begins with the self. As you say, one just has to be wide-awake to possibility. Although the journey can be started by the most surprising circumstances, the experience is in how far you travel.

While staying in a secluded mountain cottage in the Jirisan Mountain area in South Korea in the summer of 2009, my weeklong visit was thoroughly disrupted by the surprise appearance of a small stray pup. Although timid at first, his temperament was resolute and steadfast in his ownership of the place; he belonged there. So it was his space that needed to be seen, and his pace that marked time. Both were foreign to me at first, but this new perspective was rich with surprise. Later that summer, in Mumbai, it was the seamless movement of daily comings and goings amid the limits of crimped and cramped spaces that offered promise alongside the persistence. At the time, I had been carrying around in my head an abstract image about the mix of art, ideas, and life, and here was visible presence of it all coming together in a fluid culture moving within a liquid structure.

It seems that it is in the "making" where good stuff happens, whether making headway, making opportunities, or making meanings. Often the source and circumstance of an invitation into an artistic encounter is not always obvious. But here in the lockup, making art is part of the task. It's the curious mix between what's scratched on the cell walls in permanent view and what histories from the past are still to be seen anew. Although we can't change the past, we can certainly question what the history might mean. For me, a critical edge also needs to be seen to be a creative wedge that can help open up other possibilities. This is what we do best in the arts, as the creative impulse draws, dances, depicts, and deploys, depending on what is at hand and what's on your mind. As you say, the social imagination is the place where the possible can happen, a place of "resisting fixities, seeking the openings," where "we relish incompleteness, because that signifies that something still lies ahead" (2003, pp. 22–23).

Although creativity often flourishes when unencumbered, there are social limits that help us make meaning from liquid artistic insights. In other words, art can reveal what we don't know by changing what we do know. Therefore, looking forward so as to look again at the past and present requires a creative urge to reveal a critical insight—and this capacity is within the reach of everyone. As you say, "Art can't change the world, but it can change someone who can" (2002, personal communication).

This happens as invitations to curiosity awaken a new awareness of the possibility to see things differently, and then to do something about that vision.

As I think about what is seen and suggested immediately around me, amid the clues and the questions, it is in the immense world of otherness where you have been such an important travel guide. No matter where I happen to be, or what I happen to see, I am compelled to act, and my internal conversation that began with the ideas you taught me continues to change me. As my former high school English and History teacher, John Turner, once said, this is what happens when teaching becomes reaching.

—Graeme Sullivan

And the Stage Belongs to... the Philosopher

Scott Noppe-Brandon

To live a creative life, we must lose our fear of being wrong.
—Joseph Chilton Pearce, in J. Cameron, *The Artist's Way*

Dear Maxine,
   We both have Lincoln Center Institute, this institution I work for and of which you are the philosopher-in-residence, embedded in our hearts. Talking about your decades-long ideological guidance at the Institute is a discussion too vast ever to be fully captured in words and a conversation that can never have an end, for your influence will remain here long after we are all just photographs in the archives of a future world.
   I want to speak about just one of your many facets, the one that struck me first, when we first met back in 1987 and I realized that my admiration of a thinker whose books I'd devoured was taking shape in reality, becoming an admiration for a human being—a brilliant one, but one made of flesh and blood nonetheless. (I didn't know yet that this human being would honor me by becoming a friend.)
   That facet of you is your stage presence. Surprised? Would it make you smile if I told you that many of us, your friends and devotees, think of you as the rock star of the lecture stage?
   It was July 1987, backstage at the Juilliard Theater. I was waiting to hear you address the educators, and, throwing you a few covert glances, I saw that, much to my amazement, you were nervous! Could this be? The redoubtable Maxine nervous? Our friend Mark Schubart introduced you, and I watched you, purse and Kleenex in tow, saunter across the stage toward the podium—and undergo a transformation. Somehow, miraculously, the further you moved away from the wings, the larger your presence became, and by the time you had begun to speak, you and the stage were one organism. Had I not been a dancer, perhaps I never would have gotten it, but in those first moments, I knew: Maxine understands the stage. Is her manner studied? I doubt it. Instinctive? No, a better word comes to mind: it is natural, in the same way that I imagine it came naturally to Plato to hold the attention of his students as they strolled under the trees of Greece, un-self-conscious, creating a new universe of ideas, just as you were to do a mere thought in time later.

When your presentation ended, you walked back toward the wing, and with each step the rock star reverted back to regular Maxine Greene. You turned to Mark and me and asked: "Was I okay?"

Soon after, Mark relinquished the role of introducing you as the annual speaker at LCI's Summer Session; that pleasure became mine. And you know, I've been your "warm-up act" for 22 years now (I have the singular distinction of being the person who has introduced you more than anyone else), and I never tire of watching that transformation. Perhaps it is because I never lost the dancer in me, executive chair or not, and the stage holds enormous fascination for me. Perhaps it is because after 22 years of standing ovations, you sometimes still ask: "Was I okay?"

You're more than okay. Few lecturers who have met with a similar measure of success retain such generosity when speaking. Your use of references to illustrate a point is second to none. You weave together examples of plays, passages of novels, snippets of poems, thoughts from papers and everyday life. Few who listen to your speeches have read your sources, let alone owned them intellectually. Yet we are never made to feel as if it matters. You always make us part of your story; we're included in your thought process, and this makes you accessible. People always know who you are, as we found out when we co-presented at some very atypical events, such as the Council on Medical Student Education in Pediatrics, where the conference was titled *Releasing the Imagination* and based on your book of that name. Future pediatricians eager to hear about the imagination—not bad, my friend.

Recently, a dancer who works here as a teaching artist said something that made me think of you: she had been talking about the importance of stillness within the movement in her work, and I asked her to define that "moving stillness." She said that would be as difficult, if not impossible, to define as stage presence. Bingo! I thought. But while stage presence may not be easily defined, its impact is easily felt.

The impact you have had in my life is a reflection of the impact you have had in thousands of lives. I have spoken to teachers, artists, students, and first-time attendees at your lectures and the informal salons and workshops you offer in your home, and I can say this without undue poetic license: Your role, for those of us who wanted to hear and understand you, has been not only intellectual but spiritual. It has helped to not only articulate our ideas but give form to how we perceive ourselves in the world. Inasmuch as it is possible to become a human extension of an institution, you are the soul of this Institute. Plain words, but true.

—Scott Noppe-Brandon

A Performance for Maxine

JEAN TAYLOR, BARBARA ELLMANN, AND HILARY EASTON

Dear Maxine,

We have been thinking about what we would create if we were to develop a performance piece for you. We would want the work to metaphorically incorporate many of the ideas we have learned from you, along with some of the many aspects of you, personally, that we cherish. Here are some of the elements we might include in the piece:

* The performers would be men, women, and children of all sizes, ages, ethnicities, and shapes, and maybe even a dog (for added diversity).
* The people onstage would often engage in unison movement, but we would highlight the ways in which they each looked different doing the same thing.
* Conversely, there would also be times when the performers were doing very different actions at the same time, acting as individuals within the larger group.
* We feel it would be essential that there be repetition of sections or material, so the audience could look with new eyes at portions of the performance they would know increasingly well.
* Everyone will wear a hat and carry a purse.
* There will be sections in the piece with the following subtitles:
    The (Trans)action: A pure movement section, using a vocabulary of leaning, catching, and carrying, with the performers both supporting and being supported.
    The State of Wide-Awakeness: The projection on the back wall is Mondrian's *Broadway Boogie Woogie*. Performers enter carrying stacks of books and newspapers, hats on and purses in hand. They speak fragments of the following text, which they repeat, layer, and deconstruct: "There are times in my own life when, half deliberately, I take a kind of restless action to uncouple from the familiar in the midst of ordinary life, just in order to see" (Greene, 2001, p. 710).
* During this section the performers will reorder and reorganize the stacks of books and papers, building columns of varying heights and moving these stacks upstage to create the look of a New York City skyline. The projection will fade to Van Gogh's *Starry Night* and then to a photograph of your living room.

Have You Seen?: Each dancer/actor will come forward individually to ask the audience, "Have you seen _____," filling in the blank with a variety of books, artworks, performances, newspaper or journal articles, poems, or movies that the performers are thrilled by—just like you, Maxine, always using so many resources as prompts for wide-ranging conversations and ideas.

The Creative Process: A large number of individual performers will each build something with blocks and sticks, sometimes congregating to look and remark upon one person's creation before moving on to acknowledge the work of another. Ultimately, all the performers will gather upstage to look at the projection of Matisse's *Red Studio*.

As always, Maxine, you are an essential inspiration, and we look for your advice and encouragement to complete the project. Is your dance card full next week? Can we come over for lunch?

Love,
Jean, Barbara, and Hilary

Learning to Learn

JOHN TOTH

> For us education signifies an initiation into new ways of seeing, hearing, feeling, moving. It signifies a special kind of reflectiveness and expressiveness, a reaching out for meanings, a learning to learn
> —Maxine Greene, *Variations on a Blue Guitar*

Dear Maxine,

I am writing this letter to thank you for the many ways in which your philosophy has affected my life as an artist and teacher. It was 27 years ago the first time I heard you deliver one of your lectures on aesthetic education. As the keynote speaker at a Lincoln Center Institute Summer Session, you defined aesthetic education as having "kinds of experiences associated with reflective and conscious encounters with the arts" (Greene, 2001 p. 3).

What struck me the most about your presentation was that this comment perfectly describes my own method as an intermedia artist. This creative method for teaching that you presented was not what I expected. I had not yet considered how teaching art could have as its objective an aesthetic experience for all of the students. Although I had read John Dewey in art school, who confirmed my own understanding of art as being about experience, it was your words that moved the aesthetic experience out of the studio and into the everyday classroom (Dewey, 1934). I had not yet considered the act of teaching art as involving the same methods I used in creating a work of art.

Thank you for initiating me into "new ways of seeing, hearing, feeling, moving" (Greene, 2001, p. 7) and thinking as an artist and educator. It seems clear to me now, after teaching aesthetic education for 27 years, that the "reflectiveness" and "expressiveness" you identify creates a unity between body and mind (Greene, 2001, p. 7). These words guided me in developing a unit of classroom study designed to address both the technical skills and creative objectives inherent in the work of art we were studying. Finding activities that started with the most basic skills to complete the creative task (usually geared toward solving a personal problem or issue) allowed untrained students to express their ideas or feelings in a way that mattered to them. In essence, the work of art is a generator of both art activity and higher-order thinking.

As a teaching artist, I learned to engage students in an inquiry process that was guided by questioning. You taught me to ask meaningful questions of my students that allowed for their personal experiences to be considered. I stopped asking questions that I knew the answers to and started asking questions guided by your signature "what if" questioning: "What would you feel and think if *you* were standing on the hill in Van Gogh's *Starry Night*?" Thank you for a philosophy that demands a student-centered approach. Through thoughtful noticing and active participation in the elements of the work of art, we all came to find new meaning.

New meanings also began to emerge from your works in unexpected ways for me. Thank you for shaking the foundation of my rather myopic view that aesthetics was about taste—that is, knowing what I liked and disliked. Thank you for introducing a process of noticing through inquiry that allows for a suspension of judgments in taste long enough to experience and discuss a work of art.

Thank you for the epiphany that came when I discovered that this aesthetic method brought new meaning to my own life. Thank you for the surprise when I discovered that works of art that didn't fit into my narrow list of favorite artworks were not always the best works to teach from. Often during class museum visits, students would wander over to works of art that were not on their designated tour list. They would start by asking engaging questions of one another—without teacher intervention.

Over the years your lectures focused and refocused on imagination, seeing, feeling, thinking, and breaking away from conventional ways of perceiving. Your summer lectures had the most wonderful affect on my life. You planted a seed both in my teaching and in the way that I make art. Because of your writing and the references you made to poets, artists, writers, and philosophers, you instilled a deep desire within me to pursue doctoral studies. I fell deeply in love with philosophy. Kant, Dewey, Benjamin, and even Rilke started making sense to me; I *had* to change my life. And I did change.

Lastly, after reading *Variations on a Blue Guitar* so many times, I began to truly understand the underpinning of your philosophy—social justice. While accountability and standards place more and more control over what administrators, teachers, and students can and cannot do, the arts, as you suggest, are not a frill. They open new ways of learning.

> We see it as integral to the development of persons—to their cognitive, perceptual, emotional, and imaginative development: We see [art] as part of the human effort (so often forgotten today) to seek a greater coherence in the world. We see it as an effort to move individuals (working together, searching together) to seek a grounding for themselves so that they may break through the "cotton wool" of dailyness and passivity and boredom and come awake to the colored, sounding, problematic world. (Greene, 2001, p. 7)

Thank you, Maxine, for being the standard-bearer for the advocacy of the arts in the schools for so many years. You feed the children, teachers, administrators, and artists with words that bring meaning and purpose to our lives. I have been humbled by your knowledge and inspired by your thinking, but mostly I applaud the dignity you bring to humanity. I think I am beginning to learn.

Best wishes,
—John Toth

Epilogue

"Coming Together to Act on the Possibility of Repair"

Conversations with Maxine Greene

> [It is our] incompleteness that summons us to the tasks of knowledge and action . . . putting an explanation into words, fighting a plague, seeking homes for the homeless, restructuring inhumane schools.
> —Maxine Greene, *Releasing the Imagination*

I am honored by the invitation to write an epilogue for this remarkable collection of letters to Maxine. However, I here am resisting any totalizing account of Maxine Greene's immense and impassioned contributions to education, the arts, and the innumerable individuals whom she has touched over the years. For those who have heard Maxine's unmistakable voice in her writings, classrooms, and conference settings—or in her living room that serves as a salon for myriad discussions about education, the arts, social imagination, and responsibility—know that she refuses stasis, conclusions, summations.

In fact, I discussed this writing invitation with Maxine. Few, I believe, would be surprised at her reaction: "I can't say exactly where I'm headed, but I do know I'm *not finished*. No epilogue here, no endings, no eulogies, please" (Maxine Greene, in conversation, 12-06-09). Here, then, I attempt to honor Robert Lake's revised request, as editor of this collection, to engage in conversations with Maxine about how she might wish her scholarship to continue to be discussed, extended, and even reimagined.

Indeed, Maxine and I have been engaged in conversations since 1974, and—lucky for me—we live and teach in the same city and institution. We have been meeting regularly for years, most recently in relation to a current project that we both describe as in-process attempts to examine broad social, cultural, and historical implications of divergences and congruences in our lives as women academics. So I was delighted to have yet another reason to engage in our conversational interludes.

Here I have culled slivers of our past and more current discussions from my audiotape transcriptions of our own project exchanges thus far. I hope to offer several glimpses into Maxine's descriptions and positionings of her scholarship. By extension, I have extracted some conversational segments where she also gestures toward ways she hopes her work might continue to influence future generations of students, teachers, administrators, artists, and education and community activists in their attempts to consider needs for and possibilities of "fighting a plague, seeking homes for the homeless, restructuring inhumane schools."

When we do talk in person, rather than by e-mail or the telephone, we most often sit at Maxine's dining-room table. She usually sits facing the wide living room windows that are framed by several orchid plants that lounge against the glass for support. Maxine's living and dining rooms, too, are filled with vases of flowers from her most recent visitors. Always flowers.

And as we talk, we both often gaze at the trees that rise above the steady stream of joggers, dog walkers, and museum-bound tourists who parade under her third-floor apartment windows. I usually sit to Maxine's left, close to the corner of the table, mostly so that we can hear each other and so that the audiotape might record most of our words. And because our conversations are in the spirit of the original Latin meaning of *conversation* as "*wandering together with*," we typically first engage in meandering, stream-of-consciousness forays into our own and others' current daily work. We tend to do lots of talking about teaching and news of our shared institution. And we constantly toss each other questions about what's happening with people and ideas in the broad field of education in which we both teach and learn. All of these spontaneous and seemingly random conversations most often veer toward examining our particular and highly divergent biographical journeys toward "becoming women academics."

In our most recent talks, however, mindful of Maxine's rejection of any traditional "epilogue" to this collection, I invited Maxine to describe her ongoing work as well as her hopes and desires for its continuance:

> The only thing that means anything to me is what I do tomorrow, I guess. I can't change what I've already done. It's done, and some people like it and some don't. I would hope that some would still read some of what I wrote, but it most likely will eventually disappear. A couple of people will remember a couple of things.
>
> But I have to keep believing that if you can get people to think beyond what is taken for granted as "natural," to disrupt or over- come what they have internalized as given, to even make themselves

capable of outrage at violence and inequities—not only to recognize and *name*, but also to work to change these, for example—you're doing as much as anybody could. (Conversation, 11-9-09)

Of course, most of us would maintain that Maxine has done as much *and* more as anybody could. She continues to teach, write, and lecture about her convictions that educators and students need to be become more self-conscious about multiple schemata needed to interpret current and huge life and world complexities. We must do so, she argues, in order to become more responsible in the choices we make among available ways of seeing and interpreting the world. But she also insists that education—in contrast to technical-rational versions of institutions called schools—involves processes of meaning-making among individuals in micro and macro contexts and in settings riddled with unequal power relationships, paradoxes, contradictions, and mandates. Education also involves resisting the standardization and measurement of "effective" teaching and learning while, at the same time, acknowledging and honoring varying goals and desires, differing social and cultural constructions of who and what counts in pedagogical and learning processes.

> It's a matter of breaking with the natural attitude, the passive acceptance of the way things are, of what those around us keep insisting is normal. . . . We have to move beyond the moments of mere passive empathy, working through if, at all possible, our own feelings of unease, of helplessness or blindness, along with our longings to take refuge somehow at the center. It's what I draw from Schutz, that emphasis on "wide-awakeness." Consciousness is not an inner state. Acts of consciousness grasp the appearance of things, jut into the world. Consciousness is always OF something, never empty. So, wide-awakeness, for me, is not just awareness, but more like Freire's ability to name the world and *act* on it. I am so concerned about apathy, withdrawal, paralysis. (Conversation, 7-26-09)

Indeed, Maxine often quotes Dewey in saying that "facts" are repellent until one uses imagination to resist passivity and acceptance of "the norm" as well as to envision possibilities and to act to bring those possibilities to fruition. In relation to "wide-awakeness," Maxine conceptualizes actions taken in "naming" the world as grounded in what she calls social imagination. Maxine has described social imagination as "the capacity to invent visions of what should be and what might be in our deficit society, on the streets where we live, in schools" (Greene, 1995b, p. 5). She most recently elaborated:

Social imagination has to do with the recognition of the need for and the shaping of a social vision. It has to do with the possibilities of desirable changes in the social world—the fight for justice, for equality, for a decent and humane way of living together. I want people to become wide-awake enough to come together to act on the possibility of repair. (Conversation, 11-9-09)

Maxine's conceptualization of social imagination involves her drawing upon literature and the arts as means by which to both realize and act upon "desirable changes in the social world." Initially in her academic career, aspects of those desirable changes had to do with her struggles for acceptance as an educational philosopher:

I was what many called too "literary." My writing was described as not the writing of a philosopher but of an artist. They said it wasn't "philosophy writing." But Kierkegaard talked about his writing as indirect communication, like literature. You engage with it.

In using literature, my focus is on what happens in the relationship, when an act of consciousness—that is, imagination, perception, belief, indignation—grasps a paragraph or phrase, transforms it into an experience, or an event in the flow. I use literature because it brings you in touch with the problematic, with the ambiguous, with vast uncertainties. I do think that if you can engage kids with literature or painting, they possibly can break with what they take for granted or with the given. I hope so.... And that's where learning has to begin, doesn't it? I always say the teacher who comes into class with *Hamlet* already solved is not a sympathetic character to me. (Conversation, July 26, 2009)

Indeed, literature and the arts for Maxine are immediate means to demonstrate that "realities" always are changing, always yielding unpredictable and unrepeatable moments and interpretations in classrooms, in faculty meetings, in collaborative learning attempts or performances, for example. And Maxine never fails to push—to insist that we educators not only recognize but also directly attend to complexities and yes, oppressions, in educators' and students' myriad social and cultural realities.

So, it's too always a question of keeping the desire aflame. How do we become conscious of our incompleteness, how do we resist the systems, resist constant effort to thrust us into categories or render us into objects, functionaries, clerks. If we are to keep curriculum alive and unfinished, emergent..., we as educators have to be motivated by the unanswered questions, by the continual need to choose ourselves.

And yet, we also have to attend to how we are caught up in things, how we *are* in the world—and how that could stop those questions that we need in order to keep becoming. (Conversation, 4-5-03)

During our conversations, Maxine and I sometimes talk our way through a late Saturday or Sunday afternoon. As I sit at her dining room table, or sometimes side by side with Maxine in her study, I never take for granted the brilliance of her insights, the sharpness of her humor, the vast reach of her reading and analyses of national and world events or current examples of literature and the performing and visual arts. Always aware of the privilege that I enjoy in sitting and conversing with Maxine, I cannot help but wish that I could enliven this "non-epilogue" with the actual Brooklyn inflections in her voice, the clarity of her perceptions, and the depth of her insatiable questioning.

As the sun begins to nestle into the trees, we often are still puzzling, for example, about local and contingent responses to tensions between the ongoing, never-ending, unpredictable, and unrepeatable project called education and the now-mandated standardized expectations of institutions called schools. Clearly, Maxine has taught so many of us not only to question but also to look closely into the multiple texts of and local responses to our students' and our own social and cultural realities. Because of Maxine's scholarship as well her "being in the world," myriad educators have become vitally concerned with the unpredictable, unrepeatable "texts" of students' and educators' social, cultural, and historical realities that constantly *interrupt* any "smooth," linear, predetermined, and always-able-to-be-measured notion of curriculum, teaching, and learning. Again, Maxine passionately advocates for literature and the arts as aspects that can spur versions of "social imagination" that support such possible acts of interruption:

> So, my thought is if you are lucky enough to have a significant experience with a work of art, then I want to say that you're released to have it come in touch with your identity in different ways, with alternative ways of being, where there's a possibility of empathy that wouldn't have existed otherwise. I figure my job is not art appreciation. My job is to try to suggest what can flow from this. It doesn't mean you learn math better. The important part of that experience is that it does something—it has to do with the way you're in the world. You see better, you attend differently—you have some new ways of envisioning and acting on the world. (Conversation, 4-10-05)

Further, what thousands of educators continue to learn from Maxine is how she herself chooses to engage in constant and often difficult processes of meaning-making, dialogue, and reflexive questionings of her own actions in the world. She does so, she says, because:

> In attending to how things could be otherwise, I don't ever want to sound like I have a "solution." But I keep trying to choose the possible *against* the limits, because I am most afraid of numbness. (Conversation, 12-19-09)

In accepting the invitation to engage Maxine in interactive deliberations about how she might wish her work to be viewed and utilized, I knew that even though I wanted to share Maxine's own thoughts about her lifelong educational commitments and intellectual passions, I also could say what I knew she would not.

I believe that Maxine's own vast curiosities about the world as well as her formidable intellect elevate educators and students away from the familiar—away from numbness—and out *into* the world. And as such, she enables us to consider our own possibilities to choose, to forge connections with/in and across difference in order to act, even in the face of our own incongruities, contradictions, insecurities, and unknowingness.

Such is the immutable influence, I believe, of this educational philosopher who, through her "non-philosophy writing, teaching and lecturing," has inspired generations of educators and students to work together to take actions against the "plagues" of habit, indifference, passiveness, and alienation. The gift that Maxine Greene has offered and continues to confer on the whole worldwide field of education is her passion for forging ways to "come together to act on the possibility of repair," a possibility that she herself so magnificently has envisioned, embodied and enacted.

Dear Maxine. Thank you.

—Janet L. Miller

References

Ahmed, S. (November, 2008). *On being directed by happiness.* Lecture presented at Center for Gender & Sexuality Studies, New York University.

Anzaldúa, G. (1987). *Borderlands/La frontera: The new mestiza.* San Francisco: Spinsters/Aunt Lute.

Apple, M. (n.d.). Untitled & unpublished manuscript.

Arendt, H. (1958). *The crisis between past and future: Eight exercises in political thought* (Denver Lindley, trans.). New York: Penguin.

Arrowsmith, W. (1971). Teaching and the liberal arts: Notes toward an old frontier. In D. Bigelow (Ed.), *The liberal arts and teacher education: A confrontation.* Lincoln: University of Nebraska Press.

Asher, N. (2005). At the interstices: Engaging postcolonial and feminist perspectives for a multicultural education pedagogy in the South. *Teachers College Record, 107*(5), 1079–1106.

Ayers, W. C., & Miller, J. L. (Eds.) (1998). *A light in dark times: Maxine Greene and the unfinished conversation.* New York: Teachers College Press.

Barros, A., & Macy, J. (1996). *Rilke's book of hours: Love poems to God.* New York: Riverhead Books

Beatty, W. (Producer/Director). (1981). *Reds* [Motion Picture]. United States: Paramount Pictures.

Bell, Q. (1972). *Virginia Woolf: A biography.* New York: Harcourt Brace Jovanovich.

Belenky, M. F., Clinchy, B. M., Goldberger, N. R., & Tarule, J. M. (1986). *Women's ways of knowing: The development of self, voice, and mind.* New York: Basic Books.

Bishop, E. (1976). *Elizabeth Bishop: The complete poems, 1927–1979.* New York. Farrar, Straus and Giroux.

Blanchot, M. (1995). *The writing of the disaster* (A. Smock, trans.). Lincoln: University of Nebraska Press. (Original work published 1980)

Bode, P. (2006, April 21). *Art classes shouldn't be the first to go. Amherst Bulletin.*

Britzman, D. P. (2009). *The very thought of education: Psychoanalysis and the impossible professions.* Albany: State University of New York.

Brooks, G. (1998). Paul Robeson. In Freedomway (Eds.), *Paul Robeson: The great forerunner* (p. 235). New York: International Publishers.

Buber, M. (1958). *I and thou.* (Ronald Gregor Smith, trans.). New York: Scribner.

Butler, J. (2004). *Precarious life: The powers of mourning and violence.* London: Verso.

Cage, J. (1973). *M: Writings '67–72*. Middletown, CT: Wesleyan University Press.

Cage, J. (1983). *Composition in retrospect*. Middletown, CT: Wesleyan University Press.

Cameron, J. (Producer & Director). (1997). *Titanic*. [Motion picture]. United States: 20th Century Fox.

Cameron, J. (1992). *The artist's way: A spiritual path to higher creativity*. New York: Putnam.

Chodron, P. (1997). *When things fall apart: Heartfelt advice for difficult times*. Boston: Shambala Press.

Cohen, L. (1992). Anthem. On *The Future* (CD). New York: Columbia.

Cole, K. C. (2003). *Mind over matter: Conversations with the cosmos*. New York: Harcourt.

Copjec, J. (2004) *Imagine there's no woman: Ethics and sublimation*. Boston: MIT Press.

Derrida, J. (1994). *Specters of Marxism: The state of debt, the work of mourning, and the new international* (P. Kamuf, Trans.). New York: Routledge.

Dewey, J. (1930). "In response." In *John Dewey: The man and his philosophy* (H. Holmes, Ed.) (pp. 173–181). Cambridge, MA: Harvard University Press.

Dewey, J. (1934). *Art as experience*. New York: Peregee.

Dewey, J. (1944). *Democracy and education*. New York: The Free Press. (Original work published in 1916)

Dewey, J. (1964a). Human nature and conduct. In R. Archambault (Ed.), *John Dewey on education*. Chicago: University of Chicago Press. (Original work published 1922)

Dewey, J. (1964b). What is freedom? In R. Archambault (Ed.), *John Dewey on education* (pp. 81–88). Chicago: University of Chicago Press.

Dewey, J. (1969). *The early works, 1882–1898* (Vols. 1–5). Carbondale: Southern Illinois University Press.

Dewey, J. (2004). My pedagogic creed. In D. J. Flinders & S. J. Thornton (Eds.), *The curriculum studies reader* (2nd ed.) (pp. 17–23). New York: Routledge Falmer. (Original work published 1897)

Dickens, C. (1885). *Barnaby Rudge*. Philadelphia: Lippincott.

Dils, A. H., & Stinson, S. W. (2008). Toward passionate thought: Peer mentoring as learning from and with a colleague. In T. Hagood (Ed.), *Legacy in dance education: Essays and interviews on values, practices, and people* (pp. 153–168). Youngstown, NY: Cambria.

Dils, A. H., & Stinson, S. W. (in press). Teaching research and writing to dance artists and educators. In T. Randall (Ed.), *Proceedings of the Congress on Research in Dance 2009 Special Conference*, 25–27 June 2009, DeMontfort University, Leicester, UK. Champaign: University of Illinois Press.

Dimitriadis, G., & McCarthy, C. (2001). *Reading and teaching the postcolonial: From Baldwin to Basquiat and beyond*. New York: Teachers College Press.

Duckworth, E. (2006). *The having of wonderful ideas*. New York: Teachers College Press.

Dunlop, R. (2002). From Canto. In *The Body of My Garden* (p. 108). Toronto: Mansfield Press.

Eastman, B. (Producer), & Attenborough, R. (Director). (1993). *Shadowlands* [Motion picture]. Spelling Entertainment Group, Los Angeles, CA.

Edelman, L. (2004). *No future: Queer theory and the death drive.* Raleigh, NC: Duke University Press.

Eisner, E. (2002). *The arts and the creation of mind.* New Haven, CT: Yale University Press.

Emerson, R. W. (1982). *Ralph Waldo Emerson: Selected essays.* (L. Ziff, Ed.). New York: Penguin.

Freire, P. (1970). *Pedagogy of the oppressed.* New York: Seabury Press.

Freire, P. (1995). *Pedagogy of the oppressed.* New York: Continuum. (Original work published 1982)

Freire, P. (1998). *Teachers as cultural workers: Letters to those who dare teach.* Boulder, CO: Westview Press.

Fruchter, N. (1998). Pursuing public space: Maxine Greene and sameness in utter diversity. In W. Ayers & J. Miller (Eds.), *A light in dark times: Maxine Greene and the unfinished conversation* (pp. 229–240). New York: Teachers College Press.

Gallop, J. (2000). The ethics of close reading: Close encounters. *Journal of Curriculum Theorizing, 17* (3), 7–17.

Giarelli, J. (1998). *Maxine Greene: The literary imagination and sources of public education.* In W. Pinar (Ed.), *I am not yet: The passionate mind of Maxine Greene.* London: Falmer Press.

Gordon, A. (1997). *Ghostly matters: Haunting and the sociological imagination.* Minneapolis: University of Minnesota Press.

Greene, M. (1965). *The public school and the private vision.* New York: Random House.

Greene, M. (1967). *Existential encounters for teachers.* New York: Random House.

Greene, M. (1969). Against invisibility. *College English, 30*(6), 430–436.

Greene, M. (1971a). Curriculum and consciousness. *Teachers College Record, 73*(2), 253–269. Reprinted in William F. Pinar (Ed.), *Curriculum theorizing: The reconceptualists* (pp. 299–317). Berkeley, CA: McCutchan, 1975.

Greene, M. (1971b). Teaching for aesthetic experience. In B. Reimer (Ed.), *Toward an aesthetic experience* (pp. 20–44). Washington, DC: Music Educators National Conference Proceedings.

Greene, M. (1973). *Teacher as stranger.* New York: Wadsworth.

Greene, M. (1975, October 23). *Education, freedom and possibility.* Inaugural lecture as William F. Russell Professor in the Foundations of Education. New York: Teachers College, Columbia University.

Greene, M. (1977). Toward wide-awakeness: An argument for the arts and humanities in education. *Teachers College Press, 79(1),* 119–125.

Greene, M. (1978). *Landscapes of learning.* New York: Teachers College Press.

Greene, M. (1979). Liberal education and the newcomer. *Phi Delta Kappan, 60*(9), 633–636.

Greene, M. (1986). In search of a critical pedagogy. *Harvard Educational Review, 56,* 427–441.

Greene, M. (1988). *The dialectic of freedom.* New York: Teachers College Press.

Greene, M. (1993a). Diversity and inclusion: Toward a curriculum for human beings. *Teachers College Record, 95*(2), 211–221.

Greene, M. (1993b). The passions of pluralism: Multiculturalism and the expanding community. *Educational Researcher, 22*(1), 13–18.

Greene, M. (1993c). The plays and ploys of postmodernism. *Philosophy of Education Yearbook*. Retrieved December 26, 2009, from http://www.ed.uiuc.edu/eps/PES-Yearbook/93_docs/Greene.HTM#fn2.

Greene, M. (1995a). *Metaphors and responsibility*. Accessed October 11, 2009, from http://www.yale.edu/ynhti/pubs/A18/greene.hhtml.

Greene, M. (1995b). *Releasing the imagination*. San Francisco, CA: Jossey-Bass.

Greene, M. (1999). Reflection on *Teacher as Stranger*. *Books of the Century Catalog*, retrieved from http://www.ed.sc.edu/museum/exhibitions/leaders/greene.html.

Greene, M. (2001). *Variations on a blue guitar*. New York: Teachers College Press.

Greene, M. (2003). The arts and social justice. In P. Sahasrabudhe (Ed.), *Art education: Meaning dimensions and possibilities. Keynote addresses. The 31st InSEA World Congress, August 2002* (pp. 21–25). New York: Center for International Art Education Inc., Teachers College, Columbia University.

Greene, M. (2006). Prologue: From jagged landscapes to possibility. *Journal of Educational Controversy, 1*(1). Retrieved November 9, 2006, from http://www.wce.wwu.edu/Resources/CEP/eJournal/v001n001/a005.shtm.

Greene, M. (2007a). The arches of experience. In L. Bresler (Ed.), *International handbook of research in arts education* (pp. 657–662). Dordrecht, The Netherlands: Springer.

Greene, M. (2007b). The Maxine Greene Foundation for Social Imagination, the Arts & Education. Retrieved December 21, 2009, from http://www.maxinegreene.org.

Greene, M. (2008a, March). *Pedagogies of thought*. Paper presented on the occasion of her 90th birthday at Teachers College, Columbia University, New York.

Greene, M. (2008b, March). *The poet, the city and curriculum*. Paper presented at the American Association for the Advancement of Curriculum Studies (AAACS) conference, New York.

Hancock, M. (Director & Producer). (2001). *Exclusions and awakenings: The life of Maxine Greene* (Documentary). New York: Hancock Productions.

Harper, R. (1972). *The existential experience*. Baltimore, MD: Johns Hopkins University Press,

Henderson, J. G., & Gornik, R. (2007). *Transformative curriculum leadership* (3rd ed.). Upper Saddle River, NJ: Merrill/Prentice Hall.

Henderson, J. G., & Hawthorne, R. D. (1995). *Transformative curriculum leadership*. Englewood Cliffs, NJ: Merril.

Hoey, P. (2008, March 19). Maxine Greene: The importance of personal reflection. Philosophy meets public education. *Edutopia*. Retrieved from http://www.edutopia.org/maxine-greene.

Huebner, D. (1999). Religious metaphors in the language of education. In V. Hillis & W. Pinar (Eds.). *The lure of the transcendent: Collected essays by Dwayne Huebner* (pp. 358–368). Mahwah, NJ: Erlbaum.

Jaggar, A. (1989). Love and knowledge: Emotion in feminist epistemology. In A. Jaggar & S. Bordo (Eds.), *Gender/Body/Knowledge* (pp. 145–171). New Brunswick, NJ: Rutgers University Press.

King, J. (Ed.). (2005). *Black education: A Transformative research and action agenda for the new century.* Washington, DC/Mahwah, NJ: AERA/Lawrence Erlbaum.

Kliebard, H. (1992). The Tyler rationale. In H. Kliebard (Ed.), *Forging the American curriculum: Essays in curriculum history and theory* (pp. 153–167). New York: Routledge. (Original work published 1970)

Kristeva, J. (1982). *Powers of horror: An essay on abjection* (L. F. Céline, trans.). New York: Columbia University Press.

Lambert, L. (1995). *The constructivist leader.* New York: Teachers College Press.

Lambert, L., & Gardner, M. E. (2009). *Women's ways of leading.* Dog Ear Publishing, LLC.

Lear, J. (1999). *Open minded: Working out the logic of the soul.* Cambridge, MA: Harvard University Press.

Lear, J. (2008). Seminar presentation, Fudan-UIUC Advanced Training and Research Seminar on Philosophy of Education, College of Education, University of Illinois, Champaign, IL, July 7–9, 2008.

Levinas, E. (1969). *Totality and infinity: An essay in exteriority.* (Alphonso Lingis, trans.). Pittsburgh, PA: Duquesne University Press.

Lodge, D. (2002). Consciousness and the novel. In D. Lodge (Ed.), *Consciousness and the novel* (pp. 1–91). New York: Penguin.

Lorde, A. (1984). *Sister outsider.* Freedom, CA: Crossing Press.

Luce-Kapler, R. (1998). The slow fuse of aesthetic practice. In W. Pinar (Ed.), *The passionate mind of Maxine Greene: "I am . . . not yet"* (pp. 148–159). New York: Falmer.

Luce-Kapler, R. (2003). *The gardens where she dreams.* Ottawa, ON: Borealis.

Mayer, J. (2004). Apprehending the thought of (all) others in classrooms. In L. Coia, N. J. Brooks, S. J. Mayer, P. Pritchard, E. Hellman, M. L. Birch, & A. Mountain (Eds.), *Democratic responses in an era of standardization* (pp. 179–197). Troy, NY: Educator's International Press.

McNiff, S. (2004). *Art heals.* Boston: Shambhala Publications.

Merleau-Ponty, M. (1962). *Phenomenology of perception.* New York: Humanities Press.

Michaels, A. (1996). *Fugitive pieces.* Toronto: McClelland and Stewart.

Miller, G. W. (2009, July 13). It's just as you suspected: Rhode Island's got issues. *Providence Journal*, pp. A1 and A4.

Miró, J., & Rowell, M. (1992). *Joan Miró: Selected writings and interviews.* New York. Da Capo Gap Press.

Morrison, T. (1970). *The bluest eye.* New York: Penguin.

Morrison, T. (1993). Nobel Prize lecture. In S. Allen (Ed.), *Nobel lectures, literature 1991–1995* (pp. 41–56). Singapore: World Scientific Publishing.

Murdoch, I. (1999/1957). Metaphysics and ethics. In P. Conradi (Ed.), *Existentialists and mystics: Iris Murdoch's writings on philosophy and literature* (pp. 59–75). New York: Penguin.

Neruda, P. (1971). Nobel lecture. In S. Allen (Ed.), *Nobel lectures, literature 1968–1980* (pp. 49–64). Singapore: World Scientific Publishing.

Neumann, A., & Peterson, P. (1997). *Learning from our lives: Women, research, and autobiography in education.* New York: Teachers College Press.

Nieto, S. (2008). *Dear Paulo: Letters from those who dare teach.* Boulder, CO: Paradigm.

Obama, B. (2006). *The audacity of hope: Thoughts on reclaiming the American dream.* New York: Three Rivers Press.

Oliver, M. (1992). The swan. In *New and selected poems* (pp. 78–79). Boston: Beacon.

Pedraza, P., & Rivera, M. (Eds.). (2005). *Latino education: An agenda for community action research.* Mahwah, NJ: Erlbaum.

Phillion, J., & He, M. F. (2004). Using life based literary narratives in multicultural teacher education. *Multicultural Perspectives, 6*(3), 3–9.

Pinar, W. F. (1975). Currere: Toward reconceptualization. In W. F. Pinar (Ed.), *Curriculum theorizing: The reconceptualists* (pp. 396–414). Berkeley, CA: McCutchan.

Pinar, W. F. (Ed.). (1998). *The passionate mind of Maxine Greene: "I am not yet."* London: Falmer.

Pinar, W. F. (2004). *What is curriculum theory?* Mahwah, NJ: Erlbaum.

Puar, J. (2003). *Terrorist assemblages.* Raleigh, NC: Duke University Press.

Rilke, R. A. (2000). *Letters to a young poet* (J. M. Burnham, trans.). New York: MJF Books.

Rose, M. (1995). *Possible lives: The promise of public education in America.* New York: Houghton Mifflin.

Roth, P. (1997). *American pastoral.* New York: Houghton Mifflin.

Sameshima, P. (2007). *Seeing red—a pedagogy of parallax: An epistolary bildungs-roman on artful scholarly inquiry.* Amherst, NY: Cambria Press.

Sameshima, P., Vandermause, R., & Chalmers, S. (2009). *Climbing the ladder with Gabriel: Poetic inquiry of a methamphetamine addict in recovery.* Rotterdam, The Netherlands: Sense.

Sartre, J-P. (1981). *The words: The autobiography of Jean-Paul Sartre* (B. Fretchman, trans.). New York: Vintage Books.

Schubert, W. H. (2009). *Love, justice, and education: John Dewey and the Utopians.* Charlotte, NC: Information Age Publishing.

Simon, C. (1971). Anticipation. On *Anticipation* [Recording]. New York: Elektra.

Steiner, G. (1989). *Real presences: Is there anything in what we say?* London: Faber & Faber.

Stevens, W. (1982). *The collected poems of Wallace Stevens.* New York: Knopf.

Stinson, S. W. (1985). Curriculum and the morality of aesthetics. *Journal of Curriculum Theorizing, 6*(3), 66–83.

Stinson, S. W. (1998). Maxine Greene and arts education. In W. F. Pinar (Ed.), *The passionate mind of Maxine Greene: "I am...not yet"* (pp. 221–229). Bristol, PA: Falmer.

Talk of the Town. (1989, August 14). *New Yorker, 65*(26), 23.

Thoreau, H. D. (1947). I am a parcel of vain strivings tied. In C. Bode (Ed.), *The portable Thoreau* (p. 228). New York: Penguin.

Torres, C. (1998). *Education, power, and personal biography. Dialogues with critical educators.* New York: Routledge.

Tyler, R. W. (1949). *Basic principles of curriculum and instruction.* Chicago: University of Chicago Press.

Ward-Hutchinson, B. (2009). Teaching from the outside in. *Journal of Dance Education, 9*(2), 52–60.

Willis, G., & Schubert, W. (1991). *Reflections from the heart of educational inquiry: Understanding curriculum and teaching through the arts.* Albany: State University of New York Press.

Wordsworth, W. (1940). *The poetical works of William Wordsworth.* Oxford, UK: The Clarendon Press. (Original work published 1893)

Zander, R., & Zander, B. (2000). *The art of possibility.* New York: Penguin.

About the Editor
and Contributors

Jacqueline Ancess is co-director of the National Center for Restructuring Education, Schools, and Teaching (NCREST) at Teachers College, Columbia University. Her research and publications focus on urban school reform, small high schools, teacher learning, performance assessment, and accountability.

Peter Appelbaum first read *Teacher as Stranger,* and first met Maxine Greene, during his doctoral studies at the University of Michigan in the 1980s. He is now professor of education, director-at-Large of Undergraduate Curriculum, and the director of the sTRANGELY fAMILIAR mUSIC gROUP at Arcadia University, Philadelphia.

Roslyn Arnold is an honorary professor in the Faculty of Education and Social Work at the University of Sydney. She has also been Dean of Education at the University of Tasmania. Her publications include *Mirror the Wind* (a selection of poems) and *Empathic Intelligence: Teaching, Learning, Relating,* for which Maxine Greene kindly wrote the Foreword.

Nina Asher is the J. Franklin Bayhi Endowed Professor in the College of Education at Louisiana State University. She writes in the areas of postcolonialism, feminism, multiculturalism, and Asian American studies in education. She is co-director of LSU's Curriculum Theory Project and is also on the faculty of the Women's and Gender Studies Program.

Rikki Asher began melting crayons on radiators at age 5. She is director of art education at Queens College, and Faculty Aesthetic Education Consultant with the Lincoln Center Institute. She has taught in the Bronx, England, Greece, Harlem, India, Mexico, and Nicaragua.

William Ayers is distinguished professor of education at the University of Illinois at Chicago (UIC), where he teaches courses in interpretive and qualitative research, urban school change, and teaching and the modern predicament. He is currently the vice president of the curriculum division of the American Educational Research Association and has publications in a wide range of journals and books.

Louise Berman is professor emerita, College of Education, University of Maryland, College Park. Her field is curriculum studies. Her major interests are alternative value bases for the development of curriculum and compatible research designs and world cooperation in education.

Donald Blumenfeld-Jones has taught at Arizona State University since January 1991 where he specializes in curriculum studies, ethics, and the arts and education.

Patty Bode is director of art education for Tufts University in affiliation with the School of the Museum of Fine Arts, Boston. She earned her doctorate in language, literacy and culture from the University of Massachusetts—Amherst with Sonia Nieto as her advisor, where she focused on multicultural art education.

Clyde Coreil is a professor in the ESL Department at New Jersey City University and the editor of the *Journal of the Imagination in Language Learning*, although he values far more the MFA in playwriting from Carnegie Mellon University.

Suzanne de Castell has been privileged to know Maxine Greene for nearly 30 years, and she hopes for another 30. Professor of curriculum and instruction in the Faculty of Education at Simon Fraser University, Suzanne's work spans literacy, technology, gender, digital game studies, and multimodal analysis of communicative interaction.

Roger Dell is the director of the Farnsworth Art Museum in Maine. He has also been the director of education at the Honolulu Academy of Arts, Chicago Museum of Contemporary Art, and Fitchburg Art Museum (Massachusetts). He is currently an instructor in the Museum Studies Program at the Harvard Extension School.

Gene Diaz is an associate professor in the Graduate School of Arts and Social Sciences at Lesley University and is presently serving as interim associate provost of the university. She is a visual artist and ethnographer who teaches courses in curriculum theory, ethnographic research methods, and arts-based action research.

Greg Dimitriadis is professor of sociology of education at the State University of New York at Buffalo. He is interested in the potential value and importance of non-traditional educational curricula (e.g., popular culture), programs (e.g., arts-based initiatives), and institutions (e.g., community centers) in the lives of disenfranchised young people.

Bernardine Dohrn, clinical associate professor of law at Northwestern University and director and founder of the Children and Family Justice Center, is a child advocate who teaches, lectures, and writes about children's law, juvenile justice, the needs and rights of youth, and international human rights.

Hilary Easton is a choreographer and performer whose work has been widely presented in New York City and nationally. Ms. Easton is an educational consultant for the New York Philharmonic's School Partnership Program and VSA arts, has been a teaching artist and professional developer for Lincoln Center Institute, and has taught at Connecticut College and Princeton University.

Kieran Egan was born in Ireland some years ago, was educated largely in England, began a Ph.D. degree in philosophy of education at Stanford University, and completed it at Cornell. He is currently a professor of education at Simon Fraser University in British Columbia, Canada.

Elliot Eisner is the Lee Jacks Professor Emeritus of Education and professor emeritus of art at Stanford University. His research interests focus on the development of aesthetic intelligence and on the use of methods from the arts to study and improve educational practice.

Barbara Ellmann is an abstract painter and has made public artworks for the City of New York. A museum educator at the Museum of Modern Art and the Whitney Museum of American Art, she is also a teaching artist for the National Partnership at the Kennedy Center. She has been a member of the faculty of Lincoln Center Institute since 1980, where she met Maxine. They have been friends ever since.

Michelle Fine, a distinguished professor of social psychology, women's studies and urban education at the Graduate Center, City University of New York, has taught at CUNY since 1990. Her research focuses on youth in schools, communities, and prisons, developed through critical feminist theory and method.

David Flinders is a professor in the School of Education at Indiana University, Bloomington. He is a former AERA vice president for Division B: Curriculum Studies, and has served as president of the American Association for Teaching and Curriculum. His interests include curriculum theory, secondary education reform, qualitative research methods, and cluster ballooning.

Noreen B. Garman is professor, administrative and policy studies, in the School of Education at University of Pittsburgh.

Jim Garrison is a professor of philosophy of education at Virginia Tech in Blacksburg, Virginia. His work concentrates on philosophical pragmatism. His awards include the John Dewey Society Outstanding Achievement Award and has been president of the Philosophy of Education Society and the John Dewey Society.

James M. Giarelli is professor of philosophy and education at Rutgers Graduate School of Education, faculty coordinator of the South African Initiative, and associate editor of *Educational Theory*. He has published widely on social philosophy, ethics, and educational theory and co-edited *Civic Education for Diverse Citizens in Global Times: Rethinking Theory and Practice* with Beth C. Rubin.

Ming Fang He is a professor of curriculum studies at Georgia Southern University. She currently advises doctoral students, directs doctoral dissertations, and teaches graduate courses in curriculum studies, multicultural education, and qualitative research methods.

James Henderson is a professor of curriculum studies in the School of Teaching, Learning and Curriculum Studies at Kent State University. His research activities and publications address democratic curriculum leadership and its implications for educational transformation, artistry, and professional development.

Chris Higgins is an assistant professor of educational policy studies, University of Illinois at Urbana-Champaign. His latest publication, *The Good Life of Teaching: Toward a Virtue Ethics for Teachers* (forthcoming), examines how work contributes to the practitioner's own quest to lead a rich, meaningful, and excellent life.

John Holyoke currently manages programming in many schools working with Lincoln Center Institute. Prior to this, he was a practicing teaching artist. John worked as a writer/director and actor in Seattle and New York. He was a co-founder and co-artistic director of the critically acclaimed Compound Theater in Seattle.

Madeleine Fuchs Holzer is director of educational development at Lincoln Center Institute for the Arts in Education. As a former director of arts in education at the New York State Council on the Arts, she has published poetry, articles in education, and co-edited a book on the Institute's work in teacher education.

Glenn Hudak is a professor at the University of North Carolina Greensboro, where he teaches cultural and philosophic foundations of education. He is currently working on two projects: a chapter on autistic youth, desire, and sexuality for a larger collaborative project on sexuality education; and a book on the pedagogical dimensions of philosophic and psychoanalytic thinking for educators.

Kathy Hytten is a professor in the Department of Educational Administration and Higher Education at Southern Illinois University, Carbondale. She is the 2008–2009 president of the American Educational Studies Association.

Lorraine Kasprisin is professor of educational philosophy and president of the Educational Institute for Democratic Renewal at the Woodring College of Education at Western Washington University. She is the founding editor of the *Journal of Educational Controversy*.

Herbert Kohl was a Henry Fellow at Oxford in philosophy. He began his teaching career in Harlem in 1962. In his teaching career, he has taught every grade from kindergarten through college.

Wendy Kohli is professor of curriculum and instruction in the Graduate School of Education at Fairfield University. She is the editor of *Critical Conversations in*

Philosophy of Education and has contributed widely to this area of study through a broad range of publications, teaching, and service.

Craig Kridel is the E.S. Gambrell Professor of Educational Studies and curator of the Museum of Education at the University of South Carolina. His research interests include progressive education, history of educational film, and biographical research.

Gloria Ladson-Billings holds the Kellner Family Chair in Urban Education and is professor of curriculum and instruction and educational policy studies at the University of Wisconsin-Madison. She is a former president of AERA and has published widely in her field.

Robert Lake is an assistant professor at Georgia Southern University, and teaches both undergraduate and graduate courses in multicultural education from both a local and global perspective. He has also worked with the U.S. Department of State's International Leadership in Education Program (ILEP) as an academic advisor and cultural events facilitator.

Linda Lambert is professor emeritus, California State University, East Bay, and president of Lambert Leadership Development. Her books include *The Constructivist Leader* (1995, 2002) and *Women's Ways of Leading* (2009).

Nancy Lesko is the Maxine Greene Professor at Teachers College, Columbia University, where she teaches curriculum studies and gender studies. Recent publications include "The Pedagogy of Monsters: Scary Disturbances in a Doctoral Research Training Course" in the *Teachers College Record*.

Rebecca Luce-Kapler is professor of language and literacy in the Faculty of Education, Queen's University, Canada. She has an ongoing fascination in exploring the biographies of women through poetry. Her research encompasses writing processes, technologies, and pedagogies. Her most recent project is working with senior-aged women on reading and writing literary memoirs.

Susan Mayer is a learning and curriculum theorist, who focuses on the pedagogical implications of developmental, cultural, and individual diversity for democratic classrooms. Her research explores the construction of shared understandings. Susan lectures at Brandeis University and Northeastern University, and is writing a book on the distribution of interpretive authority in schools.

Martha McKenna is provost and professor of the arts at Lesley University and president of the board of the National Arts and Learning Collaborative. As chair of the National Task Force on Higher Education of the Arts Education Partnership in Washington, she authored the report *Working Partnerships: Professional Development of the Arts Teaching Workforce* (2007).

Deborah Meier is currently on the faculty of New York University's Steinhardt School of Education, as well as a board member and director of New Ventures at Mission Hill School, director and advisor to the Forum for Democracy and Education, and on the board of the Coalition of Essential Schools. Meier has spent more than 4 decades working in public education as a teacher, writer, and public advocate.

Jennifer Milam is an assistant professor at the University of Akron in Elementary/ Middle Grades Curriculum. Jennifer's primary research interests are curriculum and cultural studies at the intersections of race and ethnicity in teaching, learning, and teacher education.

Maureen Miletta is professor emerita at Hofstra University, where she taught in the Department of Curriculum and Teaching for 23 years. She is the author of *A Multi-age Classroom: Choice and Possibility* (1996) and co-editor of *Classroom Conversations: A Collection of Classics for Parents and Teachers* (2009). She has been a director of the Maxine Greene Foundation since 2003.

Heidi Miller is program manager of Teaching Artists and Strategic Alliances at Lincoln Center Institute. She is involved in the training and professional development of the Institute's teaching artists, as well as the development and implementation of its Consultancies and National Educator Workshops, both nationally and internationally.

Janet Miller is professor of English education, and program coordinator of English Education/The Teaching of English at Teachers College. She authored *Creating Spaces and Finding Voices: Teachers Collaborating for Empowerment* (1990); *Sounds of Silence Breaking: Women, Autobiography, Curriculum* (2005); and *A Light in Dark Times: Maxine Greene and the Unfinished Conversation* (1998).

Sonia Nieto is professor emerita of language, literacy, and culture at the School of Education, University of Massachusetts, Amherst. Her publications and more about her may be found at http://www.sonianieto.com/index.html.

Nel Noddings is professor of philosophy and education at Teachers College, Columbia University, and Lee L. Jacks Professor of Child Education Emerita at Stanford University. She has been a friend and colleague of Maxine Greene for many years.

Scott Noppe-Brandon is executive director of Lincoln Center Institute (LCI), the leading organization in developing skills of imagination through guided encounters with the arts. A noted speaker and author, Scott has helped start numerous public schools and is an ardent campaigner for arts and imagination in education.

JoAnn Phillion is professor of curriculum and instruction at Purdue University. Her research interests are in narrative approaches to multicultural education and teacher education. She teaches graduate courses in curriculum theory and multicultural education, and undergraduate courses in pre-service teacher development.

William Pinar teaches curriculum theory at the University of British Columbia, where he holds a Canada Research Chair. He is the author, most recently, of *The Worldliness of a Cosmopolitan Education: Passionate Lives in Public Service* (2009).

Eugene Provenzo is a professor in social and cultural foundations of education at the University of Miami. He is the author of a wide range of books on history, education, technology, and cultural studies. Most recently he has served as the editor in chief of *The Sage Encyclopedia of the Social and Cultural Foundations of Education* (2009).

Molly Quinn is associate professor in curriculum studies at Teachers College, Columbia University, New York, and author of *Going Out, Not Knowing Whither: Education, the Upward Journey and the Faith of Reason* (2001). Much of her scholarship engages spiritual and philosophical criticism toward embracing a vision of education that cultivates wholeness, beauty, compassion, and social action.

Shaireen Rasheed is an associate professor of philosophy in the School of Education at Long Island University. She had the good fortune to have Maxine Greene, Nel Noddings, and Rene Arcilla as her dissertation advisors. Some of her related publications include her book *An Existentialist Curriculum of Action* (2006), which contextualizes Maxine Greene's educational pedagogy within an existentialist tradition.

William Reynolds teaches in the Department of Curriculum, Foundations and Reading at Georgia Southern University. His two most recent books are *Expanding Curriculum Theory: Dis/positions and Lines of Flight* (2004) and *The Civic Gospel: A Political Cartography of Christianity* (2009). His current interests are curriculum as Deleuzian philosophy, film studies, religion, and political theory.

Teresa Rishel is an associate professor in curriculum and instruction at Kent State University. She received a Ph.D. in curriculum studies from Purdue University. Teresa researches adolescent suicide in terms of sociocultural relationships; and the effects of the hidden curriculum on academic performance and school behavior, and school issues of power, alienation, and the role of curriculum.

Mike Rose has taught in a range of educational settings, from kindergarten to job training and adult literacy programs, over the last 40 years. He is currently on the faculty of the University of California, Los Angeles, Graduate School of Education and Information Studies.

Pauline Sameshima's work centers on curriculum, learning system design, technology integration, collaborative and creative scholarship, eco-responsive pedagogies, and innovative forms of knowledge production and acknowledgment. She teaches at Washington State University in the Cultural Studies and Social Thought in Education Program.

William Schubert is professor of education and coordinator of the Graduate Curriculum Studies Program at the University of Illinois at Chicago.

Julie Searle lives in Berkeley, California, where she teaches writing, literature, and history at Martin Luther King Jr. Middle School. She has written about arts-based education and social justice issues. She previously worked at The Poetry Center and at Intersection for the Arts in San Francisco.

Pamela K. Smith spent over 30 years in Ohio teaching and working as an administrator in one of the state's small urban schools. She is a professor of social foundations in the Department of Teacher Education at Eastern Michigan University.

Nick Sousanis is pursuing his doctorate in art education at Teachers College, Columbia University. He is also the founding director of the University of Michigan's Work: Detroit Gallery. His educational comics can be seen at www.spinweaveandcut.blogspot.com.

Shirley Steinberg is an associate professor at McGill University in the Department of Integrated Studies in Education. She is also the director of the Paulo and Nita Freire International Project for Critical Pedagogy and is the author or editor of many books and articles.

Susan Stinson is professor of dance at University of North Carolina Greensboro, where she teaches undergraduate and graduate courses in teacher preparation, research, and curriculum. She has presented her scholarly work nationally and internationally and published in multiple journals and book chapters related to dance, the arts, and education.

Lynda Stone is professor of philosophy of education, director of graduate studies, and area chair of Culture, Curriculum and Change (CCC) at the University of North Carolina, Chapel Hill. She teaches courses in the Ph.D. in Education, CCCs, and the Master of Arts in Teaching programs. She is also the current president of the John Dewey Society.

Graeme Sullivan is professor of art education, Teachers College, Columbia University. He is the author of two books and numerous articles published in the United States, United Kingdom, Europe, Australia, and Asia that explore the cognitive practices of artists and the creative and critical approaches used in studio-based research.

Jean Taylor received a grant from the Maxine Greene Foundation for *The Wild Hair Living Room Tour*, a performance and community event held in living rooms, lofts, and salons. She is a teaching artist for Lincoln Center Institute for the Arts in Education and teaches theatrical clowning for the New School for Drama and the Barrow Group Theatre.

Julie Teel is an associate professor in the Department of Teacher Education at LeTourneau University in Texas. Her interests include all matters concerning teacher education, the arts in education, and field experiences locally and globally for pre-service teachers.

Barbara Thayer-Bacon, professor, teaches graduate courses on philosophy and history of education, social philosophy, and cultural diversity for the University of Tennessee. Her primary areas of scholarship as a philosopher of education are feminist theory and pedagogy, pragmatism, and cultural studies in education.

John Toth teaches art at Hunter College in the School of Education. He completed his Ph.D. in media and communications at the European Graduate School in Leuk Stadt, Switzerland, in 2005. He has worked as a teaching artist for Lincoln Center Institute for 25 years and for 11 years in the education department at The Museum of Modern Art.

Leonard Waks earned a Ph.D. in philosophy at the University of Wisconsin in 1968, and taught philosophy at Purdue and Stanford before joining the educational faculty at Temple University, where he is now professor emeritus of Educational Leadership. He is the general editor of the Leaders in Educational Studies: Intellectual Self-Portraits series.

Cathryn Williams is director of Strategic Alliances at the Lincoln Center Institute and oversees the institute's relationship with key partners outside the local K–12 system. In addition, Cathryn oversees the management and professional development of the institute's teaching artists. During her 20-year association with the institute, Cathryn has been a dance teaching artist first, then a field representative, observing and advising artists in all disciplines.

George Willis has been a professor of education at the University of Rhode Island since 1971. Among his books are *Reflections from the Heart of Educational Inquiry: Understanding Curriculum and Teaching Through the Arts* (1991, edited with William H. Schubert) and *Curriculum: Alternative Approaches, Ongoing Issues* (2007, 4th ed., written with Colin J. Marsh).